Anonymous

**A Complete History of the Origin and Progress of the Late War**

from its commencement, to the exchange of the ratifications of peace, between

Great-Britain, France, and Spain on the 10th of February, 1763 - Vol. 1

Anonymous

**A Complete History of the Origin and Progress of the Late War**
*from its commencement, to the exchange of the ratifications of peace, between Great-Britain, France, and Spain on the 10th of February, 1763 - Vol. 1*

ISBN/EAN: 9783337224776

Printed in Europe, USA, Canada, Australia, Japan

Cover: Foto ©ninafisch / pixelio.de

More available books at **www.hansebooks.com**

# ADVERTISEMENT.

THE author of the following sheets hath endeavoured, to the utmost of his abilities, to give the Public a succinct and impartial History of the present war.——No slave to faction, no dupe to prejudice; he hath represented facts as they really happened. It is the business of history to record; not to flatter. The condour of the public is requested for a work, the design of which is certainly commendable: How it is executed the reader must determine.

A COMPLETE
# HISTORY
OF THE
ORIGIN and PROGRESS
OF THE
# LATE WAR,
From its Commencement,

TO THE

Exchange of the Ratifications of Peace,

BETWEEN

GREAT-BRITAIN, FRANCE, and SPAIN:

On the 10th of FEBRUARY, 1763.

AND TO THE

Signing of the Treaty at HUBERTSBERG,

BETWEEN

The King of PRUSSIA, the EMPRESS-QUEEN, and the Elector of SAXONY,

On the 15th of the fame Month.

IN WHICH,

All the BATTLES, SIEGES, SEA-ENGAGEMENTS, and every other Transaction worthy of public Attention, are faithfully recorded; with political and military Observations.

IN TWO VOLUMES.

LONDON:
Printed for J. KNOX, near Southampton Street, in the Strand.
MDCCLXIV.

# A HISTORY OF THE WAR.

## CHAP. I.

*Origin of the war. Acts of hostility committed by France in America. The french incroachments there. The english ambassador remonstrates against their proceedings. Major Washington's expedition. Monckton reduces Beausejour, and other forts in Nova Scotia. Other transactions in America, till the end of 1754. General Braddock appointed to command in chief, and arrives in Virginia. He marches against Fort du Quesne. Is defeated by the french. Consequences of his defeat. Reflections.*

TO enquire into the origin of the war, it will be necessary to look back almost to the peace of Aix la Chapelle, in the year 1748; for we shall find, that very soon after that treaty, the french laid the foundations for a future war. In order to perceive this more clearly, I shall take a particular view of the proceedings of France in North America (the country in which the late commotions first began) from the abovementioned time.

In the year 1749, some english american traders commenced a traffic with the indians, on the banks of the river Ohio. The french knowing the importance of that country, were desirous to prevent us from trading, or having any communication with those indians; they threatned them with the confiscation of their goods, and imprisonment of their persons, if they did not retire, from what, they were pleased to call, their master's territories. Many of the traders immediately withdrew, on receiving this insolent menace; but several others, knowing their own just right, had more spirit; and continued their traffic as usual, notwithstanding the threats denounced against them: and accordingly in 1750, the marquis de la Jonquiere, at that time governor of Canada, sent several detachments of troops to the Ohio, to put their former threats in execution; which they did by seizing four english traders, and confiscating their goods, sending them prisoners to Quebec, from whence they were brought to Rochelle in France, and there detained in prison. These englishmen soon after their arrival at Rochelle, wrote to the earl of Albemarle, our ambassador at Paris, complaining of the ill usage they had received: upon which, that minister wrote a letter to the earl of Holdernesse, secretary of state to the king of England; of which the following is an extract.

" Paris, march 1, 1752.
I must acquaint your lordship, that in the month of november I received a letter from three persons, signing themselves, John Patton, Luke Irwin, and Thomas Bourke; representing to me, that they were englishmen, who had been brought to Rochelle, and put into prison there, from whence they wrote; having been taken by the french subjects, who seized their effects, as they were trading with the english, and other indians on the Ohio, and carried prisoners to Quebec; from whence they have been sent over to Rochelle,

Rochelle, where they were hardly used. Upon this information, I applied to M. St. Contest, and gave him a note of it; claiming them, as the king's subjects, and demanding their liberty, and the restitution of their effects that had been unjustly taken from them.

These three persons, I find by the paper your lordship has sent me, are of the number of those demanded of the french by Mr. Clinton, and named in M. de la Jonquiere's letter. I have wrote to a merchant at Rochelle to enquire after them, and to supply them with money, to make their journey hither, if they are not gone; that I may receive from them all the informations necessary. On my seeing M. St. Contest next tuesday, I will represent the case to him, in obedience to his majesty's commands, that la Jonquiere may have positive orders, to desist from the unjustifiable proceedings complained of; to release any of his majesty's subjects he may still detain in prison; and make ample restitution of their effects. And I shall take care to show him the absolute necessity of sending instructions to their several governors, not to attempt any such encroachments for the future."

And on the 8th of march lord Albemarle further writes to the earl of Holdernesse.

" I am now to acquaint your lordship, that I saw M. Rouille yesterday; and that having drawn up a note of the several complaints I had received orders to make of la Jonquiere's conduct, I delivered it to him, and told him, in general, the contents of it; insisting on the necessity, for preserving the good understanding betwixt his majesty and the most christian king, of sending such positive orders to all their governors, as might effectually prevent, for the future, any such encroachments on his majesty's territories, and committing such violence on his subjects, as had been done in the past.

I added

I added to my remonstrance, that I hoped they would be taken into consideration quickly; that he might be able to give me an answer next week, or as soon afterwards as he possibly could. This minister told me, he would use his best endeavours for that purpose; assured me it was the intention of his court to prevent any disputes arising, that might tend to alter the present correspondence between the two nations; and that I might depend upon such orders being sent to their governors accordingly.

Of the three men I mentioned to your lordship in my letter of last week, that had been brought prisoners from Canada to Rochelle, whom I sent for to come to Paris, two of them are arrived, and the third is gone to London. I will take such informations from them, as may be necessary for my own instruction, to support their receiving satisfaction for the injuries that have been done them."

At the same time that my lord Albemarle mentioned the above affair to M. de Rouille, he delivered to him a memorial containing his complaints, of which the following is a part.

" As to the fort which the french have undertaken to build on the river Niagara, and as to the six englishmen who have been made prisoners; lord Albemarle is ordered by his court to demand, that the most express orders be sent to M. de la Jonquiere, to desist from such unjust proceedings, and in particular, to cause the fort above-mentioned, to be immediately razed; and the french and others in their alliance, who may happen to be there, to retire forthwith: as likewise, to set the six englishmen at liberty, and to make them ample satisfaction for the wrongs and losses they have suffered; and lastly, that the persons who have committed these excesses, be punished in such a manner as may serve for an example to those who might venture on any like attempt."

It

It is necessary here to add a remark or two on this perplexed and intricate affair; concerning which, so much falshood has been propagated. It is very plain that, although several just demands were made by lord Albemarle to the french minister, yet none of them (except the releasing the three men at Rochelle) were complied with: even to this day the fort at Niagara has not been demolished. No satisfaction was made to those englishmen who were taken prisoners, for the losses they sustained; nor any restitution made for the effects that had been seized. And as to the positive orders which were to be sent to all their governors in North America, and to de la Jonquiere in particular, for them to desist from any the like attempts or encroachments for the future, every one knows the french never thought of complying with this demand, since they continued without interruption their encroachments; and were so far from desisting from the same, that they even carried them every day further and further, till at last it came to an open war between the two nations.

It is one of the first and best of political maxims, for every nation to resent the wrongs done them vigorously and without delay. But, to the misfortune of their country, the ministry in England did not follow that method to have its injuries redressed. 'Tis true, my lord Albemarle demanded every thing that it was reasonable to expect the french could grant. But there certainly is a wide difference between demanding, and having those demands granted. The only article complied with was, the releasing the three englishmen at Rochelle. Now it is natural here to enquire into the reason, why the british ministry did not insist upon having the other articles, mentioned in the lord Albemarle's memorial, complied with instantly, and a stop put to the many encroachments which the french were making in America. We know this should have been done: and we know it was not done. To enquire

-into

into the secret springs and causes of this neglect, must be left to those who are more acquainted with the affairs of state: but thus much I may venture to say, that one of the principal ones was the dread and fear which the ministry in England had, of being drawn into a war with France; the reasons for this fear, I think, are very evident.

The márquis de la Jonquiere, governor of Canada, died in march, 1752, just as he was preparing to march a considerable body of troops to the Ohio, with design to continue their encroachments on that river. The marquis du Quesne, successor to Jonquiere, no sooner arrived at Quebec, in the middle of the year, than he hastened to continue what his predecessor had begun; and gave the command of the troops designed for the Ohio, to the sieur de St. Pierre, who began his march in the latter end of 1753, and wintered in a fort which he built on the Beef River. In the month of october, during his stay at this post, he received a letter from Mr. Dinwiddie, lieutenant governor of Virginia, dated the 31st, complaining of sundry late hostilities; and desiring to know, by what authority an armed force had marched from Canada, and invaded a territory indubitably the right of his britannic majesty. Major Washington was the bearer of this letter. He returned with the following answer from Monsf. Legardeur de St. Pierre, dated at the fort on Beef River, the 15th of december, 1753.

"Sir,
As I have the honor to command here in chief, Mr. Washington delivered me the letter, which you directed to the commandant of the french troops. I should have been pleased if you had given him orders, or if he himself had been disposed, to visit Canada and our general; to whom, rather than to me, it properly appertains, to remonstrate the reality of the king my master's rights to lands situated along the

the Ohio, and to dispute the pretensions of the king of Great-Britain in that respect.

I shall immediately forward your letter to Monsf. le marquis du Quesne. His answer will be a law to me: and if he directs me to communicate it to you, I assure you, sir, I shall neglect nothing that may be necessary to convey it to you with expedition.

As to the requisition you make (that I retire with the troops under my command) I cannot believe myself under any obligation to submit to it: I am here in virtue of my general's orders; and I beg, sir, you would not doubt a moment of my fixed resolution to conform to them, with all the exactitude and steadiness that might be expected from a better officer.

I do not know that, in the course of this campaign, any thing has passed that can be esteemed an act of hostility, or contrary to the treaties subsisting between the two crowns; the continuation of which is as interesting and pleasing to us, as it can be to the english. If it had been agreeable to you, sir, in this respect, to have made a particular detail of the facts which occasion your complaint, I should have had the honor of answering you in the most explicit manner; and, I am persuaded you would have had reason to be satisfied.

I have taken particular care to receive Mr. Washington with all the distinction suitable to your dignity, and to his quality and great merit. I flatter myself that he will do me this justice, and join with with me in testifying the profound respect with which
   I am, Sir,
    Your most humble
    And most obedient servant,
     LEGARDEUR DE ST. PIERRE."

On receipt of this resolute answer, Mr. Dinwiddie made instant complaint to the court of Great-Britain; and laboured what he could to rouze the Virginians into a vigorous oppofition. He wrote alfo to the neighbouring governors, importuning the aid of the other colonies, for repelling the invafion, and erecting a fort at the confluence of the Ohio and Monangahela. An immediate junction in fuch meafures became abfolutely requifite for the common fecurity. But the colonies, inattentive to the inconveniencies of an endlefs frontier, contemned the power of Canada, and confided in the number of their inhabitants. They were fo entirely ignorant of the fituation and importance of the inland country; that when application was made to Virginia for fuccours, conformable to directions from the miniftry in England, fome of our provincial affemblies, particularly thofe of Penfilvania and New York *, feemed even to queftion his majefty's right to the lands ufurped by the french. Others, to avoid their fhare in the burden, framed the moft trifling excufes. New York, however, voted 5000 l. currency in aid of Virginia; which, confidering her own fituation, and approaching diftreffes, was no ungenerous contribution.

But the Virginians proceeded in their refolution of marching a body of troops to the protection of their frontiers: and paffed an act in February, 1754, for the raifing 10,000 l. and 300 men. The command was given to col. Wafhington, a young gentleman of great bravery and diftinguifhed merit.

He

---

* Extract of governor Morris's meffage to the affembly of Penfilvania, 22 November, 1755.

You would not admit, that the french encroachments and fortifications on the Ohio were within our limits, or his majefty's dominions, then by feeking an excufe to avoid doing what was required of you.

Extract of the addrefs of the general affembly of New York to lieutenant governor de Lancy, 23 April, 1754.

It appears, by other papers, your honor has been pleafed to communicate to us, that the french have built a fort at a place called the French Creek, at a confiderable diftance from the river Ohio, which may, but does not by any evidence or information appear to us to be an invafion of any of his majefty's colonies.

He began his march at the head of his little army, about the 1st of may. On the 28th he had a skirmish with the enemy, of whom ten were slain, and about twenty were made prisoners. But col. Washington finding himself too weak, waited for further reinforcements; during which time he was alarmed with the news, that a great body of french and indians were marching against him. It seems the marquis du Quesne, governor general of Canada, had appointed the sieur de Contre-Cœur to command the french troops on the Ohio, who being acquainted with the skirmish which col. Washington had with a party of french, resolved to send the greatest part of his forces, under the sieur de Villiers, to dislodge col. Washington from his little camp, which he had formed, and which was called fort Necessity. In obedience to these instructions, Villiers accordingly marched at the head of near 1000 french and 200 indians against the english. On the 3d of july, he came in sight of fort Necessity. The english troops not amounting to above 200 men, were a handful compared to the number of the enemy; but they fought bravely for upwards of three hours, nor did they give over before they had slain near 200 of the enemy; but col. Washington, observing their great superiority, who began to hem him in on all quarters, found himself under the absolute necessity of submitting to the disagreeable terms that were offered him.

In this action we had 30 killed and 50 wounded. The french, as I have said before, were assisted by a considerable number of indians, who had been long in the english alliance. And many of them were known to be of the six nations. On the surrender of our camp, they fell at once to pillaging the baggage and provisions; and shot several of the horses and cattle.

Against this conduct col. Washington remonstrated; but all his arguments made little impression upon them.

them. Thus the french remained mafters of the field; the indians were rivetted in their defection; and the frontiers of the colony expofed, through the ill-timed parfimony of the provinces. The enemy on the other hand wifely improved the prefent advantage, and erected forts to fecure to themfelves the quiet poffeffion of that fertile country. To fhew the negligence of the province of Penfilvania, we need only take notice, that foon after Wafhington's defeat, a thoufand of the back inhabitants prefented a petition to the affembly, praying, that they might be furnifhed with arms and ammunition for their defence; but the petition was rejected with fcorn. Our indian allies have often defired us to build forts, to which their wives and children might fly in time of danger; and fent down to the governor of Penfilvania, begging he would direct the building a ftockade, or wooden fort, in which they offered to defend themfelves and the englifh from the incurfions of the enemy; but the affembly, to be confiftent with themfelves, and to fhow that they were religioufly bent on the ruin of their country, refufed to give any money to this purpofe, and gave the indians for anfwer, that if they were afraid of the enemy, they might retire further down, and come within the fettled parts of the province. Thus the nobleft opportunity was loft that could have been offered, of keeping our indians fteady, and for building a fort at a fmall expence, in a pafs fo commodioufly fituated between the mountains, that it would have effectually covered and defended two of our frontier counties, from the inroads of the french and their indians.

I fhall here take notice of an inftruction fent from his majefty to the feveral governors of North America; whereby the earl of Holderneffe fignified his majefty's commands, that in cafe the fubjects of any foreign prince fhould prefume to make any encroachments in the limits of his majefty's dominions, or to erect forts on his majefty's lands, or to commit any
other

other act of hostility; and should upon a requisition made to them to desist from such proceedings, persist in them, they should draw forth the armed force of their respective provinces, and use their best endeavours to repel force by force.

It was in consequence of this message, that the governor of Pensilvania in particular, urged the assembly of that province, to raise the necessary sums for their own defence, with so much warmth, but which, as I have before said, they refused to do; although at that time the province was in the utmost danger.

At the beginning of a war, every transaction and affair, which at another time would be reckoned immaterial, is of great importance to be known. It is for this reason that I have, and shall continue to be, very particular in giving distinct accounts of all our american affairs; as this war, contrary to all others, has been more critical and important there, than any where else. I shall now mention the affairs of Nova Scotia, in which province we find the french committed repeated hostilities; and with their usual impudence seized all that part of Nova Scotia, beyond the bay of Fundi, from the river Chignecto, to that of St. John, making the first the limits of that province. Mr. Cornwallis was at that time governor of it; and M. de la Jonquiere commanded in chief in Canada, who openly and readily avowed the unjust proceedings of the french. But this affair will be much clearer laid open by the following memorial, which contains a recapitulation of the conduct of France in that province; stating many interesting particulars in a just and clear light. It was delivered to the marquis de Puysieulx at Paris, by the earl of Albemarle, the 7th of june, 1750.

" The underwritten ambassador extraordinary and plenipotentiary, from his majesty, the king of Great-Britain, has orders from the king his master, dated Hanover, the 26th of last month, to represent to the
court

court of France, how much he is surprized at hearing the violent proceedings of the french in America, under the authority and direction of M. de la Jonquiere, who has readily avowed them.

M. Cornwallis, governor of Nova Scotia, informs the duke of Bedford, by a letter dated the first of may this year, that the french have taken possession of all that part of Nova Scotia, beyond the bay of Fundi, from the river Chignecto to that of St. John, making the first the limits of that province.

They have reduced Beaubassin to ashes, and carried to the other side of the river the inhabitants with their effects; compelled them to take up arms, and formed them into companies; so that the sieur Lacorne, a french officer has at that place under his command, a body of 2500 men, made up of regular troops, canadians and indians.

The sieur de Lacorne and father Loutre, a french missionary, have made use of repeated and innumerable promises and menaces, in order to persuade all the inhabitants of the province to leave the country.

The inhabitants declare openly their abhorrence of these proceedings; but the sieurs de Lacorne and Loutre, threaten them with a general massacre from the indians, if they remain in the province. They support and protect openly the indians, our declared enemies; who inlist under the banners of France. They detain the king's subjects, his officers and soldiers, prisoners. They excite the king's french subjects to a rebellion; and those who remain loyal, they threaten with destruction. They send their indian slaves all over the country, where they are guilty of all sorts of outrages.

They have set fire to the towns acknowledged by themselves, to appertain to his majesty.

Governor Cornwallis sent the sieur Lawrence, major of foot, with a detachment to Chignecto; where he arrived the 20th of last april. They saw the
french

french set fire to the town of Chignecto, french colours planted on the ditches; and the sieur de la Corne at the head of his detachment, braving major Lawrence; and declaring, that he would defend to the last, that ground as belonging to France.

The sieur de la Corne having sent to desire a conference with the sieur Lawrence, the latter, accompanied by two captains of foot, went to meet him, and demanded by whose orders he had thus come into his majesty's territories, and committed such acts of violence. The sieur de la Corne answered; it was by those of M. de la Jonquiere, who had also commanded him to take possession of Chippodi, John's River, Man-rem, Cooke, Pitcordiack, and of all that country, as far as the river, which was on the the right hand of major St. Lawrence, as belonging to his most christian majesty; or at least, that he was to keep and defend it as such, till such time as the limits were settled by commissaries appointed for that purpose.

Though the sieur Lawrence had under his command a detachment of regular troops, very little inferior to that commanded by the sieur Lacorne, he forbore committing any hostilities, in obedience to the king's orders for that purpose.

The king cannot persuade himself that these acts of violence have been committed with the knowledge of the court of France, and he is so fully convinced of his most christian majesty's equity, and his desire to maintain a good understanding between the two crowns, that he assures himself the most christian king will readily show his disapprobation of such conduct.

Governor Cornwallis has never made, nor designed to make any settlements out of the limits of the peninsula, which the french before never pretended to belong to them: The king having had no intention, in forming a settlement in his province of Nova Scotia, to encroach on the rights of his most christian majesty,

jesty, or to take forcible possession of a country, of which the king had referred the right of propriety to the decision of the commissaries appointed for that purpose; before it was possible for them to have met in order to proceed to the settling of the limits.

The under written ambassador has orders to demand, that the conduct of M. de la Jonquiere be disavowed: that positive orders be sent him immediately to withdraw his troops, and the indians under his authority from the places which belong to Great-Britain; that amends be made for the acts of violence which have been committed, and the damage which the king's subjects have suffered: and his majesty is persuaded that the court of France will make no difficulty, to give the underwritten ambassador the duplicate of the orders, which will be sent to the governor of Canada, that he may transmit them to his court. Done at Compeigne the 7th of july, 1750. Signed,

ALBEMARLE."

In answer to this memorial, the marquis de Puysieulx wrote the following letter to the earl of Albemarle, dated Compeigne, july 23, 1750.

"SIR,

In the memorial, which your excellency has given me concerning the complaints of M. Cornwallis, governor of Arcadia, are contained many facts, so contrary to the equity of his majesty, the instructions of M. de la Jonquiere, and that if they are found to be such as they are represented, the king will take care justice shall be done to his britannic majesty's subjects, and will give such fresh orders, as will prevent the rise of any dispute of what kind soever between the two nations; his majesty being thoroughly persuaded his britannic majesty will give, on his side, orders to the same purpose.

Give

Give me leave, sir, to tell you I cannot be prevailed upon to believe, but that the facts are exposed with too much exaggeration, and from my knowledge of M. de la Jonquiere's prudence, and the instructions which he has, I am sorry M. Cornwallis has not applied for redress, before he had made complaints to his court. I sent your memorial, as soon as I received it to M. Rouille, and desired he would take the proper steps, to be informed in a speedy and precise manner, of what has passed at Canada, so as I may be enabled to give your excellency a more positive answer. I have the honour to be, &c.

Signed, PUYSIEULX.

P. S. Might not M. Cornwallis have attempted to form settlements on the places that are in dispute, or even on the king's territories?"

Soon after the earl of Albemarle received this letter, the french ministry gave him a copy of a letter wrote from M. Rouille, to M. de la Jonquiere; in which he was directed to forbear committing hostilities on the subjects of England.

But Mr. Cornwallis had not force enough to drive them from their encroachments; and it was very plain that they would remain in them, in spite of all the remonstrances and memorials, that the english ambassador might make at Paris; for we find the french made no motions with design to quit the country they had seized; till they were drove out by the New England troops in 1755; of which more hereafter. But before I take my leave of the affairs of this province for the present, it is necessary to take notice of a memorial delivered at Paris to my lord Albemarle, (as a further answer to the complaints of England) the 15th of september this year, in which they deny most of the facts laid to their charge; and speaking of the limits of the province in the most evasive and quibbling manner.

To

To return : I left col. Washington, just defeated, returning home (after having been obliged to submit to the disagreeable terms imposed on him) and he arrived safe at Williamsburg, after a most tedious and hazardous march.

As yet the affairs of North America had gone on but very badly, and wore a dismal countenance. The french were every where advancing, and always with success; our frontiers were all open to the enemy, and nothing to defend them; in such a calamitous condition, something must be done, but what to determine on, was difficult to know: our colonies were, singly, so weak, that a junction was at that time absolutely necessary, and accordingly resolved on. By his majesty's orders, the 14th of june was appointed for a grand congress of commissaries from the several provinces to be held at Albany, as well to treat with the indians of the six nations, as to concert a scheme for a general union of the british colonies. Messengers had been dispatched to the indian chiefs to request their attendance; but they did not arrive till the latter end of the month; and the Mohawks, who lived but 40 miles distant, came in last. This occasioned various speculations; some imputed it to fear, least the french in their absence, should fall upon their countries. But the most probable reason of it was: that the indians imagined, that by exciting our jealousy of their wavering disposition, at so critical a juncture, the more liberal would be the presents made them by the several governments. But they arrived at last, though in smaller numbers than was expected, or had been usual on those occasions: though they had been very well pleased with the presents made them, which were much more considerable than had been ever known: in their speech to Mr. de Lancey, the lieutenant governor of New York, they spoke with great vehemence, and very severely upon our negligent and indolent behaviour; extolling the better conduct of the french in fortifying

ing and maintaining their garrisons. And recriminated upon us the desertion of our fort at Saraghtoga the last war; lamented the defenceless condition, of our frontier city of Albany; and earnestly exhorted us for the future to defend ourselves with more spirit. The indians being dismissed, the conferences were continued till the 11th of July: the commissioners being, both for abilities and fortune, some of the most considerable men in North America: in the conclusion of their debates, a plan was concerted for a general union of the british colonies, and creating a common fund to defray all military expences; and a representation of their present state drawn up; which was agreed to be laid before the king's ministers. But this scheme was never put in execution.

During the sitting of the congress at Albany, Mr. Shirley, governor of Massachuset's Bay; a gentleman, of whom I shall have much to say in the sequel; proposed to the assembly of that province the building a strong fort near the head of the river Kennebeck, in order to protect the province from the incursions of the french, and the indians; which the assembly agreed to; and provided pay and subsistence for 800 men, to be raised on that account. Accordingly in the summer, Mr. Shirley proceeded to the eastern parts of the province, with the troops raised for that purpose; and with the consent of the indians, built fort Western and fort Halifax upon the river Kenebeck, the former about 37 miles from the mouth of it; and the other, about 54. Of this service, Mr. Shirley transmitted an account to England, and at the same time represented the imminent danger, which he apprehended the neighbouring province of Nova-Scotia was exposed to from the fortifications, and other encroachments of the french upon the isthmus, and the peninsula there, and St. John's river in the bay of Fundi; as also, from the sudden attacks, which might be formed against it from St. John's island, Louisburg and Quebec. In answer

answer to which Mr. Shirley received a letter from sir Thomas Robinson, one of his majesty's principal secretaries of state, containing his majesty's approbation of the service upon the river Kennebeck, with orders to communicate it to the assembly. And soon after Mr. Shirley received his majesty's commands, to concert measures, with Mr. Lawrence, lieutenant governor, and commander in chief of the province of Nova Scotia, for attacking the french forts in that province. Accordingly, by his majesty's commands, Mr. Shirley raised 2000 new england men, and received 2000 stands of small arms from England; with which force he marched, in conjunction with Mr. Lawrence (with the troops under his command which were in Nova Scotia) attacked, and reduced the french forts at Beausejour, and at Gaspereau, near Bay Verte, making the garrisons prisoners: and in a short time after, upon two of his majesty's ships of war appearing before the french fort, situated on the river of St. John's, about three miles above the mouth of it, the garrison there burst their cannon, demolished their works as much as they could, evacuated the fort, and retired up the river, to their other settlements upon it. By reason of the time that was necessary to prepare for this expedition, the service was not executed till the 19th of june, 1755.

The remainder of the year 1754 was spent principally in repeated representations to the ministry in England, laying before them the bad state of the colonies; together with several schemes for their general union; assuring them, that if speedy and powerful assistance was not administered, the colonies in America would inevitably fall a prey to the ambitious designs of the court of France.

In this manner ended the year 1754. As yet both courts continued to give the most solemn assurances of maintaining the peace between the two nations inviolably; when at the same time an open and bloody war was carrying on between them in America. It
was

was very palpable, that the pretended peace (which in fact had not a being) would not laſt long, but that the war would ſoon ſpread into Europe. In America there happened no affair of great conſequence; but, as in the beginning of a war every thing is of ſome conſequence, becauſe it is at the breaking out of one, I have been obliged to purſue the thread of affairs in America ſtep by ſtep, and to give the moſt particular accounts of, even ſome matters which at firſt ſight the reader will imagine but of little moment, which he will find by the ſequel, were of importance enough to have a place in hiſtory, as they tend very much to the clearer underſtanding of what follows. This was the firſt war, in which Great Britain may be ſaid to have engaged purely for the defence of her american colonies; they certainly well deſerve all the expence, pains, and care that their mother country can take of them. Since ſhe will, in the end, be repaid with an hundred fold for whatever ſhe can expend in their defence. Although Great Britain finds, that its very being as a nation, depends upon her colonies, ſtill we ſee (or at leaſt we have good reaſon to think ſo) that the french know the value of them much better than us. They make (comparatively ſpeaking) more of Canada, which is a mere barren rock, in compariſon with our colonies, than we do of all our noble ſettlements in North America. Nor can we here conſider their ſituation at the cloſe of the year 1754, without being aſtoniſhed at the negligent remiſſneſs of the engliſh miniſtry, to ſuffer theſe valuable territories, which make ſo conſiderable a part of his majeſty's dominions, to remain in ſo open and defenceleſs a condition. They may ſay in juſtification of themſelves, that the colonies have ſtrength enough to defend themſelves: but then they ought to remember, that, it is not in their power to make uſe of the ſtrength they have, ſince every one knows, that while they all continue in ſeperate provinces, without any connection with one another, they may easily fall a prey to the combined and more formidable strength of the french and their indians. Is it not surprising, that, while the french were advancing on all sides, after they had defeated the troops under Washington; and seized all that valuable tract of country, situated on the Ohio and its branches; and were continually receiving reinforcements from old France; after all this, it is not, I say, a mark of the utmost negligence, treachery or stupidity in the e——h m——y, never yet to send any troops or forces to America, to defend his majesty's rights against the unjust usurpations and invasions of the french?

We find that the french began the new year in America, with their usual diligence and activity; and having the advantage of great reinforcements from old France early in the year\*; bid very fair for

---

\* Extract of a letter, dated Philadelphia, jan. 2, 1755.

"Sir,

Since my last, we have five days ago received certain intelligence, that a body of nigh 6000 men, of the best troops of France, selected and sent over upon this particular service, are just arrived at the lower fort on the Ohio, and are employed, even in this rigorous season, in fortifying that country. In september last, the french men of war that brought them over, were seen not far from the entrance into the river St. Lawrence, into which, we are now certain they all went, and landed at Quebec. After a short stay in that city, they were seen by our indian traders passing the lakes Oswego and Erie, in a prodigious number of battoes, of which the several governors received notice, though we did not then conjecture that it was an armament from old France; till now that we are too certain of it.

Notwithstanding this, our assembly continues as obstinate as ever; nor have we as yet any probability of their giving any money for our defence, although we hear they are to adjourn in two days. The governor has beseeched them to consider the defenceless state of the province, and establish a regular militia, but in vain. He also observes, that the activity of the french at this rigorous season cannot but convince the world, that they have formed some grand design with regard to this continent, and that they have made their
first

for pushing our colonies much further, especially as they had not a single regiment from Europe to defend them; and their enemies were continually receiving supplies; which together with their advantageous situation for a war, having little or no frontier to defend, made them much more than a match for the english colonies, who have such an immense one, without any thing to defend it with. Thus we find the french advanced with such hasty strides, that at the beginning of this year, their camp and forts upon the Ohio, and the parts adjacent, were not more than 225 miles, horizontal distance, from the city of Philadelphia, and only about two days march from some of our back settlements.

At last we find that a general was appointed to command in America; his majesty constituted general Braddock generalissimo of all the troops which were in, or should be sent to America; and accordingly this general arrived in Virginia in february; and as soon, as he possibly could, sent expresses to the several governors to meet him, in order to have a consultation on the business of the approaching campaign. This convention, by appointment of the general, was held at Alexandria in Virginia. After much debating it was agreed, that for the preservation of Oswego, and reduction of Niagara, Shirley's and Pepperel's regiments should proceed to lake Ontario; on which lake, one or more armed vessels of about 60 ton each should be built, to command it. This part of the service was committed to Mr. Shirley's care; while general Braddock attacked

first attack upon Pensilvania, as being in the center, and being not only the most plentiful, but the most defencelefs and unwieldy of all his majesty's colonies. Having once got footing here, they will issue forth upon the other colonies on either side; and as they have such a large body already in the field, we apprehend it is their design, early in the spring, to fortify the passes in the mountains; and if they accomplish this, and can find provisions, they will be able to stand against three times their numbers."

fort du Quefne; and the provincial troops, commanded by general Johnfon, marched to inveft Crown Point.

Purfuant to thefe refolutions, general Braddock, at the head of 2200 men, began his march againft fort du Quefne, and arrived at fort Cumberland in his way thither, the 10th of may; from thence to fort du Quefne is not lefs than 140 miles: Mr. Braddock began his march from the former on the 10th of june; leaving the garrifon under the command of col. Innes. From the time the general marched from fort Cumberland, we may begin to date the mifcarriage of the expedition, which proceeded from a thoufand different reafons, which it is now my bufinefs to fhow.

Innumerable were the difficulties he had to furmount, in a country rugged, pathlefs, and unknown, a-crofs the allegheney mountains, through unfrequented woods, and dangerous defiles; but thefe dangers were doubly encreafed, by the difappointments which the general met with in almoft every thing he had to do with the provinces. We find he complains very much of this in his letters to the miniftry in England, efpecially in one, wherein he particularizes all that had been promifed him; amongft which was the quarter-mafter-general, who affured him that he might depend on 2500 horfes, and 200 waggons from Virginia and Maryland; of which he only received 20 waggons and 200 horfes. In like manner did all his expectations come to little, merely through the difaffection and negligence of all the perfons with whom he had any dealings. We may conceive the difficulties which Mr. Braddock met with in this terrible march, when we confider that he was obliged (to ufe his own expreffions) to be continually employed in making a road, as he proceeded with infinite labour a-crofs mountains and rocks of an exceffive heighth, which are fteep, and divided by torrents and rivers.

In

In spight of all these difficulties, general Braddock was obliged to set forward, on his march against fort du Quesne, which he did, as I have said, on the 10th of june, with his little army in two divisions : at the head of the first, consisting of 1400 men, was the general himself, with the greatest part of the ammunition and artillery : the second, with the provisions, stores, and heavy baggage, was led by col. Dunbar, (a man of great prudence and military judgment) with about 800 men, with orders to follow the general as fast as the service would admit. The general having by this means lessened his line of march, proceeded with great expedition, in hopes of being able to attack the enemy before they were joined by a detachment of 500 regular troops ; insomuch that he left the rear near forty miles behind. On the 8th of july he encamped within 10 miles of fort du Quesne; and on the 9th, in his march through the woods towards that fort, was attacked by a body of french and indians ; the former in the front, and the latter on each side, in ambuscade, which began with a quick and heavy fire upon the vanguard, under lieut. col. Gage, from the indians. Immediately the main body, in good order and high spirits, advanced to sustain them. Orders were then given to halt and form into battalia. At this juncture, the van falling back upon them in great confusion, a general pannic seized the whole body of the soldiery, and all attempts to rally them proved utterly ineffectual ; but being rallied by their officers, with much difficulty they gave one fire ; and even after they had fell back on the main body, they were with unspeakable difficulty once more rallied by their officers, and stood one fire from the enemy, but then without returning it, both regiments fled with the utmost terror and precipitation, deserting their officers ; all of whom, and the general, exerted their utmost activity to relieve the troops from their universal surprise and disorder : but they were equally deaf to intreaties and commands. During this scene of confusion, they expended their ammunition in the wildest, and most unmeaning fire. Some discharging their pieces on our parties, who were advanced from the main body for the recovery of the cannon. After three hours spent in this melancholy situation, enduring a terrible slaughter from (it may be said) an invisible foe, orders were given to sound a retreat, that the men might be brought to cover the waggons: these they surrounded but a short space of time; for the enemy's fire being again warmly renewed from the front and left flank, the whole army took to immediate flight; leaving behind them all the artillery, provisions, ammunition, baggage, military chest, together with the general's cabinet, containing his instructions, and other papers of consequence *. So great was the consternation of the soldiers, that it was impossible to stop their career, flying with the utmost precipitation three miles from the field of action; where only one hundred men began to make a more orderly retreat.

What the real strength of the enemy was, is to this day uncertain; but it has been very confidently reported, that they had upwards of 2000 regular forces, including the canadian militia, which in that country is equal in usefulness to the regular troops from old France; besides considerable numbers of indians, who were planted in ambuscade, and from whom our men suffered by far the most. On our side the loss was very great; but more particularly so, in the death of several officers of great merit, who sacrificed their lives for the service of their country, with singular and heroic bravery. The general, after having five horses shot under him, received a wound in his lungs through his right arm, of which he died in four days. His secretary, eldest son of major general Shirley, a

* The french sometime after published a large memorial, containing the conduct of the british ministry; and as vouchers to the facts advanced in the memorial, they published all the papers which they found in Mr. Braddock's cabinet.

gentleman

gentleman of a very good character, was killed on the spot, by a shot through his head. Sir Peter Halket, colonel of the 44th regiment, was killed, with several other officers of distinction. Mr. Orme, capt. Morris, both aid-de-camps, were wounded; as was lieut. col. Gage and Burton; besides many other officers both killed and wounded, who, if it had pleased God to have spared their lives, would in all probability hereafter have been useful ornaments to their country.

To what causes this unhappy defeat is to be ascribed, has been matter of much inquiry, and animated many debates. Some of the officers charged the defeat to the cowardice of the men; but in a representation they made to Mr. Shirley, by order of the crown, they in some measure apologize for their behaviour; alledging, that they were harrassed by duties unequal to their numbers, and dispirited through want of provisions: that time was not allowed them to dress their food: that their water (the only liquor they had) was both scarce and of a bad quality: in fine, that the provincials had disheartened them, by repeated suggestions of their fears of a defeat, should they be attacked by indians; in which case the european method of fighting would be entirely unavailing. These were some of the many mutual complaints on both sides; but there were some partial and ill-designing persons, who, contrary to the general knowledge and opinion of all that were in the least acquainted with the general's conduct; laid the ill success of the day to his door; but when we come to consider well the difficulties he met with, together with the positiveness of his orders, it will clearly appear, that very little of Mr. Braddock's conduct was through his own choice, but actual necessity. Many inconsiderate people have attacked the general's military capacity, alledging that the loss of the battle was owing to his rashness; but I have been assured by several creditable gentlemen, who were eye-witnesses

nesses of Mr. Braddock's actions that day, that he did most incomparably well in every order which he gave, and in all his management of the march over the mountains to the moment he was killed, no man could possibly shew greater military skill, or even more knowledge of the nature of the service on which he was sent: and as to the clamours that were raised against him in England, it was no more than would always attend a general who commanded in North America, that was attended with ill success, by reason of the predominancy of the spirit of party, which breathes throughout all the english colonies, more, if possible, than in their mother country.

On the death of this brave though unfortunate general, the command of the troops devolved on col. Dunbar, who commanded the rear party, several miles short of the place of action. When the routed troops joined Dunbar's men, the terror diffused itself through the whole army. In this scene of dreadful confusion, the commander nor any of his officers were listened to or regarded; insomuch, that the men, fearful of an unpursuing enemy, had wasted all their ammunition, and so much of their provision, for accelerating their flight, that Mr. Dunbar was obliged to send for 30 horse loads of the latter, before he reached fort Cumberland: where he arrived in a few days, with the shattered remains of the english troops.

In this melancholy manner ended so important an expedition. This defeat had the worst consequences imaginable; as it gave so much spirit and alacrity to our enemies afterwards; and went a great way in keeping the indians firm to their new allies: so on the contrary, we suffered by the battle, as much as the enemy gained; from that time, the indians in our interest, despised us as not able even to protect ourselves, and much less them; and that in a country where we were so much more numerous than the french.

french. But the indians were not the only people terrified by Mr. Braddock's defeat; an univerfal pannic feized on all our colonies, out of which they did not foon recover, and which confequently muft have been of the greateft differvice to our caufe. Many perfons in England have taken great pains to find out by whofe ill conduct this battle was loft. But with a very little reflection it will appear plain, that no fingle perfon was the reafon of it; but a chain of a thoufand different accidents, and blunders in the minifters who planned the expedition, and the difaffection of the provincials to the fervice. The capital miftake of all, was the landing the troops at firft in Virginia, whereas they ought certainly to have been landed in Penfilvania; for Mr. Braddock could get neither provifions nor carriages in Virginia, both of which he might have had in great plenty in Penfilvania; and what was as material, the fhortnefs of the rout to fort du Quefne, by way of Penfilvania, which would have fhortened their march at leaft fix weeks, and might have been performed with half the fatigue and expence of that, by way of Virginia. But in every fcheme which was planned by the then miniftry in England, we find fo much fhort-fightednefs and fuch manifeft weaknefs, that we cannot at all wonder at the ill fuccefs which attended their adminiftration.

Let me afk any impartial perfon, in what manner he thinks the affairs of England could be carried on, when one minifter had the fupreme direction of the cabinet, and when that minifter's only pretenfions for the high employments he poffeffed, was a parliamentary intereft; without being acquainted with the true interefts of the nation he governed, or poffeffing abilities to promote them.

CHAP.

## CHAP. II.

*Affairs in Europe. Preparations for war. King's meſ-*
*ſage to the parliament. Addreſſes. Commons grant the*
*king one million on account. King's ſpeech. Parlia-*
*ment prorogued. King goes to Hanover. Mirepoix,*
*the french ambaſſador, ſets out for France. King lands*
*in England. Parliament meets. King's ſpeech. Ad-*
*dreſſes. Treaties with Heſſe Caſſel and Ruſſia. Changes*
*in the miniſtry. Reflections.*

AT the beginning of the year 1754, the ſtate of affairs in Europe was much different from what it was in America; where war in reality was as much carried on as ever it was afterwards; but in Europe peace was avowed between the two nations; and while both kingdoms thought of preparing for that war, which moſt able men ſaw was nigh, ſtill the miniſters of each proteſted to each other, that war was the furtheſt from their thoughts; which aſſurances, on the part of England, I believe were extremely true; for though the proceedings of the french, even at that time, ought to have rouſed the britiſh mininiſtry to reſent it in the moſt enforſive manner; yet they knew very well, that to keep themſelves in the power they enjoyed, it was neceſſary that the nation ſhould not be led into a war with France; for then (as always was the caſe) the miniſtry in England muſt conſequently fall in pieces.

In purſuance of ſuch a plan, we find them practiſing the loweſt arts, and putting up with the greateſt injuries, ſooner than reſent in a juſt and rigorous manner, the wrongs their country had received. The french took notice of this deſpicable behaviour, and reſolved to turn it to their good: inſomuch, that, no ſooner did they find who they had to deal with, but they continued their encroachments in America with
double

double diligence. At laſt, however, theſe peaceable miniſters were obliged, whether they would or no, to ſee the preparations that were making in all the ports of France, which they could not poſſibly do, without being alarmed; they as uſual, applied to the french ambaſſador at London; but his anſwers to their applications being too frivolous and quibbling, to be depended upon; they were obliged for ſafety ſake to arm, in their own defence. This meaſure, though too late, was certainly right, and might have been more effectual, had it been made uſe of earlier.

At this time, the duke de Mirepoix was employing all his abilities, to prevent the juſt reſentment of Great Britain againſt his nation, for the hoſtilities committed by the french in North America; with the moſt religious aſſurances that his court was ſincerely inclined to adjuſt finally and expeditiouſly all diſputes ſubſiſting between the two crowns in the new world\*.

By ſome trifling preparations which they made at Calais, Dunkirk, &c. they endeavoured to perſuade us, that they intended an invaſion of England; but I think nothing in the world can be plainer, than that the french at that time had as much thoughts of of invading the moon, as ever they had of invading England. The nation was greatly alarmed; and twenty fiſhing boats on the coaſt with a camp in a maritime province of France, we found ſufficient to affrighten us into an immenſe expence to guard againſt that danger which never was to come.

On the 25th of march, his majeſty ſent a meſſage to the houſe of commons, in which he obſerves, That the preſent ſituation of affairs

---

\* Vide the memorial which the french ambaſſador delivered to the britiſh miniſtry, the 5th of january, and the anſwer to it. This and many other curious pieces which I have quoted, are to be ſeen in the memorial publiſhed by the court of France, under the title of " The conduct of the engliſh miniſtry."

having

having made it necessary for him to augment his forces by sea and land; and to take such other measures, as might best tend to preserve the general peace of Europe, and to secure the just rights and possessions of his crown in America; as well as to repel any attempts whatsoever that may be made to support or countenance any designs which may be formed against his majesty and his kingdoms; his majesty did not doubt of the concurrence and support of that house, in making such augmentations, &c. as the honour of his crown, the true interest of his people, and the security of his dominions might require, in the present critical conjuncture of affairs.

In answer to this message, the lords and commons both presented most loyal, dutiful and affectionate addresses to his majesty.

But what was of more consequence, was the following resolution, which passed the house of commons on the 26th, in consequence of the above message and addresses: "That the sum of one million be granted to his majesty upon account, towards augmenting the forces by sea and land; and taking such measures for the security of his majesty's dominions, as may be necessary in the present conjuncture."

No other material business was transacted this session. On the 25th of april his majesty came to the house, and having given his consent to such bills as were ready; he made a gracious speech to both houses; after which, the lord chancellor, by his majesty's command, prorogued the parliament to the 27th of may.

In this manner ended this session of parliament; in my account of it I have been as brief as possible; and indeed I should have omitted saying any thing of it, but I could not with propriety have made such omission, as it had a manifest connection with the war. For the future I design to give no further account of the affairs of the parliament of England, than has

any

any material connection with the military part of this history. In the session, of which I have just spoke, we find much unanimity and steadiness in following his majesty's will; and the grant of one million on account, shows that the commons had a very good opinion of his majesty's designs and measures (at this time) in repelling the encroachments that were making in his dominions. It was very remarkable in this session, to see the loyalty and affection of those members in the house, from whom no such extraordinary fidelity was expected; more particularly at this time.

His majesty having formed a design of visiting his german dominions this year, set out from St. James's on the 28th of april, about five o'clock in the morning: he went over Westminster bridge in a post chaise, through St. George's fields, over London bridge, and proceeded for Harwich, where he embarked; and in a little time landed safe at Helvoetsluys in Holland, in his way to Hanover. Before his majesty's departure, he appointed several noblemen and others lords justices for the administration of the government, during his majesty's absence; at the head of whom was his royal highness the duke.

The only act of importance they did, was the ordering the duke de Mirepoix, the french ambassador, to depart the kingdom in 24 hours: he received these orders on the 22d of july, and set out for France on the 24th, at four o'clock in the morning, for fear of being insulted by the mob. Matters between the two nations were come to such a crisis, that it would have been a jest for the ambassador to have stayed any longer.

On the 16th of september his majesty landed at Margate from Holland, and the same day arrived safe at Kensington; being convoyed in his passage by my lord Anson, with the following ships:

Ships

| Ships. | Guns. | Men. |
|---|---|---|
| Windsor | 60 | 400 |
| Falmouth | 50 | 350 |
| Romney | 44 | 280 |
| Greyhound | 24 | 160 |
| Centaur | 24 | 160 |
| Wasp | 10 | 70 |
| Wolf | 10 | 70 |

I have before said that the parliament was prorogued to may 27; after several adjournments, it met the 12th of november. In his majesty's speech he mentioned two treaties which he had concluded with the empress of Russia and the landgrave of Hesse Cassel, which soon after occasioned a warm debate in the house of lords; for the duke of Marlborough stood up and moved for an address of thanks; in which motion there were several expressions which seemed to imply an approbation of those treaties: this was, by several, objected to; but the motion was seconded by the earl of Marchmont: many amendments were proposed, and it occasioned a long debate, in which the duke of Marlborough, the earl of Marchmont, the duke of Bedford, the duke of Newcastle, the lord chancellor, and the earl of Granville, spoke for the motion; and the earl Temple, the earl of Pomfret, and the lord Talbot against it: also, the earl of Hallifax spoke particularly against the treaties; but upon the question's being put, the motion was agreed to without a division.

In the address of the commons were these expressions, " And we think ourselves bound in justice and gratitude to assist your majesty against insults and attacks that may be made against any of your majesty's dominions, though not belonging to the crown of Great Britain," which occasioned a very long debate; but it was agreed to at last, though not without being thought by many, a little extraordinary. The
assurances

assurances of assistance which were made his majesty, the reader will find hereafter were fully made good.

I am now come to give the reader an account of a transaction which occasioned much discourse; I mean the treaties with Hesse Cassel and Russia; a measure as much praised by some, as it was condemned by others. The following is an extract from that with Hesse Cassel, signed at Hanover june 18.

I. The prince of Hesse engages to hold in readiness 8000 men, of which 1400 are to be horse, during four years from the signing this treaty, for the service of his britannic majesty, to march immediately after being required, if for the defence of the low countries; and within two months, if for the defence of England or Hanover. To be commanded by hessian officers, and to swear fidelity to the king of Great Britain, upon their being first mustered by an english commissary.

II. Each battalion of foot to have two field pieces.

III. His majesty engages to pay for every trooper or dragoon 80 crowns banco, and for every foot soldier 30 crowns banco.

IV. The king engages to pay, during this treaty, an annual subsidy of 150,000 crowns banco, the crown reckoned at four shillings and ninepence three farthings, english money, from the time of signing the treaty, till the troops shall be required to march, and 300,000 crowns from their being required to march, till they enter into the pay of his majesty; and from their entering into such pay, the landgrave to enjoy an annual subsidy of 150,000 crowns. When the troops shall be again sent back, the subsidy shall be again raised to 300,000, which shall be annually paid from the time of their entering the landgrave's territories to the expiration of the treaty.

V. If these troops are required to serve in Germany, they shall be put on the same foot with his majesty's forces; and if in England or Ireland, on the same foot with his british forces.

D      VI. If

VI. If any of these troops shall be cut off, or the artillery lost or destroyed, his majesty shall defray all expences of recruiting and remounting them, and make good the loss of the guns.

VII. The king shall keep these troops in his service during all the time of the treaty, and employ them where he pleases, provided it be not on board the fleet, or beyond the seas.

VIII. The king shall send back these troops if the landgrave should be attacked, paying them a month's pay, and furnishing them with transport vessels at his own expence, affording him the succour of such other troops as the case shall require, to be continued till entire security is obtained. The landgrave of Hesse also engages, that if his majesty shall be attacked, he will yield him all the succour in his power, and continue it till an advantageous peace shall be concluded.

IX. To claim the succours stipulated by this treaty, it shall suffice, that either of the parties are attacked by force of arms, without having used open force against him who attacks him.

X. This body of 8000 shall be augmented to 12000, if his majesty shall require it, on the same conditions; the additional body of 4000 men to be ready six months after demanded, and the subsidy for them to commence from the time of the demand.

XI. This treaty shall subsist for four years.

XII. The ratifications to be exchanged six months after the signature.

Such was the treaty with Hesse Cassel, and, the better to make my remarks upon it, I shall give the reader an abstract of that with Russia, signed at Petersburgh 30 september, N. S. when by comparing them together we shall be the better able to judge of the wisdom of the english ministry in concluding these two treaties.

Treaty

## Treaty with Ruffia.

I. Recites, that the emprefs has, for the mutual defence of herfelf and his majefty, at all events marched to the frontiers of Livonia, adjoining to Lithuania, 55000 men, of which 40000 are infantry of her regular troops, and 15000 cavalry; and ftipulates, that they fhall continue there as long as the prefent convention fhall fubfift.

II. The emprefs engages to hold in readinefs on the coafts of that province, during the fame time, 40 or 50 gallies with their crews, in condition to act on the firft notice.

III. Thefe troops and gallies fhall not act, except his britannic majefty or his allies are attacked, and then the commanding officer, as foon as he fhall receive his majefty's requifitions, fhall make a diverfion with 30,000 of the infantry, and all the 15,000 cavalry, and at the fame time fhall embark the other 10,000 infantry on board the gallies, in order to make a defcent, according to the exigency of the cafe.

IV. If his majefty's german dominions fhall be attacked, the emprefs will regard it as a cafe of the alliance of 1742.

V. His majefty engages to pay 500,000 l. fterling per annum, in confideration of this fervice, from the time the ruffian troops fhall, in confequence of his requifition, pafs the frontiers of their country. The payment to be always four months in advance, the firft to be on the day the troops pafs the frontiers.

VI. The emprefs takes upon herfelf the fubfiftance and payment of thefe troops both by fea and land.

VII. The emprefs engages not to recall thefe troops, even though fhe herfelf fhould be attacked by any other power; and his majefty promifes, that in fuch cafe, he will immediately furnifh the fuccour ftipulated in the treaty of 1742.

VIII. If, contrary to all expectation, a war should break out, his majesty shall send into the Baltick a squadron of force suitable to the circumstances, to act in concert with the russian army, as long as they shall be within reach of each other.

IX. A british commissary and admiral shall always assist in councils of war, with the russian commander of the auxiliary troops.

X. The russians shall be entitled to all plunder.

XI. The king engages to procure a passage for these troops through Poland, if necessary.

XII. This convention to subsist four years.

XIII. If peace be made, or the object of the diversion ceases within four years, the russian troops then to return and enjoy the succour agreed on three months. If no peace, the parties to agree on the prolongation of the convention.

XIV. The convention to be ratified within two months.

A separate and secret article.

His majesty engages to pay 100,000 l. per ann. always one year in advance, from the ratification of this treaty to the march of the troops beyond the frontier, when the payment of 500,000 l. per ann. is to commence in its stead.

Without considering the necessity, if there was any, of these treaties, and the goodness of them, we should observe, that by the fifth article of the treaty with Hesse, it is agreed, that every trooper shall first be purchased at about 20 l. sterling, and every foot soldier at about 7 l. which in all makes about 112,000 l. levy money; besides this, the landgrave is to have about 37,000 l. annually before the troops march; and as soon as they march, he is to receive 74,000 l. annually, till they enter into pay, according to that of Hanover or England; at which time the subsidy returns to about 37,000 l. annually; which again, when the troops are sent back,

is

is to return to 74,000 l. a year, during the whole duration of the treaty.

By the compact with Ruffia, the emprefs is to affift England with 55,000 troops, and to tranfport and maintain them for the annual fubfidy of 500,000 l. without any further confideration for death of men and horfes, or lofs of military ftores, and no return of them is to take place during the duration of the treaty, even though the emprefs herfelf fhould be attacked. The reader need not be told how infinitely more advantageous the treaty with Ruffia was, than that with Heffe Caffel, for it explains itfelf: who would have imagined, that we fhould ever have preferred the affiftance of 8000 heffians, before a fupply of ruffians, when the former was ten times as expenfive as the latter; but ftill this amazing folly (if I may be allowed the expreffion) afterwards appeared in the britifh councils, as we fhall fee hereafter.

If we confider the treaty with Ruffia, it will appear very plain that it was intended againft the king of Pruffia; for it is agreed by the fecond article, that thefe troops are to be held in readinefs on the frontiers of Livonia, and the gallies cruizing on that coaft: and that, on his majefty's requifition, the commanding officer fhall make a diverfion with 30,000 infantry, and 15,000 cavalry, which fpeaks in fo many words that they were defigned againft his pruffian majefty. It feems that the britifh court, was at this time very jealous of that monarch's intentions; they were fearful he intended to attack Hanover, and to guard againft this danger (whether or not it was a real one, I am not able to fay) they thought it neceffary to conclude the treaty abovementioned with Ruffia. Againft what other power could this treaty be defigned? It was impoffible that the ruffians were to attack France, or defend us againft the french, for gallies are quite unfit for the ocean; befides which, the article of their making a defcent with 10,000 men,

men sufficiently speaks that they were intended to further the operation of the land army. In short, from every article of this treaty, it appears to be manifestly intended to defend the electorate of Hanover against the supposed ill intentions of his prussian majesty. But the affairs of Europe took such a course afterwards, as made this treaty (for that purpose at least) useless. But let the merit of them be ever so much extolled, they will appear to me to be but a very short-sighted remedy for the mischief they were intended to prevent. And I freely own the management in making them, is to ointricate for me to pretend to unravel.

In the middle of november, there happened several changes in the ministry. Sir Thomas Robinson resigned the seals, and was made keeper of the rolls; in the room of lord Barrington, who was made secretary at war; Mr. Fox being removed from the war office and made secretary of state. And soon after appeared a new commission for the treasury, consisting of the following lords; the duke of Newcastle, first lord commissioner, the earl of Darlington, sir George Lyttleton, Thomas Hay, and Robert Newgent esqrs. at the same time, sir George Lyttleton was made chancellor of the exchequer, in the room of Mr. Legge. But this new set of ministers did not hold together long, for we find, that on the 16th of december, the earl of Darlington, and Mr. Hay, removed from the treasury, and were appointed paymasters general in the room of Mr. Pitt; and earl Gower sworn of the privy-council, and keeper of the privy seal; and the duke of Marlborough made master general of the ordnance: the same day, lord Anson, sir William Rowley, William Ponsonby, Thomas Villiers, Edward Boscawen, Richard Edgecumbe, esqrs. and lord Bateman were constituted lords of the admiralty.

Such were the men, who were at this time set at the head of affairs; but only a few of them were

concerned

concerned or confulted in the adminiftration of the moft material affairs of the ftate.

From the face our affairs wore at the beginning of this war, we fhall not have great reafon to exult in our fuccefs. The reader has feen the begining of a war between the two nations; and if we confider what the french made the aim and end of all their proceedings, namely, that tract of land in America, on the river Ohio (of which I have fpoke fo particularly in the former chapter) or as the french were pleafed to term it, for a " few barren acres," we fhall certainly conclude, that they in a manner got their defires accomplifhed. Indeed I have fhown how loyal and unanimous the parliament of Great Britain was in their refolutions to fupport and defend his majefty's right to the utmoft; but I believe the reader will join with me in being of opinion, that all the neceffary meafures to hinder a rupture with France from taking place, were not exerted. But this we fhall be able to judge of clearly by and by, when we come to be further acquainted with the ftate of the quarrel, when it was more advanced, from its infancy.

# CHAP. III.

*Naval affairs in Europe, during the year* 1755. *Great diligence used by both nations to equip several squadrons. Macnamara sails from Brest; and Boscawen from Portsmouth. Alcide and Lys taken. Holbourn sails from Spithead. Du Guay arrives at Cadiz. Hawke sails to intercept him. Returns without doing it. Byng sails from Spithead. Court martial on lord Harry Powlett. Boscawen arrives at Spithead. Reflections.*

THE naval affairs of the two nations were not neglected. And indeed the english were more forward by sea than by land, that is naturally their element; and, if that nation would more confine its military views by land, and exert them more by sea, they would soon convince their neighbours how impolitic it would be to break with them. But we find that both nations at this period were extremely diligent in preparing their maritime forces for any exigency of affairs that might happen. So early as january 1754, in England, impress warrants were issued by the lords of the admiralty; and in two days time upwards of 2000 seamen were taken on the river Thames; to man (as it was then given out) a squadron for the East-Indies: and the press continued with great violence in most of the ports of England, several thousand able hands were picked up, and many entered themselves voluntarily.

Neither were the french indolent; but with their usual diligence were very vigorous in their naval preparations; and in the beginning of 1755, laid a general embargo on all the ports of France, to man with the utmost expedition, a fleet which was fitting out in Brest; and so early as the first of january, sir Thomas Robinson, one of his majesty's principal secretaries of state, was informed by de Cosne, the secretary

secretary of the embassy at Paris, that seventeen men of war were ordered to be equipped at Brest; the admiral's ship to be of 70 guns, and that the greatest part of this fleet was destined for America. In the sequel we shall find, that de Cosne's advice proved true; but he was not the only one that sent this intelligence to the ministry in England, for it was repeated from many places, particularly from Paris, with many additional circumstances. And indeed the truth was, that the french exerted at this time all their diligence and industry to forward their preparations for getting a strong squadron to sea, which at that time was advancing very fast at Brest, where they worked night and day to fit the ships for sea. Nor were these armaments confined to Brest only, Rochfort and Toulon were filled with workmen; but matters were not so forward there as at Brest, the squadron at which port was expected to be ready to sail by the middle of april; but in this calculation, the french were mistaken. Many of the ships that were to compose this squadron, were to carry no more than 20 or 22 guns, as they were designed for the transporting a large body of land forces. However, although the orders from court were positive, the wind would not permit this fleet to sail till the third of may; at which time it did with so fair a wind, that it was out of sight in a short time. This grand fleet consisted of 18 sail of the line and 9 frigates, carrying 1532 guns.

On the 20th of may Macnamara the admiral, returned to Brest, with nine ships of the line, having convoyed the transports beyond the capes; and left them to proceed to Canada, according to their instructions, with a fair wind.

Now we have seen the french fleet to sea, it is necessary to return, and take notice of what had been doing in England by sea during that time. The ministry here, were very active in their naval preparations, to get the english fleet to sea as soon as that of France;

France; and indeed they were before the french by a fortnight; for admiral Boscawen sailed from Portsmouth the 19th of april, with 13 sail of the line, and one frigate, carrying 738 guns, and 5300 men.

The reader only need compare the force of these two fleets together, and he will at first sight perceive the great oversight in the ministry's sending fourteen ships to intercept twenty-seven. And yet this egregious omission in british politicks, was still out-done by the remedy which was applied to supply the former defect. That of sending six ships of the line and one frigate, under admiral Holbourn, to follow Mr. Boscawen; who did not sail till the 11th of may, when it was scarce possible for him to escape Macnamara's fleet, which had sailed but eight days before. And yet, this was the only effort made by the british ministry for several months, to counteract the vigorous armaments of the whole naval power of France.

His orders were to join Mr. Boscawen as soon as possible; but this he was not able to perform, till the 21st of june, when he met with admiral Boscawen's squadron, formed in a line before the river St. Lawrence, cruising on the banks of Newfoundland; the same ship which brought the news of this junction, also acquainted the ministry with the capture of the Lys and Alcide, two french men of war in de la Mothe's squadron: these ships having parted from the rest, fell in with the english squadron, the admiral of which ordered the Dunkirk, Torbay, and Monarque to chace; and the Dunkirk coming up first with the Alcide, hailed the captain, requiring him to put back, and come under the admiral's stern; the frenchman in reply, asked if it was peace or war; captain Howe (the commander of the Dunkirk) said he did not know, but repeated his orders; the frenchman again asked, if it was peace or war; and captain Howe again replied, he knew not, but
would

have him prepare for the worft, as he every moment expected a fignal from the admiral to fire upon him for not coming to. At the fame time, obferving fome foldiers, and land officers, with feveral ladies, ftanding very thick upon deck, he admonifhed them to go down; they foon complied, and the frenchman, not waiting for captain Howe's broadfide, immediately fired upon him. The other french man of war ftruck to the Torbay and Monarque. This is the moft probable account we had of this action; many people doubted whether there was any converfation at all between the two captains; but I have been affured by undoubted authority that there was *.

In the mean time the french were in fome pain for their fquadron in America, left it fhould be met with and intercepted in its return from thence: to remedy which, in the beft manner they were able, they fent the nine fhips with which M. de Macnamara returned to Breft, under the command of M. du Guay, a french admiral to favour their return, who fet fail from Breft on the 4th of june.

His orders were to cruife on the coaft of Portugal, to favour the return of M. la Mothe and Salvert, in cafe of bad news from America; du Guay cruifed in the Atlantic ocean, near the ftreights of Gibraltar; but not meeting with the other french fleet, which did not return till fome time afterwards, put into Cadiz; and during his ftay in that place, the englifh miniftry difpatched fir Edward Hawke on the 24th of july, with 21 fhips of the line, and five

---

* The Dunkirk's guns in this fight were all double-fhotted every round, and being yard-arm and yard-arm, did fuch terrible execution, that the officers of the Alcide could not keep the men to their quarters, and ran one of them through in order to deter the others; but all would not do, the frenchmen not liking fuch warm work; and M. le commodore himfelf, when he was brought prifoner on board the Dunkirk, told the brave captain Howe, that it was cruel to engage fo very clofe.

frigates

frigates to intercept him, in his return to Breſt, or any other french ſhips that might eſcape Mr. Boſcawen. But this meaſure was much condemned by thoſe who were knowing in ſea affairs; for, according to the advices which the miniſtry received concerning the naval armaments of the french, it was probable, that Hawke might fall in with du Guay's ſquadron of nine ſhips, joined by five ſhips from Rochfort, and ten from Breſt, (both which were ready to ſail from that port;) and ten ſhips in their return from America. By which it appears, that Hawke with 21 ſhips might very poſſibly have fell in with 35 french ones; and I believe the miniſtry that planned his expedition, had not ſo very great an opinion of engliſh courage as to ſuppoſe that Hawke would (in caſe of a battle) have come off conqueror.

Sir Edward Hawke's orders were to cruiſe off cape Finiſterre, till the french ſhips ſhould appear. If we are to judge of the wiſdom of theſe orders by the ſucceſs they met with, the reader, I believe, will not admire the prudence of them; for M. du Guay, as ſoon as he heard where Hawke was ſtationed, and what was his buſineſs, ſailed from Cadiz for Breſt; but not in the uſual tract, which he did to avoid the engliſh fleet; he ſteered directly weſt from Spain into the Atlantic ocean; when, being at a great diſtance from the coaſt, he changed his courſe, and ſtood directly for the land's end of England; by this precaution of ſailing weſt to a great diſtance, before he ſteered towards the channel, he paſſed on the outſide of all our fleet, cruiſing at cape Finiſterre, and arriving ſafe in the channel, fell in behind it with his ſquadron, and got ſafe into the harbour of Breſt, having left Cadiz the beginning of auguſt. Sir Edward Hawke not having been ſucceſsful in the cruiſe he was ſent upon, was called home, where,

however

however he did not arrive till the 29th of September *.

As to admiral Byng's expedition, or rather cruife, which he went upon the 14th of october, with ten sail of the line, being the western squadron; it did not afford much speculation for history. It is enough to say, that he returned the 22d of november, not having done any action of consequence.

I shall here present the reader with an affair, that reflected no great honour on the person chiefly concerned. I mean, the court martial on lord Harry Powlett. It seems lord Harry commanded his majesty's ship the Barfleur, one of the squadron with which sir Edward Hawke was sent to intercept the french admiral, du Guay. The case was this; in consequence of verbal orders from sir Edward Hawke on the the 23d of august, in the morning, lord Harry Powlett in the Barfleur, gave chase to a sail in the south east, which he pursued all night, and next morning was unable to find the fleet; and finding his rudder in a very bad condition, was obliged to put into port, without orders for so doing from the admiral. And for this action capt. Powlett was tried by a court martial, held on board the Prince George in Portsmouth harbour, the 20th, 21st, and 22d of october.

The following were the members that composed this court, viz.

    Henry Osborne, esq. vice-admiral of the red, president.
    Capt. Roger Martin,
    Hon. capt. John Hamilton,

---

* I should here mention a pretty extraordinary instance of the feigned politeness of our enemies the french; or rather of their pretended justice: I mean the capture which M. du Guay's squadron made, in its return to Brest, of the Blandford man of war of 20 guns, having governor Lyttleton on board for Carolina, and which was afterwards restored by order of the french court; I leave my readers to reflect on this piece of politeness.

Capt.

Capt. George Bridges Rodney,
Capt. John Montague,
Hon. capt. George Murray,
Capt. Thomas Fowke,
Capt. Richard Tyrrel,
Capt. William Lloyd,
Capt. R. Edwards.

The court having heard the evidence, and also what the prisoner had to offer, were of opinion, that he did not judge and act right in giving chace on the 24th of auguſt, to a ſail ſeen in the ſouth-weſt, when three ſail were ſeen in the north-eaſt, which might probably be part of the fleet; but it having clearly appeared to them, that his intentions were upright towards the ſervice, as he had before uſed his utmoſt endeavours to rejoin the fleet, on the ſtation it was in, when he ſeparated from it, and did afterwards uſe the like endeavours to join it on the rendezvous, they do not think this error deſerving of puniſhment, and do therefore unanimouſly only judge it proper to admoniſh him, as he is hereby admoniſhed to be more cautious in his future conduct.

As to his returning into port, the court are of opinion, that, conſidering the defects of the ſhip's rudder, his proceeding therein was very juſtifiable, and therefore they do unanimouſly acquit him of all blame upon that account; and he is hereby acquitted accordingly *.

It requires much caution to reflect on ſuch unlucky affairs as theſe. It is impoſſible for any perſon to be able to ſay, whether the court martial on lord Harry Powlett acted juſtly or not; but a private man is not to find fault with the proceedings of a court of juſtice: thus much I may be allowed to ſay, the nation was not pleaſed with their ſentence, with how much reaſon, I will not determine; but only obſerve, that lord Harry Powlett has never been employed ſince, in any ſtation of importance.

Such

Such was the determination of this unfortunate affair. The nation, in general, at this time, was eager to have every military offender feverely punifhed. At the eve of a war, examples of a juft feverity are, certainly neceffary; but more particularly fo, when a conftant train of ill fuccefs had baffled all our military undertakings. At the beginning of every war, it is neceffary to roufe the englifh from that fatal confufed inactivity, which fo diftinguifhes their councils from thofe of many other nations. But when once the fpirit of the people is raifed, it is then that englifh courage becomes fuccefsful, to the terror of their enemies.

CHAP.

# CHAP. IV.

*American affairs to the end of the year 1755. The chief command in North America falls on major general Shirley. His march to Oswego. Dunbar marches to Philadelphia. Battle at Lake George. Transactions at New York. Grand council of war. Plan of operations for the ensuing year agreed on. Reflections on the fruitless campaign of 1755.*

I Left (at the end of the first chap.) general Braddock utterly defeated by the french, and slain; on his unfortunate catastrophe, the command of his majesty's forces in North America devolved on major general Shirley, who having left New York, arrived at Albany in the beginning of july. This city was then the grand theatre for all the preparations, for the northern expedition against Crown Point, as well as that to the westward, for the reduction of Niagara. The general, on his arrival here, did not find the military preparations in such forwardness as he had reason to expect; insomuch, that he was obliged to wait at Albany on several disagreeable accounts; but his own troops were, in the mean time filing off, in different divisions from Schenactady, towards Oswego.

Oswego has long been the accustomed route, it is computed to be about 300 miles west from Albany, was formerly garrisoned by twenty-five men; but on the commencement of the late disputes the number was augmented to fifty; and early this spring fifty more were ordered up: and at the latter end of may capt. Bradstreet arrived there with two hundred, besides workmen to be employed in the naval preparations, pursuant to the scheme concerted in the congress of commissioners at Albany the last summer. On the 24th of july, general Shirley arrived at Schenactady, hectada, where he found lieut. col. Ellifon had embarked the day before, with the -th divifion of the 50th regiment, for Ofwego; and that lieut. col. Mercer with five companies of the 51ft, and one of the 50th, were ftill remaining for want of battoe-men. On the 29th, the general embarked with 97 battoes, loaded with military ftores, provifions and other neceffaries for the expedition; together with about 200 regular troops, 150 battoe men, and 40 indians, for Ofwego, leaving orders for lieut. col. Mercer to follow him as foon as poffible.

At laft, on the 18th of auguft, Mr. Shirley arrived at Ofwego. He found the works there in a very bad condition; the chief ftrength of the fort, was its being mounted with five fmall cannon, three or four pounders; it confifted of a ftone wall, and was fituated on the fouth edge of lake Ontario.

As foon as he arrived there, he took a furvey of the fortifications, and the adjacent country; and gave orders for erecting on the point, a ftrong log pallifaded fort, capable of mounting large cannon, and containing barracks for 300 men, which, from the dimenfions of its logs, might be defenfible againft three or four pounders; and, if it fhould be thought requifite to have a ftrong, regular fortification built round it another year, it would be of fervice whilft the new works were erecting; and for fecuring the place to the fouthward of the old fort, he determined, as foon as hands and time could be fpared for it, to have a fmall fquare fort of earth and mafonry, with four baftions, a rampart, parapet and ditch, containing barracks for 200 men, built on the other eminence.

General Shirley, during his ftay, received feveral accounts of the ftrength and defigns of the french at Niagara, which made him refolve upon an expedition thither; and the works of the new fort which he was building at Ofwego, were fo far advanced, that he hoped it might be ready in a few days

days to receive its artillery, he propofed to proceed to Niagara, with 600 regulars, befides the albany men and indians, and a fmall train of artillery; and having ordered the preparations to be forthwith made for the intended attempt; the 600 troops were drafted, and held themfelves in readinefs to embark. One great inducement for Mr. Shirley to perfift in the refolution he had taken to attack Niagara, was the arrival of eight battoes at Ofwego, on the 27th of feptember, containing forty barrels of flower, and thirteen of bread, which were the fpecies of provifions wanted.

The reader will no doubted be furprifed when he hears, that for all the advantages attending the Niagara expedition, yet it was laid afide by the general till the next year. The confiderations which had the greateft weight with him, to induce him to take this refolution, were thefe: that nothing more could have been done that year (fuppofing he had got the troops and artillery fafe before it) than to diflodge the french and demolifh the works, as the ftate of his provifions would not admit of his leaving a garrifon there, during the winter, for its defence; fo that an effectual poffeffion of that pafs could not have been taken that year; whereas, in the mean time, during the abfence of the veffels from Ofwego (all of which, it was neceffary for Mr. Shirley to have taken with him upon his attempt againft Niagara) it would have been in the power of the french to have tranfported a train of artillery without oppofition, a-crofs the lake to fort Frontenac, and have landed them near the eminence, behind the old fort of Ofwego, where the intended new fort was not begun to be built; in which cafe, they might not only have made themfelves mafters of Ofwego, but muft have cut off Mr. Shirley's return from Niagara; which would have been fatal likewife to the troops.

Such were the reafons given by Mr. Shirley and his friends, for not proceeding againft Niagara; certainly
the

the argument used to persuade us, that the scheme was really impossible to be executed successfully, is entirely fallacious, and its very foundation is sapped, when we come to enquire, why the works which Mr. Shirley erected at Oswego were not finished, or at least so far in fowardness, as to permit him to attempt the expedition : nor can I conceive, that it was so utterly impossible to leave a garrison in Niagara during the winter, since by the situation of that fort the french would not have been able to make themselves masters of it in that season, with the force which it was in their power to use against it. But one of the greatest objections to this change in the general's opinion is, his pretending that he could not leave the garrison in Niagara, by reason of the scarcity of provisions ; for it will be very palpable to the reader that the general did not use his utmost care in that article of providing provisions, at least in so great a degree as is pretended by his friends : it is very plain by the other parts of his conduct in this expedition, that he was well provided with every thing but provision ; and that he was not so very badly off in that regard as is pretended.

The difficulty which the general met with in forwarding the two forts, he was building, was certainly great ; but not in so great a degree as has been thought: It should be considered, that they were erected without any regular engineer, (an officer though, I should suppose Mr. Shirley might have procured) at the distance of 300 miles from any english settlement, where a larger supply of proper workmen and materials for strong fortifications could not be had ; and the bad weather retarded his expedition considerably ; besides which, part of their time was taken up in finishing a vessel then building for his majesty's service, in order to preserve the command of lake Ontario ; together with a large hospital and barracks for winter quarters, to contain upwards of 900 men ; the timber for all which, was to be cut from the

stem,

stem, and the ground on which the forts were building, to be cleared of the trees and underwood, with which it was covered.

The general having settled these matters at Ofwego, and finding a great accession of business advance, upon the death of general Braddock, began to think of leaving Ofwego, and proceeding to the colony of Massachuset's bay, of which he was governor.

Upon his departure, he left orders with the commanding officer of the garrison to finish the two forts in his absence; for although Mr. Shirley had spent so much time at Ofwego, yet these forts were not near complete; but to assist the commanding officer in furnishing and strengthening them, and the other works, he sent two engineers as early in the spring as he could.

I remarked before, that Mr. Shirley calculated these forts more for defence against musketry and small cannon of two or three pound ball, than large battering ones: for securing the forts against such as might be conveyed by the french on the lake, he depended upon having a superior naval force on the lake Ontario; on supposition that, if his majesty's vessels kept the command of the lake, it would be impracticable for the french to attack Ofwego. Having settled these matters, the general set out on the 24th of October, in a whale boat, attended by some battoes; and arrived at Albany the 4th of november.

Such was the end of the Ofwego expedition: the service which the general did there, had its uses; but he completed nothing; more might have been expected, considering the time he spent there; he certainly might (from the several accounts which we have of this transaction) have left Ofwego in such a condition, as to have had nothing to fear from a french invasion; the great difficulty of transporting cannon in that wild country, did indeed, in some measure, insure the safty of the fort; but then we

find

find that the general was ſtrangely out, in his imagining, that he rendered the lake ſecure by his naval force; he ought certainly to have left Oſwego in ſuch a condition, as to have been able to refiſt any force that the french could bring againſt it, by any road whatever, whether by land or the lake ; and this ſurely the general might have done, in the time he ſpent there.

I ſhall now purſue the account I gave of the military tranſactions under colonel Dunbar, in the ſouthern colonies. Having reached fort Cumberland, he diſpatched an indian expreſs to general Shirley, with an account of the defeat, and the neceſſary returns reſpecting the troops under his command; acquainting him, moreover, with his intention of marching to Philadelphia, and his hopes of meeting his orders at Shippenſburg. About the ſame time Mr. Dinwiddie wrote to Dunbar, propoſing a ſecond attempt on fort du Queſne; but a council being thereupon held, the members of which were col. Dunbar, lieut. col, Gage, governor Sharpe, major Chapman, major Sparke, and ſir John St. Clair, it was unanimouſly conceived, that Mr. Dinwiddie's ſcheme was impracticable. The very next day, being the 2d of auguſt, Dunbar began his march towards Philadelphia, with 1600 men, four ſix pounders, and as many cohorns ; leaving behind him the Virginia and Maryland companies, and about 400 wounded. At this ſudden departure of the forces, the Virginians were extremely diſobliged, as not only expoſing their frontiers and occaſioning the daily deſertion of their provincials ; but becauſe the enemy in flying parties, penetrated into the province, and on many of the inhabitants committed robberies and murder. Dunbar certainly acted right in retreating to Philadelphia; for this reaſon, becauſe in that province was ſeated one of the moſt conſiderable cities in all our plantations, which would have been of greater conſequence to the french to conquer, than ten times the number of ſcattered settlements

settlements in Virginia, of which that whole province consists.

Upon the advices received from Dunbar, Mr. Shirley gave orders for renewing the attempt; if the southern colonies would readily afford him a competent reinforcement: governor Morris having convened the Pensilvania assembly, he informed them of the retreat of the english army, and in a well drawn pathetic speech, pressed them to vigorous measures for the defence of their borders. They proceeded so far, as to vote the raising 50,000 l. but offering a bill for taxing the proprietary estate, an immediate rupture ensued; and in this manner broke up an assembly of as obstinate v------s, as any fellons that ever were sent over from Great Britain thither for slaves. Virginia being almost equally open to the irruptions of the enemy, four companies of rangers were ordered out, and the assembly voted 40,000 l. for furnishing 1000 men for the defence of their frontier. About the same time the council and assembly of New Jersey met, and the latter voted 30,000 l. for the public service; but as the house proposed to prolong the currency of the bills for nine years, to which Mr. Belcher (the governor) not being able to assent, 15,000 l. only, was raised, and its use restricted to keeping on foot her regiment at Oswego, commanded by col. Schuyler. At New York, the house of representatives assembled on the 5th of august, and set out with a generous spirit. They resolved to reinforce the provincial army destined for Crown Point with 400, the bill was actually passed the house for that purpose; but it afterwards dropped.

About a month before the departure of general Shirley from Oswego, major general Lyman being advanced with the troops to the carrying place, about 60 miles from Albany, was waiting the arrival of general Johnson, who set out from thence the 8th of august, with the train of artillery. Lyman had begun a fort at the landing, on the east side of Hudson's son's river, now called fort Edward. About the latter end of the month, general Johnson, with the main body, moved forward, 14 miles more northerly, and pitched his camp at the south end of lake George, before called lake Sacrament. By some indians, who had been sent as scouts, he received the following advices: that they had discovered a party of french and indians at Ticonderoga, situated on the isthmus between the north end of lake George and the southern part of the lake Champlain, 15 miles on this side Crown Point; but no works were then thrown up. To have secured this pass, which commanded the route to Crown Point, through the lake, had been a measure extremely adviseable. Mr. Johnson, informed of its importance, on the 1st of september, wrote to general Shirley, that he was impatient to get up his battoes; proposing then to proceed with part of the troops, and seize upon that pass; the french however took advantage of this delay of general Shirley's, and cut out work enough for him at his own camp.

The french fleet, which admiral Boscawen sailed in the spring to intercept, carried over, as I have elsewhere mentioned, the troops destined for the defence of Canada, with Monf. de Vaudreuil, governor general, and the baron de Dieskau, commander of the forces. The french court well apprised of the singular consequence of Oswego, had determined to reduce it. Such being the baron's instructions, he immediately proceeded to Montreal, from whence he detached 700 of his troops up the river, intending himself speedily to join them with the remainder. Just before he had made the necessary preparations, Montreal was alarmed with the news of our forming a numerous army near lake St. Sacrament, for the reduction of fort Frederick, and perhaps to penetrate into the heart of Canada. Whereupon, a grand council being held, the baron was importuned to proceed through lake Champlain, for the defence of that fortress: nor was he without great difficulty prevailed upon to alter his intended route.

It seems that the baron de Diefkau, waited in expectation of our army coming up to give him battle; but being disappointed therein, he resolved to advance against Johnson; designing, if he proved victorious, to lay waste all our northern colonies, lay the towns of Albany and Schenectady in ashes, and cut off all communication with Oswego. For the execution of which design, he embarked at fort St. Frederick, with 2000 men in battoes, and landed at the south bay, about 16 miles from the english encampment; his design was, first to attack and make himself master of fort Edward, and then attack Mr. Johnson in his camp; this he proposed to his troops, and was heard with pleasure by the regulars of his army; but the canadians and the militia were very much averse to that plan, they agreed to the attack of the general in his camp, as they expected to meet with no cannon to oppose them; in this however they were mistaken, for the english artillery was got up to the camp from fort Edward a day or two before the action, and of which the french had no intelligence. Diefkau, thus disappointed in his principal design, changed his route, and began to move against the main body at the lake. General Johnson had received advice by his indian scouts, that the enemy was marching towards fort Edward, where 250 of the New Hampshire regiment, and five companies of the New York regiment were posted, under the command of col. Blanchard; this was on the 7th of september, and the next morning a council of war was held, in which it was agreed to detach 1000 men, in order, either to succour fort Edward, or meet the french general in his return from that post, whether he was victorious or not. Accordingly this body of men marched about nine o'clock, under the command of col. Williams, an officer much esteemed for his personal bravery and good conduct.

The situation of the english was this: they were encamped on the banks of lake George, being covered on either side by a thick wooded swamp; in the front, the general had thrown up a breast work of trees felled, to which he drew up his cannon, that were afterwards of great service to him. The detachment under col. Williams was beat back by the french, about an hour and half after their departure; being much inferior to the enemy.

About eleven, the enemy appeared in sight; they marched in a very regular order towards the center of the english army, till they were within 150 yards of the breast work; when, to the utter astonishment of the english general, Dieskau made a halt for some time, which proved his ruin; the english army was in some consternation, and had the frenchman then began the attack, the fortune of the day might probably have been otherwise; but when they found the french army made this ill-timed halt, their spirits recovered, and they prepared to resist the enemy with an alacrity, which forboded the approaching victory. However, Dieskau began the attack, at the center of the english army, in good order, with his regulars: the canadians and indians were concealed among the swamps, on the flanks of the english army, and maintained an irregular and scattered fire. The first regular fire from the french were their regular's platoons, but did no great execution, being at too great a distance; on which the english artillery, commanded by capt. Eyre, began to play, when the engagement became general on both sides; the french regulars behaved well, and kept their ground and order for some time, with great resolution and good conduct; but the constant fire from the english artillery, disordered them, when their fire became very faint: they then moved to the right, and attacked col. Williams, col. Ruggles, and col. Titcomb's regiments, where they maintained a very warm fire for near an hour, still keeping up their fire in the other parts

parts of the line, but not very strong; the three regiments on the right, supported the attack so bravely, that the enemy was repulsed with considerable loss; at which time the english troops and indians leaped the breastwork pursued the enemy, slaughtered numbers, and took several prisoners; among whom, was the baron Diefkau, the french commander in chief, which made the victory on the side of the english complete; the pursuit of the enemy ended about seven o'clock. The loss of the french was upwards of 1000 men; that of the conquerors did not exceed 130 killed and 60 wounded; col. Titcomb was killed, major Johnson and major Nichols were wounded. Our greatest loss was in the detachment under col. Williams, who was killed, together with major Ashley, captains Ingersal, Puter, Ferral, Stoddert, M'Gimes and Steevens, all indian officers, with 40 indians and old Hendrik, the famous indian sachem.

It is to be remarked, that in this engagement, the indians (some of the Mohawks excepted) retired from the camp, and did not join the army till after the battle; this shows us very plain, that our good friends the indians were ready to join the conqueror, whether french or english; which I wonder at the more, as Mr. Johnson was allowed to have an universal influence over those with him in this expedition. But the general's conduct was impeached of a much greater mistake than that he was guilty of, in putting too much confidence in his indians, his not following the blow he had gained; it was objected against him, that had he pursued the enemy close, with spirit, he might with little difficulty have made himself master of Crown Point, the chief object of the expedition. It must be allowed that if we consider several expressions in the general's letter to the governors of the colonies, we shall find reason to believe, that he did not make the most of his advantage; and his seeming to be so much afraid of a " more formidable attack," makes us think that he had conceived much too great

notions

notions of the enemy he had conquered : as to his own perfonal bravery, I never heard the leaft flur thrown upon that.

Governor Shirley, as I mentioned before, arrived at New York, from Ofwego, the 2d of december; having, before he left Albany, wrote circular letters to the feveral governors upon the continent, as far weftward as Virginia, fummoning them to meet him there, in order to form a council of war, confifting (purfuant to one of his majefty's inftructions to him) of fuch of the governors upon the continent, and field officers of his majefty's troops, as could attend it. The council met the 12th, and although the invitation was general, it confifted but of few members.

Mr. Shirley opened the conference, by laying before them, his majefty's inftructions to general Braddock ; and then delivered his own fentiments to the board ; who declared their opinion in favour of Mr. Shirley's fchemes ; and, in particular, that it was moft effentially neceffary, at all events, to fecure the navigation of the lake Ontario ; but they were of opinion, that 6000 troops fhould be employed in the expedition againft the french forts upon that lake, and 10,000 in that againft Crown Point ; and as to the propofed attempt againft fort du Quefne, and operations upon the river Chaudiere, they were of opinion, they fhould be carried into execution, provided it could be done without interfering with the two principal expeditions : and after confidering the points propofed to them by Mr. Shirley, they declared it to be their unanimous opinion that, an additional number of regular troops to thofe his majefty then had upon the continent, would be neceffary for effectually recovering and fecuring his juft rights there. The refult of the council was, that Mr. Shirley, as he had received intelligence, that the french were building veffels of force at Frontenac, ordered a fnow, a brigantine, and a floop to be built, as foon as poffible at Ofwego;

and

and determined to make preparations for carrying into execution the before-mentioned plan of operations in the enfuing year, as far as the forces he then fhould have, would permit him.

Such were the refolutions taken in this council of war; who adopted Mr. Shirley's opinion in every thing, and indeed with great reafon; for certainly the plan of operations which he framed and laid before them, was drawn up in a mafterly manner, and fhowed that the author of it was perfectly well acquainted with his bufinefs, in the theory at leaft; what he was in the practice of it, I fhall have further occafion to mention hereafter.

But although the debates and refolutions in the cabinet were guided by wifdom, prudence, and forefight; the operations in the field, afforded but a melancholy profpect. How fruitlefs was the campaign of 1755! It was the misfortune of the englifh colonies to defpife their enemy: they knew their own country was populous, fertile, and great part of it well cultivated; on the contrary, Canada was barren, and uncultivated, and had not a fiftieth part of the inhabitants, which were in their own; the parallel fo advantageous to the englifh, proved almoft their ruin; exalted with thefe notions of their fuperiority, they did not confider, that the french knowing their own inferiority, were refolved to make up, by the moft unremitting diligence, what they wanted in point of numbers; for fome time the event anfwered their expectations; for furely no country was ever in a more pitiful condition, than the englifh colonies were reduced to, by means of the incurfions of the french and their indians; the defencelefs country was one continued fcene of all the horrors of war, rendered more terrible by the barbarous manner with which the indians make it. General Braddock, in whom their greateft hopes were centered, was defeated, and their enemies pouring in upon them, like an irrefiftible torrent, without any thing to oppofe them:

them: and in full poffeffion of all their formidable encroachments: all the englifh could boaft of having done (to the fouth of Nova Scotia) was the building two paltry forts at Ofwego, and they not comeplete; and the fine fpeeches made in the council of war by the commander in chief: I am fpeaking of what concerned general Shirley; Mr. Johnfon indeed, gained a victory over the enemy, which had very great confequences; but as to Mr. Shirley's expedition to Ofwego, in which he fpent fo much time and money; I cannot reflect on it without regret. The manner in which the year 1755 ended, will be remembered in the annals of America, with forrow. The weak efforts made by the englifh nation to recover its juft rights, which were fo fcandaloufly trampled upon by the french; will be a lafting difgrace to the politics of a people who make fo confiderable a figure in Europe, and who were fo able to protect their fellow fubjects in America. Indeed, with the bleffing of God, they have fince had better fuccefs in fo juft a caufe; and have exulted, with reafon, in their turn; but under different generals, directed by very different councils. It will be my bufinefs to fhew this hereafter; in the mean time, it is neceffary to take a view of the tranfactions in Europe; which fhall be the fubject of the next chapter.

## CHAP. V.

*Transactions in England in the beginning of the year. Rouillé's letter to Fox, and his answer. Treaty with Prussia. Col. York, at the Hague, demands the 6000 troops. Parliament meets. King's message. Addresses, and king's answers. Parliament address the king to bring over the Hanoverians. King's message and speech. Parliament prorogued. Hanoverians and Hessians arrive. Declarations of war. Affairs in the East-Indies. Fort Geriah taken. Reflections.*

FEW years ever opened the dawn of their contents, at a more critical time than the year 1756. The disputes between the kingdoms of England and France, was come to such a height, that a war was inevitable: although neither party chose yet to declare themselves openly, still it was very plain from the general circumstances of the two nations, that matters were come to such a crisis, as to be impossible to be healed. In America the war was become open and avowed, and it was expected to be the same in Europe every day; for all intercourse was cut off. Many discerning people were mistaken in their conjectures, when they thought they perceived a reconciliation between the two nations, near at hand, so far from it, that it was never further off. The ministry, who at this time presided in the councils of England, would have been glad to have procured a lasting peace between the french and english, could they have been able to do it without forfeiting their own honour, or what perhaps they esteemed a greater loss, their places. These gentlemen foresaw, very plain, that as soon as an irruption took place between the two courts, their power would fall to pieces, by reason of the multitude of factions and parties, which always spring up in the english

court

court at the beginning of a war : urged by thefe reafons, they would have patched up matters with the french court, more fpeedily than the intereft of their country required; if the nation had not had a truer fenfe of the injuries received from the french. In this ticklifh fituation, was the court of England, at the beginning of the year 1756.

This year, fo remarkable in the annals of Britain, was ufhered in by the ftrange letter\*, wrote by Monf. Rouillé, minifter and fecretary of ftate to the king of France, to Mr. Fox, fecretary of ftate to the king of England; it contained a pompous juftification of the french king's conduct, and complaining of the hoftilities committed by the englifh; turning the whole blame of the war on the king of England. Mr. Fox's anfwer was wrote with the fame defign, complaining of the conduct of the french court.

Before I make any obfervations on the french memorial, I fhall juft add a remark on Mr. F—'s management of this affair, fo far as it concerned his anfwer; and that is, the fcandalous manner in which the nation was difgraced by the beggarly french, in which Mr. F—'s letter was compofed, and as fuch was printed in the Paris gazette. I leave the reader to judge, whether it is becoming the honour of the englifh nation, for its firft minifter to talk to a foreign court in any other language but that of his own nation.

Never did the chicanary of the court of France appear more glaringly, than in the above memorial; nothing is more fufceptable of the moft mathematical demoftration, than that Britain was, in her own moft juft defence, forced into this war with France: ftabbed at her vitals in America, fhe was either obliged to acquiefce fupinely in the french manifold invafions there; or to put a ftop to them by repelling the aggreffion with a commencement of hoftilities. An immediate declaration of war would, perhaps, have been more confonant to the eftablifhed forms

of

\* Vide appendix.

of practice; but since the french themselves had not paid any regard to them, in their own procedure; they could, at least, with the worse grace complain of our having followed the bad example they had set us; which was not the less real, for its being the less manifest to the rest of Europe.

But to clear up beyond doubt the falsity of the allegations contained in this memorial, we need but consider the following matters of fact, relating to it. It should be remembered, that in january 1755, the french ambassador returned to London, and made great protestations of his court's sincere desire, finally and speedily to adjust all disputes between the two crowns concerning America: and notwithstanding the extraordinary preparations which were at that time making in the ports of France, her ambassador proposed, " That before the ground and circum-
" stances of the quarrel should be enquired into,
" positive orders should be immediately sent to our
" respective governors, forbidding them to under-
" take any new enterprise, or proceed to any act of
" hostility; and enjoining them, on the contrary, to
" put things without delay, with regard to the lands
" on the Ohio, on the same footing that they were,
" or ought to have been before the war; and that
" the respective claims should be amicably referred
" to the commissioners at Paris, that the two courts
" might terminate the difference by a speedy accom-
" modation."

The british court immediately declared its readiness to consent to the proposed cessation of hostilities, and that all the points in dispute might be discussed and terminated by the ministers of the two crowns; but on this condition, that all the possessions in America should be previously put on the foot of the treaty of Utrecht, confirmed by that of Aix la Chapelle; therefore, the king of England proposed, " That the
" possession of the land on the Ohio should be re-
" stored to the footing it was on at the conclu-
" sion

"tion of the said treaty, which was renewed by that
"of Aix la Chapelle; and moreover, that the other
"possessions in north America should be restored to
"the same condition in which they actually were, at
"the signing of the said treaty of Utrecht, and
"agreeable to cessions and stipulations therein ex-
"pressed: and then the method of informing the
"respective governors, and forbidding them to un-
"dertake any new enterprise, or act of hostility,
"might be treated of; and the claims of both par-
"ties reserved, to be speedily and finally adjusted,
"in an amicable manner between the two courts."
That is to say, that France should repay the injury done by open force, before the parties should enter into treaty about the claim of right, after which the possessions of both parties might be settled on the foot of a definitive agreement.

The reason for the french court's proceeding in this manner, is very palpable: nothing would have served their turn so well, as referring the case to be agreed on by the commissioners at Paris; and the reason is very plain; no sooner should we have ordered our american governors to desist from any acts of hostility, and referred our cause to negociation; but the french would have set about strengthening themselves in America, by supplies from Europe, in such a manner, that they would at this day have been superior to the english in that country; and not only have secured to themselves, the encroachments they had already made, but would in all probability have conquered all the back settlements belonging to the english colonies; or, to use the words of a french writer, have "drove the english into the sea."

Negotiations at this period extended further than just between the two crowns of Great Britain and France; the two kings of England and Prussia, at this time, thought it necessary for each other's welfare to enter into a negotiation for a treaty to keep all foreign troops from entering the empire; which were

F                                                       speedily

speedily brought to a conclusion; for a treaty was signed between these two powers, on the 16th of January, this year: the reasons given by the british ministry for taking this measure, were chiefly centered in the design, to keep the french from invading the electorate of Hanover; which it was very natural to expect they would really do, after they had threatened it in all the courts of Europe. The substance of this treaty was as follows:

I. That Great Britain with her allies, and Prussia, shall mutually assist each other, in endeavouring to keep all foreign troops from entering the empire.

II. That Great Britain shall pay 20,000 l. as an indemnification for the captures of that merchandize, which was taken on board prussian bottoms, and sold during the last war, and in return, that Prussia shall pay the Silesia loan.

The reader will perceive, that the most important article of this treaty is, that Great Britain and her allies, and Prussia, shall mutually assist each other in endeavouring to keep all foreign troops from entering the empire. And here it is necessary to recall to mind, the treaty concluded the last year with Russia, by which, as I before shewed, the Russians were to act in Germany, agreeable to the directions of his britannic majesty. From this it appears, that these two treaties with Russia and Prussia are, at least, seemingly contradictory to each other; for by the russian treaty, the russians are to march into Germany, for the purposes of that treaty; and by the prussian treaty, they are excluded from entering the empire, being foreign troops. I know to this, many specious political arguments are used by the friends of the english ministry, to persuade the world, that these two treaties are not in the least opposite and contradictory to one another, being solely designed for the protection of Hanover against the french; but I must confess, that in my humble opinion, nothing can be more seemingly inconsistent; I say seemingly,
for

for we know not what private reasons, (there certainly can be no public ones) might induce the english ministry to have concluded this treaty. In short, this is one of those surprising turns in the political world, which astonishes every one, as it leaves every one in the dark, and which nothing but time can make appear in its true light,

The situation of affairs in Europe were at this time extremely critical; every day produced some new reasons to believe, that a war was become inevitable between Great Britain and France; and it was much feared, that the quarrel between these two nations would involve the rest of Europe in the war; by reason of the open declarations, which France every where made of her intentions, to march an army into the electorate of Hanover; which it was thought would engage some of the german princes in the quarrel, as soon as any french troops invaded the empire. In the North, matters did not bid so fairly for war, as every thing was peaceable in those kingdoms; but the scene of negotiations on the continent of Europe at this time, was the Hague; where the ministers of the two belligerant powers were using their utmost endeavours to procure an interest in the republic, for their respective masters. It was then (the 13th of february) that col. York, the king of Great Britain's ambassador at the Hague, delivered to their high mightinesses an important memorial, importing, "That although his master had convinced all Europe of his desire to maintain the general peace that had lately subsisted; yet he found himself threatened with a war being kindled in his own dominions. That France was at that time making immense preparations of all kinds, particularly on the northern coasts, which were evidently designed against Great Britain; and which the french ministers at the several courts of Europe had confirmed, by their declarations. That these motives had obliged the king to demand the 6000 men, to be sent over to his assistance, affiftance, which the republic was bound to do by treaty; and that the neceffary fhipping for their embarkation, would be got ready immediately."

This memorial gave a clear and juft account of the great preparations which France was at this time making on all fides. It is true, their deftination was not then known; but, they were certainly very alarming to the court of Great Britain; there were at leaft 40,000 men affembled in Flanders, under the command of two marfhals of France, thefe troops were pofted there, for two reafons; the firft to be ready to annoy England, and fecondly to awe the dutch; for the french ambaffador at the Hague, threatened the ftates general with an invafion, if they complied with the demands of Great Britain, in relation to the 6000 men. All the ports of France at this time refounded with the noife of preparations, which tended to invade Great Britain: troops from all the inland parts of the kingdom were continually. fwarming towards the northern coaft. Indeed, in this cafe, it is natural for the reader to afk how it came about, that England was at this time fo deftitute of national force; for really it does not appear, but that the kingdom was not fo very weak, as to make it neceffary to call in the affiftance of the troops, which Holland was by treaty obliged to furnifh; but ftill as the dutch were bound to fuccour us, it was judged a neceffary meafure to demand the fupply of 6000 men, as we might by that means perceive how they ftood affected towards the englifh.

The truth was, thefe phlegmetic friends were fo much under the influence of France, that upon the french ambaffador's prefenting a memorial to the ftates general, on account of the demand made by England, they refufed to fend the fuccours, although they were bound fo to do by treaty; nor will they furprife us much, when we confider the quantity of french gold that was made ufe of to procure this refolve, which reflected fo much difhonour on the ftates

of

of Holland; but France is never without her pensioners at the Hague.

Matters were become so warlike between the two nations, that many in England really believed, that the french intended to invade us; it is very plain that the ministry did not think themselves perfectly secure, from a message which his majesty sent to the parliament, in which he acquainted them, that he had received sure advice of a design formed by France to invade his kingdoms, which his majesty had great reason to believe true, from the immense preparations making on the coast of France: that his majesty had, with their advice, augmented his forces, and made a requisition of a body of hessian troops, to be brought over, as they are obliged to be by treaty: that his majesty doubted not, but he should be supported on this occasion by his parliament, in opposition to any such daring attempts.

Never did any parliament shew more unanimity than was discovered on reading this message; it was agreed, without any opposition, that an address of thanks should be presented to his majesty, assuring him of their inviolable attachment to his person and government, against the hostile attempts of France.

In return for so much loyalty and affection, his majesty answered, " That he thanked them for their
" repeated assurances of their unalterable zeal,
" duty, and affection to him, on this occasion, and
" has the utmost confidence in their vigorous sup-
" port."

As I have several times mentioned the alarm that prevailed in England, to so great a degree, of a french invasion, it will be necessary to acquaint the reader, that the parliament was now so much of opinion that the nation was really in danger, as to address the king, to bring over a body of the hanoverian troops, for the protection of the kingdom, against the designs of France; to which his majesty returned the following answer. " I am always very
" glad

" glad to do any thing that is agreeable to my parli-
" ament, and for the benefit and fecurity of my peo-
" ple; and as both houfes defire that a body of my
" german troops fhould be brought over hither, to
" affift in defence of this kingdom, in the prefent
" critical conjuncture, I will give immediate orders
" for that purpofe."

I cannot pafs over an affair which made fo great a noife half Europe over, as the addrefs of the britifh parliament. It is difficult to fay, what could poffefs the nation with fuch an univerfal dread of an invafion, as at this time ran through all degrees of people, from the higheft to the loweft. Every true briton, that loves his country and efteems its honour, will look back upon it with deteftation. Will it not be recorded to the difhonour of the britifh nation, that fhe was forced to afk the affiftance of the electorate of Hanover, to defend herfelf againft an imaginary danger; for it is well known, that all the mighty preparations of France, were, at this time, deftined for a different expedition, which afterwards fully appeared: and this difgrace is yet more fully difplayed, when we confider, that at this time, very few englifh troops were abfent in the Eaft or Weft-Indies, or the american colonies. Would it not have been more honourable in the nation, to have raifed an army of the natives to defend their own country, than to call in the affiftance of foreigners; and after all the noife and buftle that was made in trumpeting out the danger the nation was in, when it was pretended that a concatination of events foretold this danger, that after all, it fhould turn out a mere ftratagem of the french court, to deceive the englifh miniftry.

As I am now mentioning the affairs of the parliament this feffion, for the fake of perfpicuity, I will continue my account till the end of the feffion; firft taking notice of the meffage which his majefty fent to both houfes, the 11th of may, fignifying, " That
" his

"his majesty being desirous to be prepared against all attempts and designs whatsoever, that may be formed by his enemies in the present critical conjuncture, and considering that sudden emergencies may arise, which may be of the utmost importance, and be attended with the most pernicious consequences, if proper means should not be immediately applied, to prevent or defeat them; his majesty hoped, that he shall be enabled by his parliament, to concert and take such measures as may be necessary to disappoint or defeat any enterprises or designs of his enemies, and as the exigency of affairs may require." To this message both houses presented the most loyal and dutiful addresses; but what was much more conducive to the design in his majesty's message, was the famous resolution of the house of commons, in consequence of this message, whereby they granted his majesty one million upon account; a generosity hardly to be paralleled; and this vote was in fact the most important piece of business performed this session of parliament. On the 27th of may, his majesty made a speech to both houses of parliament; the following is the most material passage:

"The injuries and hostilities, which have been for some time committed by the french against my dominions and subjects, are now followed by the actual invasion of the island of Minorca; which stands guarantied to me by all the great powers of Europe, and in particular by the french king. I have therefore found myself obliged, in vindication of the honour of my crown, and of the rights of my people, to declare war in form against France. I rely on the divine protection, and the vigorous assistance of my faithful subjects, in so just a cause."

After this speech, the lord chancellor signified his majesty's pleasure, that both houses should severally adjourn

adjourn themselves until june the 18th, which they accordingly did; and on that day they again adjourned themselves to july the 15th; but on the 7th they were prorogued to auguſt the 17th, which put an end to the ſeſſion.

Thus ended this ſeſſion of parliament, that had been even more generous than any former ones, of late years at leaſt. I have given the reader this abſtract of parliamentary affairs together for the ſake of brevity; as to the affair of Minorca, which his majeſty mentions in his ſpeech, I muſt deſire the reader's patience for a little while, before I can give an account of an affair equally inglorious to my country and diſagreeable to me. I ſhould remember to obſerve, that during this ſeſſion, that is on the 3d and 8th of may, the following votes were paſſed:

That there be granted to his majeſty, for the charge of 6544 foot, with the general officers and train of artillery, of the heſſian troops, from february 23d, 1756, to december 24 following, together with the ſubſidy purſuant to treaty, 163357 l. 9 s. 9 d.

May 8. For the charge of 8605 foot, with the general officers, train of artillery and hoſpital, of the Hanover troops, from may 11, 1756, to december 24 following, 121447 l. 2 s. 6 d.

In conſequence of theſe votes, we find that on the 13th of may, two men of war, with 45 tranſports, having 8000 heſſian foot and 900 horſe on board, anchored in Margate road, and on the 15th landed at Southampton; with a large train of artillery. They were divided into eight regiments, ten companies in a regiment, eighty men in a company; each regiment having ninety engineers, eighty-ſeven horſes, and eight field pieces. The principal officers were, the lieutenant general, count Iſenburg, knight of the teutonic order, who was the firſt in command; lieutenant general baron Diebe, knight of the ſame order, who commanded the artillery; and baron Furſtenburg, brother to the count, major generals. The troops

troops made a fine appearance, being generally ftreight, tall, and flender; their uniform was blue, turned up with red, and laced with white, in imitation of filver. The officers, who were all well made, were richly dreffed in blue, laced with gold, with that on their hats remarkably broad. They were quartered in the neighbouring towns, where they obferved the ftricteft difcipline.

On the 21ft, the hanoverians landed at Chatham, to the number of 10,000 men, and began their march in two divifions; the firft for Maidftone, and the other for Canterbury. They were received with great civility, and behaved with remarkable regularity. At Maidftone, fome little difturbance happened, and complaint being made to the commanding officer, " Point me out the man," faid he, " and prove him " the aggreffor, and you fhall fee him hanged im-" mediately;" but this was thought too fevere, and no particular man was pitched upon. Thefe hanoverians, and the heffian troops were thought at that time to be fome of the beft foldiers in Europe; and we have fince found them to behave with the greateft honour and bravery.

Amidft all thefe preparations for war, which had really brought on an open rupture between the two nations; all Europe was furprifed that neither of the belligerent powers had yet declared war in due form. It was a matter of aftonifhment to the generality of mankind, to fee two powerful kingdoms at open war, without any public univerfal manifefto concerning the reafons for their attacking one another. At laft however, his britannic majefty thought it neceffary to obferve this ufual decorum, and accordingly declared war againft France on the 17th of may; and that of France againft England was on the 9th of june.

Such were the ftate of affairs between the two nations in Europe, at the time war was declared. In the Eaft-Indies, matters went on much fafter, and
more

more prosperously to the english; it was the beginning of this year, that the famous pyrate Tulagee Angria was conquered, and rooted out of his strong hold at fort Geriah, by the english forces under colonel Clive. But before we can give any account of the action itself, it will be necessary to say something concerning so extraordinary a man, as him we are speaking off. It seems that some years ago, the ancestors of Angria were viceroys to the great moghul, and governed a fine country on the Caromandel coast, where they lived with great splendor and opulence; and by means of the great riches they amassed, were enabled for a considerable time to throw off their allegiance to the moghul; but were afterwards reduced to obedience by a sovereign prince, whose dominions lay to the south of those of Angria, who was called the south raja; this prince imposed a tribute on Angria, which was regularly paid for some years, till Tulagee Angria refused, about the year 1754; at which, the south raja was highly provoked; and to chastise the insolence of Angria's behaviour, marched an army into his country, and blocked up all his towns; the most considerable of which, were the ports of Zivanchi, Antiguria, Dabul, and south Rook. And to enable himself the more readily to destroy his enemy, he sent to the english at Bombay, to desire them to assist him, in his conquest of Angria.

With this request the english complied; and admiral Watson commanding at that time in the East-Indies, he assisted at a council of war held at Bombay on the 6th of february. The land forces were under the command of colonel Clive. The admiral attacked Geriah on the 12th, and it surrendered on the 13th.

In the fort were found 250 iron and brass cannon of all sizes, and a prodigious quantity of ammunition of all sorts, provisions, rich goods, and many other commodities. The garrison consisted of about 300 men,

though

though there were above 2000 in the fort. In silver rupees were found about 100,000 l. and in other effects near 30,000 l. The admiral left about 300 of the East-India company's troops, as many seapoys, and 3 or 4 of the company's armed vessels in the harbour, for the defence of the place, as it was judged to be extremely well situated for the interest of the company, and very tenable.

In this successful manner ended the expedition against Angria; which was of infinite service to the East-India company's affairs, as it rooted a notorious pyrate from his fortress of the greatest consequence to him. It is thought that col. Clive got above 100,000 l. by this affair, and the admirals and other officers were equally fortunate in this important conquest. The french in this part of the world looked with a very envious eye upon this success; as no doubt they did not care to see the exaltation of a company, who were the enemies of that nation, and who were every day excelling them in their trade. This was the first warlike expedition of consequence in the East-Indies this war.

# CHAP. VI.

*Naval affairs in the beginning of* 1756. *Hawke sails from St. Hellen's. Rumours of a french invasion. Holbourn sails for north America. Boscawen from St. Hellen's. Hawke with his fleet arrives at Spithead. Preparations at Toulon. State of the affairs of Europe. The french fleet sails from Toulon. Siege of St. Philip's. Byng sails from St. Hellen's. Battle off Minorca. Fort St. Philip's surrenders. Reflections. Hawke takes the command from Byng. Lord Tyrawley arrests general Fowke. Byng and Fowke arrive in England.*

IT has with great reason been made a matter of wonder, that the french monarchy has been able for near a century past, to produce at the same time such powerful armaments both by sea and land. No other nation in Europe has been so powerful at sea and land at the same time as France, except England; and the naval strength of England has never stood such severe trials as that of France. The power and resources of a nation are best discovered by its losses; every war that has happened between France and England, since Charles the first's time, has never failed to be more ruinous to the former than the latter; and many times has been entirely destroyed, more particularly at the end of the war of 1740. The arms of Great Britain were not so successful the beginning of this war, neither by sea nor land, as the greatness of our preparations might have inspired us with the hopes of. At the beginning of this year particularly, all the ports of England resounded with the noise of naval armaments; the rigorous method of pressing men to man the fleet was now adopted with the utmost severity, and many thousands of able hands were picked up throughout all England; insomuch, that most part of the month of january

we

we had a noble fleet riding at Spithead, besides several strong squadrons at sea, to protect our own trade and annoy that of the enemy. The naval affairs, though they are always of importance, and necessary to be known, towards a perfect understanding of the present quarrel between the two nations, yet, during the beginning of 1756, we meet with few squadrons, that sailed from british ports, whose motions are any ways instructive to the reader; the most material one at this time was, sir Edward Hawke's expedition. The lords of the admiralty having been informed that six french men of war had sailed from Brest, ordered admiral Hawke on the 27th of february to put to sea immediately, but he was detained till the 12th of march by contrary winds, on which day he sailed with the East-India ships, to convoy them 150 leagues westward of Ushant. He was then ordered to return to cape Ortegal, and cruise in the bay, to prevent the french ships putting to sea from Brest or Rochfort, or to intercept the aforesaid french squadron. This squadron consisted of eleven ships of the line and one frigate.

Sir Edward Hawke, according to his instructions cruised till the beginning of may, for the french, but unluckily was not able to effect any thing. He returned to Spithead the 8th with part of his squadron.

During the first part of this year, the french had by all the arts and means in their power endeavoured to persuade the english, that they really intended to invade them. It is even to this day a doubt, whether the french, at the time we are speaking of, had ever really determined to attempt an invasion. The preparations they made were certainly considerable; and it was confidently talked of, at most of the courts of Europe, that England was in great danger. It was at this time the common topic of conversation; those who were most persuaded of the reality of the french designing to invade us, said even in a positive
manner,

manner, (and the advices that were received from the Hague on this head corroborated exactly with that opinion) that the plan for invading Great Britain was propoſed by M. de Belleiſle, who offered to undertake the execution thereof; but that he had been violently oppoſed by M. de Seychelles. The marſhal's plan, was not to attack any of the powers on the continent, and particularly to leave Hanover quiet; but at the ſame time to aſſemble three large armies on the frontiers of Alſace, Flanders, and Languedoc; in order to keep the powers in Europe in awe and ſuſpence. Then ſeriouſly to attempt an invaſion of Great Britain or Ireland, or both, by getting together as many veſſels as poſſible in different ports, with every thing neceſſary for an embarkation. And he further adviſed the french king, not to ſend out any large ſquadrons of men of war, but only ſome light cruiſers to cover the arrival and departure of their tranſports; to give notice of the motions of the engliſh, and to carry ſupplies to their colonies; however, at Breſt he thought it neceſſary to have a very large fleet ready to give umbrage to the engliſh, and to ſerve as occaſion ſhould require. This was Belleiſle's plan, and although we find that it, in general was rejected, ſtill ſome motions of the french looked as if they had adopted part of it; the marſhal, and the prince de Soubiſe, ſoon after began their circuit at Dunkirk, and from thence went from port to port quite to Breſt, forwarding the preparations that were making all along the coaſt, ſeemingly to invade us.

Whether they really intended to put their threats in execution or not is unknown, yet they certainly gained one point of importance by theſe means; they deceived the attention of the britiſh miniſtry, and were thereby enabled to render ſucceſsful their deſigns againſt another quarter; beſides which, the expence their preparations put the engliſh to, in counteract-
ing

ing their defigns, was to be fure of great confequence.

It was on account of thefe preparations on the coaft of France, that, we were always obliged to keep a fquadron of men of war in the Downs; and for the greater fecurity, commodore Keppel failed on the 7th of april to cruife off Cherburgh with a fquadron of five fhips, to burn the flat bottomed boats, which the french were building, and to pick up any ftraggling tranfports that might fall in their way, the latter of thefe ends was pretty well anfwered by the commodore's fuccefs.

The naval ftrength which the englifh had at this time in America, was very fmall, in proportion to the great importance of that ftation: and the miniftry in England was much blamed for not keeping regularly and conftantly a ftrong fquadron of men of men of war in that part of the world, to refift and annoy the operations of the french. At laft, however, admiral Holbourn failed from Plymouth, with feven fail of fhips to convoy the tranfports, containing the reinforcement of troops that were juftly thought neceffary to repair the bad ftate of the britifh empire there, by checking the progrefs of France.

But in Europe, the naval equipments were more confiderable; admiral Hawke, as I have before mentioned, was before Breft with a confiderable fleet, to relieve which, admiral Bofcawen failed from Spithead with twelve fail.

So formidable an armament failing to the coaft of France, would naturally lead us to expect fome attempt of importance. But this was not the cafe, the french miniftry, by alarming us with the fear of an invafion, put us to fuch an immenfe expence to keep their fleets in harbour, and even this, we were feldom able to perform, for the french feveral times flipt through the englifh fleets lying before Breft. The principal reafon that has been given by the britifh miniftry for putting the nation to fo great an expence

merely

merely to coop our enemies up in their harbours, was, to hinder them at this time from sending succours to America. Admiral Hawke, as I said before, soon after arrived at Spithead with a small squadron.

Several other squadrons were fitted out, and sailed as cruisers, convoys, or squadrons of observation; but as their destination was not so important, I have for brevity sake omitted mentioning them. But I must now begin to take notice of a much more important affair, and which will require a more minute enquiry into the first appearances of the designs of our enemies: I mean the conquest of Minorca by the french.

It will be here necessary for me to trace out some advices which the ministry in England received concerning the preparations of the french in the port of Toulon; for from thence we must afterwards conclude, whether they had reason to believe that the french intended an invasion of the island of Minorca, or whether they only meant it as a feint to draw the attention of the english from the channel, that they might thereby be able to effect their grand design against Great Britain itself.

So early as the month of august 1755, the ministry in England had intelligence, from different parts, of the armament at Toulon. They were expresfly informed, that orders had been sent thither, to equip with expedition, all the new ships, and to get the old ones also in a condition for service: that these orders were then pursued with great diligence, and that they were to take on board several companies of land forces, besides marines. That since the arrival of two expresses at Toulon, which had caused the holding of two extraordinary councils, attended by the principal officers of the marine, the hands which were at work in fitting out nine ships there, were doubled, and six other ships of the line put in commission, and ordered

dered to be equipped with the former nine, so as to be able to put all the 15 sail to sea before the 18th or 20th of august, and to be victualed only for three months. This intelligence was in part confirmed by the earl of Bristol, the english ambassador at Turin, who informed the ministry, that all the master builders were commanded to repair immediately from the ports of Provence, &c. to Toulon; and that a body of 20,000 french troops were prepared to form a camp at Valence in Dauphine: these advices were exactly confirmed by consul Birtles, from Nice. But consul Banks, in his letters from Carthagena, dated the 20th and 27th of august, is still more explicit; " Masters of french vessels from Toulon," says he, " report, that there are in that port 26 men of war of the line, viz. 18 new ships built since the peace, and 8 old ones, which are all fitting for sea; also 12 frigates, and a great many smaller vessels, which are in like manner fitting out; besides six ships of the line on the stocks; some of which are ready for launching: that he had received intelligence of 180 battalions of soldiers marching into Roussillon with great diligence; and that these troops were designed against Minorca, to be transported thither in merchant ships, now at Marseilles, and to be convoyed by all the men of war in the port of Toulon."

These advices were constantly repeated: not a month passed, without innumerable assurances being received at the secretary of state's office, from lord Bristol, general Blakeney, general Fowke, sir Ben. Keene, and, in short, all the consuls in the Mediterranean, concerning the great preparations which were carrying on at Toulon. Sir Ben. Keene wrote to Mr. Fox, particularly assuring him, " that the french designed to invade Minorca." Nothing could be more circumstantial than the repeated advices which the english ministry received of the designs of France. But let us see what were their measures to oppose such formidable preparations.

There were at this time in the Mediterranean a small squadron of three ships of the line, and five frigates, under commodore Edgecombe; but no fleet was ordered to sail from England, for the protection of Minorca, till the 8th of march; when a squadron was directed to be under the command of vice-admiral Byng, and to be ready by the 11th. It is impossible to account for the negligence of the english ministry, in not thinking of this valuable island before so late a date: it is also as unaccountable, that they should not believe any of the advices, which their correspondents all over Europe gave them, of the reality of the design of the french, in making such immense and early preparations at Toulon. Had they believed the truth of these advices, they certainly would have taken care that their administration should not be tarnished with the loss of so important a fortress as that of St. Philip's: it is very well known, how lightly they treated the notion of an invasion of the island of Minorca; they did not think it possible, that the french could procure sailors sufficient to man their fleet; if they had supposed it possible for the french to put so strong a fleet to sea from Toulon, as they afterwards fatally found to be the case, why did they not send admiral Osborn's squadron, of 13 ships of the line, and one frigate, into the Mediterranean, who sailed the 30th of january (and returned the 16th of february) to convoy a fleet of merchantmen. By sending this squadron into the Mediterranean so early, the french would naturally have been deterred from attempting the invasion; their success in which expedition, entirely depended on the negligence of their enemies.

At last however, they exerted themselves so far, as to send a fleet under admiral Byng to the Mediterranean,

( 83 )

nean, confisting of ten ships of the line *, which sailed the 7th of april.

However, in France more expedition was used. The marshal duke de Richelieu was already set out from Paris for Toulon, with the officers who were to serve under him, and arrived there the 25th of march, finding every thing in great readiness. The fleet † sailed the 12th of april, consisting of 13 sail of the line and 7 frigates.

| * Ships. | Guns. | | Captains. |
|---|---|---|---|
| Ramilies, | 90 | Byng. | Gardner. |
| Buckingham, | 70 | West, | Everet. |
| Culloden, | 74 | | Ward. |
| Revenge, | 70 | | Cornwall. |
| Captain, | 70 | | Catford. |
| Trident, | 64 | | Durell. |
| Intrepid, | 64 | | Young. |
| Kingston, | 64 | | Parry. |
| Lancaster, | 60 | | Noel. |
| Defiance, | 60 | | Andrews. |

| † Ships. | Guns. | Captains. |
|---|---|---|
| Foudroyant, | 80 | M. de la Galissoniere. Lieutenant General. Capt. M. Forger de l'Aiguille. |
| Couronne. | 70 | M. de la Clüe, chief d'Escarde. Capt. M. Gabanous. |
| Redoutable, | 74 | M. de Glandeves, chief d'Escarde. Capt. M. de Marconville. |
| Temeraire, | 74 | M. Beaumont l'Maitre. |
| Guerrier, | 74 | M. Villars de la Brosse. |
| Lion, | 64 | M. de St. Aignan. |
| Sage, | 64 | M. du Revest. |
| Orpheé, | 64 | M. du Raimondis. |
| Content, | 64 | M. Sabron Grammont. |
| Triton, | 64 | M. Mercier. |
| Hippopotame, | 50 | M. de Rochemaure. |
| Fier, | 50 | M. de Herville. |
| Junon, | 46 | M. Beaussier. |
| Rose, | 26 | M. de Costebelle. |
| Gracieuse, | 24 | M. Marquezan. |
| Topaze, | 24 | M. de Corné-Montelet. |
| Nymphe, | 24 | M. de Callian. |

The troops on board it, including a detachment of marines, in every ship of war, amounted to about 16,000 men, in 25 battalions, embarked in 200 transports: M. de Richelieu, his son, and his son-in-law; M. de Maillebois, M. du Mesnil, M. de Lannion, the prince de Beauveau, the prince de Wirtemberg, and M. de Caufons, embarked on board the Foudroyant. The troops were all in merchant ships; the grenadiers alone were in the men of war. The fleet and convoy contained at a moderate computation, near 30,000 fouls, including about 600 women; a prodigious quantity of provisions of every kind, above 800 oxen, and 3000 sheep, 100 horses, and as many mules.

The report of these immense preparations, which threatened to overwhelm the little island of Minorca, without a blow, did not in the least terrify the brave commander of the english troops in the fortress of St. Philip: no sooner did the information of the designs of the french reach general Blakeney, but he disposed all things for a brave and vigorous resistance; he prepared 40,000 fascines, and demolished all the trifling buildings which obstructed the open command of his cannon. The french landed at Cieutadella the 18th of april, from whence part of a regiment retired, evacuating the place to the enemy: Forty men, who belonged to the regiments at Gibraltar, and all the marines which were on board the men of war, then in the harbour, were commanded into the garrison, as a reinforcement; and the british squdron, six in number, sailed out; capt. Scroop having first, with 140 of his men, joined the garrison, and sent his ship, the Defiance, to sea, under the command of the first lieutenant.

I cannot omit taking notice of a patriot-like action performed by capt. Cunningham, a scotch gentleman, who being second engineer of St. Philips, when Mr. Armstrong left it, he was thereupon appointed by general Blakeney to succeed him, pro tempore, till a commission for that purpose should arrive from England;

land, of which no doubt was made; but being superseeded, he begged Mr. Blakeney's leave to retire to his regiment. The general could not refuse so reasonable a request, and Mr. Cunningham embarked for Nice, together with two children and his lady; who was there brought to bed; when Mr. Cunningham, hearing of the french designs against Minorca, and recollecting that the platforms of the batteries in fort St. Philip's were in such a ruinous condition, that they could not stand any hot service, instantly laid out all the money he was master of, about 1600l. in purchasing timber fit for repairing them, hired a a vessel, put it on board, and sailed directly with it himself for Port Mahon, leaving his lady and children at Nice. His arrival with such a supply, in such a critical conjuncture, gave general Blakeney infinite pleasure. He told capt. Cunningham, that the service he had done his country, was so considerable, that he did not know how he could be sufficiently rewarded for it; that in the mean time, to show his own sense of it, he would venture to take a very irregular step, by superseding the gentleman, who was sent to succeed Mr. Armstrong, as superannuated and unfit for duty, and appointing him in his place, not only as a testimony of his approbation of what he had done, but to engage a man of his known abilities, to exert them still further in defence of the place. We shall find hereafter that capt. Cunningham very well deserved the confidence Mr. Blakeney reposed in him; but the public spirited action which I have just now given an account of, is of itself so shining a proof of the merits of this gentleman, that any further attempt to make them conspicuous is unnecessary.

After many difficulties, the french being masters of all the forts in the island, except St. Philip's, and those adjoining to it, at length erected a battery of five 24 pounders, and five morters, over against St. Philip's, at cape Mola, near Sandy bay, on the side opposite St. Philipet fort, which was ready to play the 5th of May, but was left masked till others were ready also: this battery was well contrived, for by means of it the french commanded the harbour so much, that it would be difficult to land any succour, but within fire of it. For several succeeding days the enemy continued to erect batteries without intermission, and the besiged continued to defend themselves with as great bravery.

But I must here return to the motions which Mr. Byng made, to relieve the distressed garrison of St. Philip. I left the admiral proceeding to Gibraltar, where, after a tedious passage, he arrived may the 2d; and directly demanded of lieut. gen. Fowke, the governor, according to his instructions, a detachment from his garrison, equal to a battalion; but this demand Mr. Fowke did not think proper to comply with (although he had orders for that purpose from his majesty) till he had called a council of war, to demand the officers of his garrison's opinion on that point.

The council meeting on the 4th of may, took into their consideration three letters * from lord Barrington, his majesty's secretary at war, to the governor of Gibraltar, of the 21st and 28th of march, and 1st of april last; as also an order from the lords of the admiralty to admiral Byng of the 31st of march; and having considered the state of affairs in the Mediterranean, were of opinion, that the sending a detachment equal to a battalion would evidently weaken the garrison of Gibraltar, and be no way effectual to the relief of Minorca; for which opinion they gave several reasons, relating to the difficulty of landing them at Minorca, and its weakening the garrison of Gibraltar.

---

* Containing an order for general Fowke to make a detachment from his garrison to be sent on board the fleet, equal to a battalion.

This

This opinion of the council of war we shall afterwards find made a very great noise. But of this we must defer speaking, till other transactions naturally lead us to it. Admiral Byng having been delayed by watering, sailed the eighth from Gibraltar; he was afterwards accused of protracting this time longer than was needful. He arrived off Minorca the 19th, having been joined by his majesty's ship Phœnix, off Majorca, two days before. He dispatched the Phœnix, Chesterfield, and Dolphin a-head, to reconnoitre the harbour's mouth, and capt. Harvey to endeavour to land a letter for general Blakeney, to let him know the fleet was come to his assistance; but the enemy's fleet appearing to south east, and the wind at the same time coming strong off the land, obliged the admiral to call those ships in, before they could get near enough the entrance of the harbour to make the necessary observations. There being little wind, about five the admiral formed his line, on which the enemy stood towards him in a regular line; but tacked about seven, endeavouring to get the wind of the english fleet in the night; to avoid which, Mr. Byng tacked, in order to keep the weather gage, as well as to make sure of the land wind in the morning, being very hazy, and not above five leagues off cape Mola. At day-light, on the 20th, the two fleets were not within sight of each other. But soon after the enemy began to appear from the mast head, on which the english admiral called in the cruisers, and when they had joined him, tacked towards the enemy, and formed the line a-head, while the french were preparing to form their's to the leeward, having unsuccessfully endeavoured to weather their antagonist; but as soon as he judged his rear to be the length of the enemy's van, they tacked all together, and ordered the Deptford to quit the line: the reason which the english admiral gave for this step, was, that the english fleet might become exactly equal to the enemy's, which consisted of 12 ships of the line and 5 frigates.

frigates. At two, admiral Byng made the signal to engage, on which, rear admiral West instantly bore down on the enemy's ships opposed to his, and in going down received the fire of the french ships against him, three times, before he returned it, and then he soon obliged the two ships successively to sheer off, who were opposed to him. The admiral bore down upon the ship stationed against him, for some little time, but the Intrepid having his foretop-mast shot away, this, as the admiral gave out, obliged him and all his division to fall a-back; by this unaccountable management, the enemy's center was left unattacked, and the rear admiral's division quite uncovered; by which the french were enabled to bear down on admiral West, with the rear of their fleet, but they declined coming to a close engagement; and at last the several ships that were opposed to West's division sheered off, and bent their endeavours to destroy the rigging of the english ships, at a distance, while the english admiral was lying a considerable distance a-stern of his rear. Next morning the two fleets were out of sight of each other, and Mr. Byng sent cruisers out to look for the Intrepide and Chesterfield, who had parted in the night from the fleet, and they returned and joined them the next day.

Such was the event of this famous engagement; it is equally surprising, that Mr. Byng should shew such great conduct and knowledge in management of the fleet before he threw out the signal for battle; and that he should then seem to have lost all the merit he had gained by his former proceedings. It is allowed by those who are understanding in sea affairs, that from the time he came in sight of the french fleet, till he hung out the signal to engage, he managed his fleet with infinite dexterity and judgment, by which means he preserved the weather gage against the enemy, who were not able, during the succeeding engagement, to recover it.

On

On the 24th of may, the admiral defired the attendance of the rear admiral, &c. &c. at a council of war held on board the Ramillies, to afk their opinions concerning the future operations of the fleet; at which were prefent the admirals, and all the captains of the fhips, and general officers of the land forces. The queftions which were debated and the council's refolutions are as follows:

I. Whether an attack upon the french fleet gives any profpect of relieving Minorca?
Anf. It would not.
II. Whether, if there was no french fleet cruifing off Minorca, the englifh fleet could raife the fiege?
Anf. It could not.
III. Whether Gibraltar would not be in danger by any accident that may befall this fleet?
Anf. It would be in danger.
IV. Whether an attack with our fleet in the prefent ftate of it upon that of the french, will not endanger the fafety of Gibraltar, and expofe the trade of the Mediterranean to great hazard?
Anf. That it would.
V. Whether it is not moft for his majefty's fervice that the fleet fhould immediately proceed for Gibraltar?
Anf. That it fhould proceed for Gibraltar.

Thefe refolutions were unanimoufly agreed to, and figned by all the members of the council. And to the aftonifhment of all Europe, a fleet in every refpect equal to that of the enemy, and, confidering the fuperior courage and dexterity of the common failors, much fuperior to it, fhould fly from that of the enemy, leaving them all the confequences of a victory, riding triumphantly before Mahon, and gaining refpect to the french flag throughout all the ports in the Mediterranean. Admiral Byng, on the 25th, fet fail, and on the 19th of june arrived at Gibraltar.

braltar. As I shall have ample occasion to treat further of this affair hereafter, I shall not determine on it at present. It is now time to return to the governor of St. Philip's, bravely defending himself against the attacks of the french army.

For several days after the engagement of the 20th, the fire of both the besieged and besiegers continued very brisk; but the besieged had always the advantage, owing to the superior weight of their cannon, and skill of the engineers *. During the fore part of the siege, this was constantly the case, but after the french general changed his plan of attack †, the garrison suffered

---

\* The 13th in the morning, a very singular accident happened. In the fort, some guards parading in an under-ground gallery for safety, where, in the center was a hole to let in light, and receiving wood from a neighbouring magazine; through this hole a 13 inch shell made way, and burst among the guards without the least hurt to one man. During the whole siege, the garrison did not meet with so providential an escape. Another extraordinary accident happened in the like providential manner: a ten inch shell falling into a barrack, the habitation of capt. Lind, in the castle, and breaking every thing before it, forced its way through the floor, and burst without hurting any body, though a piece of the shell even alighted on the bed where capt. Lind and his lady then lay.

† The 27th M. de Richelieu, having altered his attack, had some time before pitched upon this day for the general one, the evening before he called a council of war, at which were present all the general officers, to whom he imparted the whole project, which was unanimously approved: M. de Richelieu then proceeded to give them their respective charges.

The plan of the whole attack being made known to the army, M. de Richelieu resolved that his own post should be in the center of the attacks on the left, and that the count de Maillebois, the the marquis du Mesnil, and the prince de Wirtemburg, should attend him to give the necessary orders for the support and success of the attacks.

It was agreed, that the signal for beginning the attack, should be given by firing a cannon and four bombs, from the battery near the signal house. All things being thus ordered, the artillery continued to batter the forts, till the 27th, at ten o'clock in the evening, when they all ceased firing: and then the battery near the signal house fired a cannon shot, and threw four bombs into the fort; upon which, M. de Monty immediately marched against Strugen

and

fered very severely; and in a little time most of the principal works in the fortifications were ruined; under

and Argyle, and successively Messrs. de Briqueville and de Sades, advanced to the attack of Kane, and the Queen's redoubt. These attacks were furious, and the defence as brave. The besieged maintained their ground for a long while, and the firing on both sides did great execution; but at length fort Strugen was taken by assault; and Argyle and the Queen's redoubt by scalade. Here the english sustained a great loss; for Mr. Jefferies, lieutenant colonel of the regiment of Effingham, who was coming to their assistance, between Strugen and Argyle, with 100 men, arrived too late, the french being masters of the forts; and whilst he attempted to retire, was taken prisoner with 15 men. Mr. Jefferies was the principal acting man in the garrison.

These three forts being taken, with several pieces of cannon and mortars, the french made instantly a lodgement in that part, which was the principal attack; mean while the other attacks were carrying on with vigour. The prince de Beauveau, having at the same time marched with his brigades against the Western and Caroline lunettes; he took possession of the covert way, and nailed up 12 pieces of cannon there; but as Kane's lunette was not taken, he could not make a lodgement here, but contented himself with cutting down the pallisadoes, destroying the gun carriages, and maintaining for some time this attack, in order to favour the principal, which was making with great bravery.

The diversion caused by all these firings, and the combination of all these various attacks gave that on the left time to ensure success; and by break of day, the french being totally masters of the Queen's redoubt, and the forts Strugen and Argyle, they posted 400 men in the former, and 200 in the latter. M. de Richelieu, M. de Maillebois, M. du Mesnil, and the prince de Wirtemburg, were all this time, as they had concerted, in the center of the attacks on the left. Several of the mines were sprung under the glacis of the Anstruther, the Queen's redoubt, and Kane's lunette, and likewise one under the gorge of Argyle, while a considerable party of the enemy were in it, most of whom were destroyed.

During these furious attacks; the brave governor and garrison defended themselves with all the intrepidity that was natural to englishmen. The West, and Caroline's lunettes distinguished themselves particularly: with such exalted courage, and exerted bravery did this fatigued part of the garrison maintain their ground, against unequal numbers, each officer and soldier emulous of glory.

The 28th, by break of day, the besiegers beat a parley, on which immediately a cessation of arms ensued; this gave them an opportunity, which they took the advantage of, to secure the lodgements

der thefe difadvantages, it was amazing to find the brave and vigorous defence made by the englifh garrifon; fo that, although the french batteries began to play on the 5th of may, yet we find that the intrepidity of the brave general Blakeney, and the courageous garrifon, the french were not able to make themfelves mafters of it before the 28th of june, on which day the garrifon furrendered on honourable terms.

The next day, june the 29th, early in the morning, the duke de Fronfac, fon to M. de Richelieu, was difpatched by him to carry to the king at Compeigne the news of the fuccefs of the laft attack againft fort St. Philip's, but not the articles of capitulation, general Blakeney, not having at that time returned his anfwer to the alterations the marfhal had made to the conditions he had propofed. M. de Fronfac was 6 days going from Minorca to Toulon, the winds having proved contrary almoft the whole time. However, he came to Lyons the 7th of july, dined at the archbifhop's, with the cardinal de Fenchion's, and fet out immediately after for Paris, where he arrived the 9th, late in the evening, and early the 10th at Compeigne; where, after having acquainted the king with all the particulars of the furrender of fort St. Philip's, he was promoted by his majefty to the poft of brigadier of his armies.

The articles of capitulation being figned, and the hoftages given, M. de Richelieu entered fort St. Philip the 29th of june at noon, and found 240 pieces of cannon fit for fervice, befides 40 that had been either ruined or nailed up during the attack; about

ments they had made, by pouring in a confiderable number of troops, into a fubterranean paffage, that had been opened by a fhell, and which was not difcovered till the day cleared up. On the ceffation of arms, a capitulation took place, wherein almoft all that was defired was granted, in confideration of the brave defence made by the gallant general Blakeney, and his intrepid garrifon.

70 mortars, 700,000 l. of gunpowder; 12,000 cannon balls, and 15,000 bombs. The garrison consisted of 2963 men, about 2300 whereof were military. The english lost during the siege only 400 men either killed or wounded, by reason of the galleries and casemattes cut in the rock and bomb proof, in which they were sheltered. So that the garrison consisted, at the time of the french landing at Minorca, of about 800 labourers, &c. and 2600 soldiers, making four regiments, viz. Rich's, Husk's, Cornwallis's, and Effingham's; but their colonels were not there; 60 of the inferior officers were also wanting, though expected from day to day; insomuch, that the besieged were commanded by three lieut. colonels only, 23 captains, and a very few subalterns.

The 8th of july, M. de Richelieu embarked on board the Foudroyant, with some of the principal officers; and the same day the whole french fleet hoisted sail, with several transports, carrying troops and artillery, and arrived safe at Toulon the 16th; where as soon as M. de Richelieu landed, he was saluted successively by the cannon of the whole fleet, and those of the forts. Some days after, all the troops arrived at Toulon and Marseilles, except those that were left at Minorca, which consisted of 11 battallions, with a detachment of royal artillery, consisting of 100 men, and three engineers. The command of these troops was given to the count de Lannion, who was soon after made governor of the island.

The king of France, to reward the bravery shown by his troops in the siege of Minorca, made several promotions, as a reward for the service of the officers at the siege.

Such was the loss of the island of Minorca: a loss which certainly stains the annals of Britain, in an indelible manner. Had the island been conquered by the french, in spite of the united efforts of the english fleet and garrison; or had not the english possessed a more powerful naval force than the french nation, the cafe would have been altered; but it is with equal grief and concern, that I am obliged to own and explain (if it wants explanation) how much the political character of Britain fuffered by this unfortunate lofs. The miniftry in England were extremely blameable in not fending a ftronger fquadron fooner into the Mediterranean; had a ftout fleet been fent thither to cruife off Toulon, before the french fleet failed, it would have been quite out of their power to tranfport an army to Minorca. For although they are able now and then to flip by a fuperior fleet lying before their harbour's mouth, yet, it would have been equally impoffible to have effected that, and abfurd to have endeavoured to do the fame, when they had 300 fail of tranfports to convoy. As to the cafe and merits of Mr. Byng, they are points fo very undetermined, and fo much difputed, that their confideration muft be deferred till I come to fpeak of his trial *.

General

* Abftract of all the ammunition expended in the fiege of Minorca, from the 30th of april, to the 30th of june, 1756.

| Shells. | Inches. |
|---|---|
| 1972 | $12\frac{3}{4}$ |
| 1385 | $6\frac{3}{4}$ |
| 1551 | $6\frac{3}{4}$ |
| 5738 | $5\frac{3}{4}$ |
| 16572 | $4\frac{1}{2}$ |
| 1032 hand grenades. | |

Total  28250

| | Inches. | No. |
|---|---|---|
| Carcaffes of | $12\frac{3}{4}$ | 73 |
| Ditto of | 10 | 41 |
| Fireballs | | 86 |

Total  200

Round

General William Blakeney, the brave defender of St. Philip's, was born at Mount Blakeney, in the county of Limerick in Ireland, anno 1672, the feat of his anceftors. He went early into the army in the beginning of the queen's war, and was an enfign with lord Cutts at the fiege of Venlo. He was long overlooked and neglected for want of friends, till at laft by the duke of Richmond's good offices, he was promoted to a regiment. He afterwards ferved againft the fpaniards at Carthagena, and commanded in Stirling caftle againft the rebels, in the late rebellion, when they laid fiege to it, and wherein his courage and conduct gained him great applaufe. He was a long time lieutenant governor of Minorca; and confidering his great merit, and unblemifhed character, was always put into the moft fevere and difagreeable employments. On his arrival in England, after his brave defence of St. Philip's, his majefty received him in the moft gracious manner; and he was foon after created a baron of the kingdom of Ireland, by the

| Round fhot. | | Grape fhot. | |
|---|---|---|---|
| Weight. | No. | Weight. | No. |
| 32 pound | 4001 | 32 pounds | 490 |
| 24 | 2061 | 18 | 171 |
| 18 | 17600 | 12 | 19 |
| 12 | 6059 | 9 | 37 |
| 9 | 1940 | 6 | 148 |
| 6 | 489 | 4 | 13 |
| 4 | 556 | 3 | 28 |
| | | 1½ | 53 |
| Total | 32706 | Total | 959 |

| Double headed fhot. | | Pounds of powder expended. | | |
|---|---|---|---|---|
| Weight. | No. | Barrels. | Weight. | Ounces. |
| 32 pounds | 152 | 3157 | 49 | 13 |
| 18 | 155 | | | |
| 12 | 3 | Reduced into pounds, make | | |
| 9 | 13 | | | |
| 3 | 9 | 353639 pounds, and 13 ounces. | | |
| Total | 332 | | | |

name

name and title of lord Blakeney of Mount Blakeney, in that kingdom.

I shall conclude all what I have to say on this subject, with a few hints on what Minorca might have been, had the conduct of Britain been such, in regard to that island, as might have been expected from the politics of a nation famous for their love of arts and sciences, and the improvement and cultivation of all their extensive dominions. The natives of Minorca at present, are computed at about 28,000; but I leave the reader to judge, how much that number would have been encreased, had the whole island and every harbour and creek in it been declared a free port, as soon as ever they fell under the subjection of England; without any sort of duties or fees, either upon importation or exportation, nor any tax upon goods of any kind, until they came into the retailer's or consumer's hands. Even then the taxes ought to have been as moderate, and collected in as easy a manner as possible, in order to have made living in the island both cheap and convenient; for very moderate taxes of this kind, with a land tax of two shillings in the pound in the time of peace, and four in the time of war, always fully and equally, and for that reason frequently assessed, would have probably produced as much as would have paid all the troops we should have been obliged to keep within the island in time of peace; and perhaps would have spared a considerable sum yearly for maintaining and improving the fortifications of all those places, which could by nature have been the most easy fortified.

And as this island lies so conveniently for trade, and communication between the richest parts of Europe, Asia, and Africa, it would certainly soon have become a general magazine, and mart for the trade of all those countries, if we had at first established the civil government and laws of England, for all british subjects and foreigners, who should come to settle in, or trade to the island; and this would have

encreased

encreased considerably the number of inhabitants. For this purpose, it would have been necessary to have established a civil as well as a military governnor, and to have made the former absolutely independent of the latter, unless when the island was in danger of being invaded, and martial law proclaimed with the consent of a counsel and an assembly, the former appointed by the crown, and the latter chosen by the people, with the approbation of the crown, or of some officer appointed by the crown, for such an approbation would be necessary to keep factious and seditious men out of the assembly.

Another improvement which certainly ought to have been put in execution, was the erecting more fortifications in the island than one single citadel, some of the cities, particularly Citudadella ought to have been as completely fortified as the nature of the ground would admit. The fort of St. Philip's ought not to have been so large, nor works so very extensive, for at present they require 8000 men to man them: the length of the late siege is no argument to the contrary, since the duke de Richelieu's conduct at the siege was so extremely faulty, that it was reported another marshal of France was ready to set out from Paris, to take the command from him, when the news came of its surrender. And as the ground on which Marlborough redoubt stands is very high, it ought certainly to have been included within a regular and strong fortification : for the further security of the harbour of Port Mahon, the intended fortification of cape Mola, ought to have been finished, and Philipet little redoubt very much enlarged : and for the security of the naval stores, Bloody Island should have been completely fortified all round, and filled with magazines, casematted, and bomb-proof.

With regard to the natural produce of the island, there are two necessary materials for our manufactories, which it is surprising were never yet produced in common in the ifland, either by the natives, or by fending people thither for that purpofe, thefe are cotton and filk; the planting of the cotton fhrub has been tried here with fuccefs, and the Maltefe produce fuch quantities of it, that they export 15,000 quintals of cotton wool yearly; therefore it feems certain, that it might be produced as freely at Minorca, and as the ifland is fo much larger than Malta, we might have expected by this time to have had large quantities of cotton wool exported yearly, had we encouraged the producing of it by allowing it to be imported duty free. As to filk, it is very probable that mulberry trees would have done very well, if planted in Minorca, as great numbers grow in the countries on all fides of it; if that had been the cafe, it would certainly be a very fine place for breeding filk worms, as they feldom have any froft or fnow, and never of any continuance; therefore the planting of fuch trees ought at leaft to have been tried, and if they had fucceeded (which is extremely probable) the pains and coft which might have been expended in the attempt would very amply have been repaid us; but fuch was the ill-management of the englifh miniftry from the time it came into our poffeffion, to the moment it was taken, that not one of thefe fchemes were ever tried. But it is now time to return to the motions of Mr. Byng's fleet.

The latter end of may commodore Broderick had been fent from England to the Mediterranean with five fhips of the line to reinforce Mr. Byng's fleet; and fome days after his failing, advice having been received by way of France of that admiral's behaviour in the engagement of the 20th of may; fir Edward Hawke, with Mr. Saunders (who had been made an admiral fome days before) and feveral captains, together with the earl of Panmure, and lord Tyrawley (appointed governor of Gibraltar, in the room of Mr. Fowke) were ordered to repair immediately to Portfmouth, there to embark on board the Antelope
man

man of war of 50 guns, and proceed to Gibraltar, where admiral Hawke had orders to take upon him the command of the fleet, together with Mr. Saunders, and send Mr. Byng and Mr. West, and some of the captains home immediately; lord Tyrawley had orders to send Mr. Fowke home at the same time, under arrest. They accordingly sailed from Portsmouth in the Antelope, on the 16th of June, and arrived at Gibraltar, the 3d of July, when sir Edward Hawke took the command of his majesty's fleet; and the Antelope sailed from Gibraltar the 9th, with Mr. Byng on board, and arrived at Portsmouth after a short passage. Mr. West repaired immediately to London, and was received by his majesty in the most gracious manner. Mr. Byng on his arrival, was immediately put under arrest.

## CHAP. VII.

*Affairs in England. In North America. Council of war at Albany. Plan of operations. Major general Abercrombie takes the chief command. Gallant action under Bradstreet. Oswego taken by the french. Reflections. Affairs in the East-Indies. Nabob of Bengal takes Calcutta. Reflections.*

THE loss of Minorca had thrown the nation into a flame. The clamour against the ministry was very great throughout the whole kingdom; all the corporations in England presented addresses to his majesty, petitioning in the strongest terms for a change of ministers and measures: and indeed, the general despondency which appeared in all ranks of men, from which, even the ministry themselves were not entirely free, owing to the loss of Minorca, and the dread of a french invasion, which had for some time rooted deep in the minds of the people, was not altogether without some reason; for without doubt, the nation was at this time in a very melancholy condition, for though the war had not continued long enough for her resources to be exhausted, yet the mean figure which we then made in the eyes of all Europe, was very mortifying to those englishmen, who had a true sense of their country's honour. The insults, the contemptuous usage, and the harsh acts of oppression, put upon the english in general, throughout all the Mediterranean, were they not known facts, would at present appear incredible. At this unhappy period, the glory of our name was sullied, not only in Europe, but wherever else they had to combat with the victorious french: In short, the privateers were the only victors which then belonged to us; and these were almost ballanced by the num-

ber

ber of ships taken by those of the french. The affairs of North America wore the same gloomy aspect that distinguished the appearance of its mother country in Europe.

There the french were still victorious, at least they were quite succesful in their plan of operations in that country, which was by any means to secure to themselves the sole trade and navigation of all the great lakes and rivers, on the back of the english settlements; to effect this, they had already made very great advances; they had usurped all the immense tract of lands on the river Ohio, and secured it for the present by the important fortress of du Quesne; they had secured another tract by building the fort at Crown Point, and fort Cohasser; they had erected a multitude of small forts on all the passes of the lakes to awe the indians and command their trade, those of Niagara and Frontenac, were the most considerable; the frontiers of the Carolina's were awed and curbed by fort Condé, besides many other forts of less consequence singly, but of great importance all together, as they connected the chain, which commanded all the frontiers of the english settlements, from Nova Scotia to Georgia. And what added greatly to the strength and formidableness of the french in North America, was the divided state of the english colonies, whereas those of the french were all connected in one general government, under the absolute military controul of the governor general of Canada. It was under these great and manifest disadvantages, that the new year, 1756, was opened in North America.

General Shirley still continued commander in chief. I left him at New York, having settled with the grand council held there, the plan of operations, which the reader may remember in my 4th chapter; he set out for Albany and arrived there the 7th of may, and continuing his preparations till the 25th, 

H 3 called

called a council of war, to advise on his future measures, and he took their opinions in every article, few of which were of importance.

He had heard some time before, that there was a design in England to supersede him; but this was uncertain, till col. Webb arrived at New York from England, bringing two letters from his majesty's principal secretaries of State, dated the 13th and 31st of march; in the latter of which, he received his majesty's orders to repair to England. On the 20th of june, major general Abercrombie arrived at New York with Otway's, and the highland regiments, from whence he went to Albany, in company with col. Webb, and the day following took upon himself the chief command of all his majesty's forces in North America. Mr. Shirley gave general Abercrombie a very particular account in writing, of the state of every part of his majesty's service under his care, with the strength of the regiments, garrisons, and works; and also gave him his sentiments and advice in regard to the expeditions which were then in agitation, against the french. One of them, as it displays a great piece of bravery, I must be more particular in mentioning. It was a very gallant action under captain Bradstreet. That officer commanding the battoes in their way to Oswego, was attacked by a party of french and indians in ambuscade; finding himself between two fires, he retired with great dexterity to a little island on the river, where, for some time, he defended himself with six men, against forty of the enemy, and obliged them to retire; being reinforced, he attacked a large body infinitely superior to his own, and gained a complete victory over them, which was owing intirely to his own admirable conduct, and the astonishing bravery of his men.

In march last the earl of Loudon had been appointed commander in chief of all his majesty's forces in

North America; and general Abercrombie sent over to assume the command, till his lordship's arrival, which was on the 23d of july, at New York. Mr. Shirley having arrived there the 4th, his lordship regardless of his ease, and the fatigues of a tedious voyage, rested there but three days; and on the 29th of july, reached his head quarters at Albany, when he took upon himself the command of the army.

Soon after his lordship's arrival, capt. Bradstreet dispatched intelligence, that he was informed the french were preparing to attack Oswego, having 1200 men for that purpose encamped, not far from the eastermost fort. Upon receipt of this intelligence, general Webb was ordered to hold himself in readiness to march for its defence, with the 44th regiment; and on the 12th of august, the troops embarked for that expedition, at Albany.

In the mean time, lieutenant colonel Mercer, commanding officer at Oswego, received repeated intelligence, that the enemy had some place or camp to the eastward of Oswego, about 30 miles from it; and particularly on the 6th of august, that there was a large encampment of french and indians about 12 miles to the eastward of that fort; on these intelligences, Mr. Mercer dispatched an express boat to the commanding officer upon the lake, who was then out upon a cruise to the westward, with a brigantine and two sloops; letting him know that he intended next day to send 400 men in whale boats to visit the enemy, and desiring him to keep to the eastward as much as he could, in order to cover the men in the boats, and hinder the enemy from approaching nearer; but by some strange neglect, or some other private reason, instead of complying therewith, they returned next day to Oswego, and in endeavouring to enter the harbour, the brigantine was driven by a gale of wind upon rocky ground, where she lay beating about 18 hours, and was afterwards forced to heave down, in order to have a falſe keel.

Monſieur Montcalm, the french general, having intelligence given him of the ſituation of the engliſh veſſels, that the brigantine was ſtranded, and the other two returned into harbour, took the opportunity of tranſporting and landing his artillery and troops in boats, within a mile and half of fort Ontario; which, as a french officer declared after Oſwego was taken, he could not have done, had our veſſels been out to the eaſtward.

Their artillery, for drawing which they tranſported 35 horſes, conſiſted of about 32 pieces of cannon, from 12 to 24 pounders, ſeveral large braſs mortars and hoyets (among which was the artillery taken from general Braddock at Monongahela) and were all brought in battoes from Portland Point, as they could not have been tranſported by land from thence, on account of the great number of ſwamps, drowned lands, and creeks in the way; their forces conſiſted of about 1800 regular troops, 2500 canadians, and 500 indians. The french troops began to fire upon Oſwego on the 11th of auguſt, which was returned with ſmall arms, and eight cannon from the fort, and ſhells from the other ſide the river.

In ſhort, the force of the french amounting to upwards of 3000 men, after a few days defence, the garriſon was obliged to ſurrender; but not before their governor col. Mercer was killed by a cannon ball.

During the whole ſiege, the ſoldiers behaved with a remarkable reſolution and intrepidity againſt the enemy, exerting themſelves in the defence of the place in every part of duty; and it was with great reluctance, that they were perſuaded by their officers to lay down their arms, after the garriſon had capitulated.

Immediately ·

Immediately after the surrender of Oswego, the french demolished the works there, and embarked with their prisoners, provisions, artillery, and booty for fort Frontenac, in their way back to Montreal, and from thence to Quebec, where the garrison was put on board a merchant ship, which set sail directly for Portsmouth in England, and exchanged them for the same number of french prisoners.

From what I have said, concerning the siege of Oswego, the reader will perceive, that the loss of that fortress, in all probability would not have happened, if they had not brought a train of artillery against it, and that was impracticable by any other means, than by water carriage on the lake; and it appeared by the behaviour of the french vessels, and from the confession of the french officers themselves, that the english vessels fitted out upon the lake were of sufficient strength to have prevented the french from transporting their artillery, &c. by water; and consequently, if the new sloop and sloop Oswego had been in a condition to have acted upon the lake, it would have rendered it quite impracticable for the enemy to have brought their artillery to Oswego, even without the occasional assistance of the whale boats. In regard to the strength of the forts at Oswego, for resisting an army furnished with cannon, it was very insufficient; and the most particular partisans of general Shirley are forced to slur over this affair, in the most plausible manner they were able, as the arguments they use for that end, are founded too much upon the general's intentions, and expectations of the service of the indians; surely he might have placed the safety of so important a post upon stronger foundations, especially, as he had all along made Oswego one of the principal articles of his management, whilst he had the chief command, and spent so much time there in person, in forwarding the fortifications; and, as I have said before, had almost finished the

transportation

transportation of provisions, enough for 5000 men for several months, to that fort; one would have thought that Mr. Shirley might have known, that these methods must all be tried in vain, unless he put the fortress itself in such a state of defence, as to have nothing to fear from any armaments which the french could make against it.

I observed before, that general Webb was ordered to march to the relief of Oswego: he was advanced as far as the german flatts, when he received an express from the commanding officer, at the great Carrying-place, august the 17th, acquainting him, that Oswego was in the hands of the enemy. In answer to which, he received orders from general Webb to employ as large a party of men as he could spare, in obstructing the passage of the Wood-creek, for 24 miles, by felling of trees a-cross it; and in a few days the general arrived there himself, and immediately sent out fresh parties to assist in stopping up the passage of the Wood-creek. Upon his arrival at the Carrying-place, there were about 1500 regular troops there, which, together with the seamen, battoe-men, &c. made upwards of 2500 fighting men, and sir Will. Johnson was then marching thither, with the albany militia. As general Webb was entirely ignorant of the strength of the french forces that had taken Oswego, or the rout they had marched, he encamped at the great Carrying-place, and threw up an entrenchment and breast-work round his camp, upon which he mounted 28 pieces of cannon.

But soon after, repeated intelligence being brought to the general, that the french had evacuated Oswego, and were marching home again; he ordered all the battoes he had with him, to be loaded with all the stores, cannon, ammunition, and provisions that were there, and proceed back again to Albany: and as to the forts at the Carrying-place, he ordered them to be pulled down, burnt, and destroyed. This was of very bad confequence; for the indians inhabiting the country round thefe forts, were no fooner left unprotected, than they wavered in their alliance with the englifh; and this meafure was alfo needlefs in another refpect, as the french who conquered Ofwego had marched back again; whereas, general Webb ftopped up the Wood-creek, and demolifhed the forts at the great Carrying-place, in expectation of the enemy's marching againft him.

This was the laft affair in which Mr. Shirley was any ways concerned, as commander in chief; I mean the lofs of Ofwego. It is very difficult to pronounce decifively on the abilities of a man, from the tranfactions he is concerned in during one year's command; at leaft this is the cafe with regard to general Shirley: with great juftnefs, and the ftricteft impartiality one may venture to pronounce, that he was an able man, though unequal in appearance to the weight of public care, which he affumed when he undertook the chief command; the greateft flaw in his conduct was the lofs of Ofwego, the prefervation of which place, he had many times declared to be the chief point he had in view for a long time; and it is natural to fuppofe, that when a general himfelf undertakes to fee any poft fortified, that fuch a fortrefs fhould at leaft be ftrong enough to refift an enemy a reafonable time; at leaft this was certainly to have been expected in regard to Ofwego: but after all the objections which have been raifed againft his conduct, yet we fhould remember, that if, upon the moft ftrict enquiry, we find he was in his command very faulty, thofe minifters in England, who permitted him to continue in it, were alfo faulty, in a like proportion, for not being acquainted with the merits of the man they promoted. It was indeed a little unufual to find a private perfon, who had been originally bred to the law, at the univerfity in Cambridge, and feeking his fortune in the

manner

manner Mr. Shirley did, rise almost at once to be generalissimo in America, with the appointments and pay of the great duke of Marlborough.

Such was the bad success of his majesty's arms in America; and in the East-Indies, affairs wore a still worse aspect: the company, by the bad management of their affairs, which is just what one would expect from the dominion of a company of traders, lost their valuable settlement at Bengal. It seems that Alvedeikam, nabob of Bengal, having died in the beginning of may 1756, his nephew, Saradjot Dollah succeeded him. This succession occasioned much discontent and trouble. Saradjot proving a most abominable tyrant, his subjects many of them conspired against him, and being discovered, took refuge in the english settlement at Calcutta. The nabob marched against that place with an army, and after making some enormous demands, laid siege to it; governor Dr-k- pretended to be a quaker, persuaded many people to send their treasures on board a ship in the river with him to save them, which many did; the governor then, with the officer next in command, set sail, and left the garrison, uncommanded, to take care of themselves. They, dispirited by this behaviour, soon surrendered, and were treated with the greatest cruelty; what 200 of them suffered in the black hole is too shocking and too fresh in every one's memory to be forgot. It was expected that the governor would have been called to account for his bad behaviour at Calcutta, in leaving the garrison to take care of themselves; but he escaped without so much as a trial; it was said for his excuse, that he was a quaker, and consequently his conscience would not allow him to fight; but supposing that was the case, yet there remains a query that will be difficult to be answered; and that is, why did the next commanding officer follow so bad an example and go away with him,

that

that gentleman was no quaker by religion, although he shewed himself to have the same aversion to fighting. It is equally a disgrace to the english East-India company, the appointing a quaker to be commander of a place of such importance, and the leaving it in such a defenceless condition: but such oversights and weak management is generally to be found in the affairs of a company of traders, who as such may be conspicuous, but as warriors contemptible.

CHAP.

## CHAP. VIII.

*Affairs in Europe. Court martial on lieut. gen. Fowke. Reflections. Recapitulation of the Affairs of Germany. Negotiations in Germany, from 1744 to 1756. Measures of the courts of Vienna, Petersburg, and Dresden. They prepare for war. King of Prussia's memorial to the empress queen, and her answer. Conduct of the court of Saxony. Of his prussian majesty. Reflections.*

IN Europe, the affairs of the british nation wore but a gloomy aspect, proceeding from the sense of those disgraces, which that brave people met with in other parts of the world; and which could not but damp the spirits of every englishman, who had the least regard for the honour and welfare of his country. During the course of the unfortunate year, 1756, England was stripped of the valuable island of Minorca, and suffered a severe disgrace under admiral Byng. In North America, the important fortress of Oswego was conquered by the french; and a general unsuccess sullied the british arms. In the East-Indies indeed, the pirate Angria was conquered, and thereby the india company received great advantages, their trade was more secure and less interrupted; but this good fortune was soon after followed by the loss of Calcutta; so that in this country, the english were far from being successful; and then adding to these instances, the success which the french met with in their small squadrons, always escaping the superior ones of the english, we may justly conclude, with repeating how much the martial credit of the nation suffered by the events which happened from the beginning of this war, to the period I am now speaking of. But to return.

The

The reader may remember, that when Admiral Byng arrived at Gibraltar, in his way to the relief of Minorca, he, pursuant to his instructions, demanded of lieut. gen. Fowke a detachment from his garrison, equal to a battalion, to take on board his fleet and carry to reinforce the garrison of St. Philip's; and that Mr. Fowke had received his majesty's orders to comply with such demand; but he, in consequence of the weakness of his garrison, called a council of war at Gibraltar, to consider whether it was expedient, as the state of affairs then stood in the Mediterranean, to obey these commands; and that it was resolved by this council of war, not to send such a detachment on board Mr. Byng's fleet. It was for disobedience to these orders, that lieut. gen. Fowke was brought before the following board of general officers, appointed to enquire into his behaviour, and who met the 10th of august, 1760, viz.

    Gen. sir Robert Rich, president,
    Gen. sir John Ligonier,
    Lieut. gen. Hawley,
    Lieut. gen. lord Cadogan,
    Lieut. gen. Guise,
    Lieut. gen. Onslow,
    Lieut. gen. Pultney,
    Lieut. gen. Huske,
    Lieut. gen. Campbell,
    Lieut. gen. lord de la Warr,
    Lieut. gen. Charles duke of Marlborough,
    Lieut. gen. Wolfe,
    Lieut. gen. Cholmondeley,
    Major gen. Lascelles,
    Major gen. Bockland,
    Major gen. lord Geo. Beauclerk.

The members of this court being sworn, and the necessary papers read, the judge advocate opened the prosecution, by accusing the general of disobedience to his majesty's orders. The nature of this court martial, did not require that many witnesses should be examined, the principal part of the proceedings was the general's defence. Having prepared it, it was read, and was as follows;

"That he received these three letters together, by the same hand, and must therefore take them together. That his orders were confused at least, if not contradictory: that if they were confused, then he could not know how to execute them; and if they were contradictory, they could not be executed at all.

My orders being confused and contradictory, I called a council of war, not to deliberate whether I should obey my orders or not, but only to take their sense, what was the meaning of them.

The whole number which I had then in garrison, was but 2700 men. I had spared to Mr. Edgecomb's ships 230, which, with 40 of my men which he had left in St. Philip's, made 270. The ordinary duty of the garrison required in workmen and guards 800 men, so that I had then only 130 men more than three reliefs. If I had made the detachment of a battalion, and put it on board the fleet, I should not then have had much more than two reliefs, and this at a time, when I believed the place was in danger of being attacked, for good reasons, which I do not think myself at liberty to mention."

When the judge advocate had finished reading the general's defence; Mr. Fowke made a speech to the court, by which he enforced what he before insisted upon, that the orders delivered to him were confused and contradictory, and that in every sense that could be put upon them, they were discretionary, that is to say, to be complied with, or not to be complied with, according as the admiral and he should, from the then circumstances of affairs, judge to be most for his majesty's service.

The reader perceives, that the general's defence consists in the supposition of his order's being discretionary

cretionary, and thefe certainly were fome queftions, which would make one think, they either were fo, or contradictory. The judge advocate being ordered to read a letter from the fecretary at war to general Fowke, began it thus:

"I wrote to you by general Stuart; if that order "is not complied with, then you are," &c. &c.

Upon which the general very naturally afked, how could his lordfhip write, "If that order is not complied with," if he had thought it an abfolute order, and not difcretionary.

Another very odd anfwer was made, during the fitting of the court, which is very worthy of being remembered to the credit of its author.

General Fowke afked the fecretary at war, "But "is it not the cuftom of your office, when fecond "orders are intended to fuperfede the firft, to men-"tion that they do fo?" In reply to which, my lord Barrington faid, "I had then been but about four "months in my office." This anfwer, I think, needs no comment.

When the queftion came to be put, to acquit or to fufpend for one year, the court was equally divided, there being eight for acquitting, and eight for fufpending; and as, in fuch cafes the prefident has a cafting vote, he gave it for fufpending. Which fentence being reported to his majefty, he thought fit to difmifs him from his fervice.

Such were the refolutions of this council of war. I muft make a few remarks on the evidence that appeared on the trial, which I fhall do with the ftricteft impartiality. General Fowke received two orders from the fecretary at war, the firft to receive lord Robert Bertie's regiment into his garrifon, and to fend a detachment on board the fleet; the fecond faid nothing about lord Robert Bertie's regiment, but repeated the other order. On the receipt of them, he directly called a council of war, and laid before them the ftate of his own garrifon, and

the

the difficulty of throwing fuccours into Minorca, and defired their opinion concerning the expediency of obeying his orders, whether it was for his majefty's fervice. The general afterwards in his defence declared, that he called this council of war, not to confider whether he fhould obey his orders, or not, but to know the meaning of them : if this was really the cafe, would it not have been natural for him to lay his orders before them, and, in one word to afk their opinions, whether they were difcretionary or abfolute; but fo far from this, there never paffed a doubt about his orders, the point in difpute amongft them was, whether they fhould be obeyed, or no.

One point, indeed, fpoke for him, which was the beginning of lord Barrington's letter, of the 12th of may. " I wrote you by general Stuart; if that or-" der was not complied with, then," this was in one fenfe faying, that the order by general Stuart was difcretionary, for his lordfhip muft know, or had at leaft great reafon to think, that Mr. Fowke had received thofe by general Stuart. But what condemns him moft of all was, his letter to the fecretary at war, dated the 6th of may, wherein he tells him, " That he had, with the advice of a council of " war, difobeyed his order, and that he had been in-" duced to act fo, on the confideration of the weak " ftate of his garrifon ;" but never once mentions that he had acted according to his judgment in obedience to his lordfhip's difcretionary orders; which he certainly would have done, had he really thought they were difcretionary. If the general thought his orders to be fo undoubtedly difcretionary, what occafion was there to call a council of war, to know their meaning? as he fays in his defence he did. In fhort, it was that fatal letter to lord Barrington, which convinced the court martial of the general's difobedience; had he not produced it, many have thought, that he would have been acquitted; but that letter
convinced

convinced them, that he himfelf thought his orders abfolute.

But to leave the gloomy affairs of England for a moment, and turn our eyes on thofe of more refplendent and magnificent eclat ; we muft accompany the reader through the principal courts in Germany, and point out the feeming fecret caufes of thofe great events, which for fome years held all Europe equally in fufpence, and aftonifhment. As the courts of Berlin and Vienna were the principals in this famous conteft, it will be neceffary (for the information of the reader) to prefent him with a recapitulation of the general affairs of Germany, antecedent to the period I am fpeaking of: and more particularly of the two courts abovementioned.

Every one, who is the leaft verfed in the hiftory of Germany, muft know, that Frederick William the IId, elector of Brandenburg, was one of the greateft and moft diftinguifhed princes of his time, both for wifdom and courage ; which were always properly employed for his own fecurity, and the benefit of his people. He entered upon the government, in the year 1640, a time when the affairs of Germany, and his own, were in a very difficult and embarraffed fituation. In the year 1687, this prince came to an amicable conclufion with the emperor Leopold, in relation to a difpute, which had long fubfifted, concerning the principality of Jagerndorff in Silefia ; the inveftiture of which had been conferred on the margraves of Brandenburg, by Lewis, king of Bohemia, about the year 1523 ; which duchy had afterwards been refumed by the houfe of Auftria, under feveral trifling pretenfions, at times when the power of the auftrian family was undifturbed, and that of Brandenburg involved in the confufion of war. In compenfation for this principality, the elector had the territory of Schwibus, in the northern part of Silefia yielded up to him, which the emperor afterwards found

found means to obtain back from his son and successor.

Frederick III succeeded his father in the electorate of Brandenburg, in april, 1688; and, like several of his predecessors, entered upon the administration of affairs, at a conjuncture, which required a prince of great parts to conduct them to advantage.

This great and magnificent prince died in the 56th year of his age, and was succeeded in all his dominions by Frederick William, prince royal of Prussia, and electoral prince of Brunswick, whose reign was no less glorious, than that of his father's, shewing, in every transaction of his life, that he was in every instance careful to maintain and support his own dignity, to secure his dominions, to make himself respected by his neighbours, to keep his troops and fortresses constantly in such a posture, as might prevent his being hurt by any unforeseen accident; and give him an opportunity, where the circumstances of things would permit it, of turning any such accident to his advantage. It was with this view, that he kept always on foot, between 80 and 100,000 regular troops well paid, and perfectly well disciplined; at the same time that he was no less careful of his revenues, as being thoroughly sensible, that if ever a war became necessary, treasure would be to the full as needful as troops.

Charles Frederick, the present king of Prussia, and elector of Brandenburg, was born january the 24th, 1712, and consequently was in the 29th year of his age, when he mounted the throne. I shall be more particular in what relates to this great monarch, antecedent to the period I shall attempt to write the history of, as he afterwards shone forth with so distinguishing a lustre, in the late war.

The very dawning of this young monarch's government drew the attention of all Europe, and gave his neighbours very just ideas of what might be expected in the progress of it. He had been but
indifferently

indifferently treated in his father's life-time, and there confequently were many who dreaded his refentments; but he punifhed no body except the counfellor Eckard, whom he ordered to depart his dominions, becaufe he had been a conftant devifer of taxes, and the principal inftrument of the late king, in laying burthens upon his fubjects; fo that in his manner of treating him, the new monarch fhewed that he could avenge the wrongs done to his people, though he was at the fame time patient under his own. He was no fooner poffeffed of the crown, than he declared himfelf a protector of learning; and by a letter written with his own hand, invited the famous Mr. Maupertuis from Paris, to take upon him the direction of the academy of Berlin; or, as the king himfelf elegantly expreffed it, to graft the flips of true fcience on the wild ftocks in the north *.

This young monarch, in the difputes he had concerning the barony of Herftall, and principality of Neufchatel, with the bifhop of Liege, and the duke of Chevreufe, manifefted to his neighbours, the firmnefs and vigour of his government. Thefe however, were but as preludes to the great ftroke of all, by which his majefty added a great part of the rich and fruitful country of Silefia to his dominions: which, as it has been confidered as the occafion of the general war of 1741, and bore a confiderable fhare in that of which I am giving the hiftory; the reader will naturally expect, that we fhould be a little more particular in the account of this fingular tranfaction.

I have already fhown, that the houfe of Brandenburg had a very fair title to the principality of Jagerndorf, and other territories in that country, which

---

\* Vide Prefent State of Europe, from which ingenious work I have taken great part of this account of the king of Pruffia, preceding the war.

the emperor, notwithstanding united to the kingdom of Bohemia; but as the elector still kept up his claim, and the house of Austria had great need of his assistance, it was found necessary to give him some satisfaction; and accordingly a treaty was set on foot at Berlin, in 1686, whereby it was stipulated, that the elector should renounce all the pretensions of his house, to the principalities of Jagerndorf, Lignitz, Brieg and Wohau, upon condition that the emperor should yield to the elector, the territory of Schwibus. The baron de Frytag, who managed this negotiation for the court of Vienna, with the elector Frederick II, set on foot at the same time another clandestine treaty with the electoral prince Frederick, who was afterwards Frederick III, elector of Brandenburg, though he is generally called Frederick I, because he was the first king of Prussia.

The nature of this secret negotiation was very dark; for there were some family disputes, in which the emperor threatened to take part against the prince, if, at the same time his father subscribed the treaty abovementioned, he did not subscribe an obligation to give up, as soon as it should be in his power the territory of Schwibus, for a small sum of money. Accordingly, when he became elector of Brandenburg, the money was offered, and the territory demanded; but all the counsellors of the new elector advised him not to part with it, as he had been compelled to make this agreement, which, in its own nature therefore was void; but the emperor Leopold insisting upon it, and threatening to use force, he yielded up the territory; but refused to confirm the renunciation made by his father, of his former right.

Thus the reader sees, in a few words, the nature of the king of Prussia's claim; he represented both Frederick II, and Frederick III, consequently the rights of both were in him; and, as the house of Austria had taken away the equivalent, he conceived he had

had a juft right to the territories formerly in the poffeffion of his family, viz. the principality of Jagerndorf, and other countries, of which he refolved immediately to take poffeffion. He had two reafons for acting in this manner, without any previous declarations made to the court of Vienna; the firft was, that the male line of the houfe of Auftria being extinct, and the power of that family thereby weakened, he thought this a favourable opportunity of doing himfelf juftice; and that he fhould be wanting to himfelf and his pofterity, or fucceffors, if he neglected it. His fecond, that the elector of Bavaria and the king of Spain forming pretenfions upon the emperor's fucceffion, he was defirous of reconciling his view of doing himfelf juftice, to the inclination he had of affifting Mary Therefa queen of Hungary, in maintaining her rights to her father's dominions, agreeable to the pragmatic fanction.

At the fame time therefore, that he ordered his troops to march into Silefia, which was in december, 1740, he declared toh e court of Vienna, that notwithftanding this ftep, he was difpofed to promote the election of the duke of Lorrain to the imperial dignity; that he was willing to advance the queen of Hungary two millions of florins; and that he was ready to employ all his forces in defending her dominions, againft all her competitors. But thefe propofitions were abfolutely rejected, upon which a war enfued. It is to be obferved, that in this article I am ftating the claims, pretenfions, and meafures of his pruffian majefty, as matters of fact; and am very far from taking upon me to decide, whether the former were well or ill founded, and confequently whether the latter were right or wrong; but thus much, I think, I may be allowed to fay, that if the court of Vienna had accepted of this propofal, the war in Germany had been prevented, and the emprefs queen had not yielded more to the king of Pruffia, than fhe was obliged to do afterwards, after all the blood

blood and treasure spent on both sides in this fatal quarrel.

His prussian majesty carried his point in the first instance; that is to say, he made himself master of Silesia, without much opposition; and the austrians having brought a great army into the field, under the command of the field marshal count Nieuperg; in the beginning of the next spring, his prussian majesty gave that army battle, the 10th of april, 1741, at Molwitz, in which, though with great effusion of blood, he gained the victory. In may, 1742, he fought the famous battle of Czaslau, in which he also claimed the victory; but both parties being now weary of the war, a treaty of peace was negotiated between his majesty on one part, and the queen of Hungary on the other, which was concluded and signed june the 11th, at Breslau in Silesia; by which the greatest part of that duchy, and the whole county of Glatz were yielded to his majesty.

But this valuable cession did not hinder him from entering into the league of Frankfort, in support of the emperor Charles VII, in consequence of which, he invaded Bohemia, and took the city of Prague, in june, 1744, won the uncontested victory of Friedburg in june, 1745, and that of Stadentz in the september following. Yet, the austrians still persisting to continue the war, presuming on the diversion to be made by a great body of russian auxiliaries, which it was supposed would have marched through Poland into his territories. But his prussian majesty took advantage of the season, and while his enemies were pleasing themselves, with the hopes of invading and ruining his country, the old prince of Anhault Dessau, with a prussian army entered their's. The king of Poland was obliged to abandon his hereditary dominions, and to retire to the frontiers of Bohemia for safety. Leipsick opened her gates to the conqueror, and though a numerous army of saxons and austrians interposed, to preserve Dresden, yet, december the 4th,

4th, 1745, they were totally defeated by the prince of Anhalt Deſſau, with half their number of pruſſian troops.

The king entered Dreſden in triumph, and having overcome all his enemies, on the 14th of the ſame month, overcame his provocation and reſentment; and in the full warmth of victory, gave them a fair and equitable peace. By which, Sileſia was again ſolemnly yielded to him; the ſaxons gave him one million of crowns for the expence of the war; his majeſty acknowledged the emperor, guarantied the dominions of the empreſs queen, and included his ally, the elector Palatine, in the ſame treaty, which was negotiated under the mediation of his britannic majeſty, and the concluſion of which, once more ſettled the tranquility of Germany.

I now come to the negotiations, which gave riſe more immediately to the war, of which I am giving an account; but the more clearly to do this, it is neceſſary to look back, a little before the peace of Dreſden, which I have juſt mentioned. I ſhall here acquaint the reader, that moſt of the facts mentioned in my account of that ſeries of projects, conſpiracies, treachery of the courts of Vienna, and Dreſden, is ſelected from the authentic pieces publiſhed by his majeſty of Pruſſia, when he poſſeſſed himſelf of Dreſden.

To come at the ſource of all theſe dark negotiations, which afterwards threw the greateſt part of Europe into a flame, we muſt look back as far as the war that preceded the peace of Dreſden. The fond hopes that the two courts of Auſtria and Saxony had conceived, upon the ſucceſs of the campaign, in 1744, gave occaſion to a treaty of eventual partition, which they concluded the 18th of may, 1745, agreeably to which, the court of Vienna was to have the duchy of Sileſia, and the county of Glatz; and the king of Poland, elector of Saxony, the duchies of Magdeburg, and Croſlen, the circles of Zullichow,

and

and Schwibus, together with the prussian part of Lusatia; or only part of those provinces, in proportion to their conquests.

Soon after the peace of Dresden, which was signed the 25th of december, 1745, there was no further room for a treaty of so extraordinary a nature, as that of an eventual partion, with regard to a power, with whom the two contracting parties lived in peace; but yet the court of Vienna made no scruple to propose to the court of Saxony, a new treaty of alliance, in which they should likewise renew the treaty of eventual partition, of the 18th of may, 1745.

The court of Saxony thought it necessary, in the first place, to give a greater consistency to their plan, by grounding it upon an alliance between the courts of Russia and Vienna. These two powers did in fact conclude a defensive alliance at Petersburg, the 22d of may, 1746. But it is easy to perceive, that the body or ostensible part of this treaty was drawn up merely with a view, to conceal the six secret articles from the knowledge of the public; the fourth of which is levelled singly against Prussia, according to the counterpart of it, found by his prussian majesty among the other state papers, in the cabinet at Dresden.

In this article, the empress queen of Hungary and Bohemia, sets out with a protestation, that she will religiously observe the treaty of Dresden; but she says a little lower, " If the king of Prussia should
" be the first to depart from this peace, by attacking
" either her majesty, the empress queen of Hungary
" and Bohemia, or her majesty the empress of Russia,
" or even the republic of Poland, in all which cases,
" the rights of her majesty, the empress queen to
" Silesia, and the county of Glatz, would again take
" place, and recover their full effect; the two con-
" tracting parties shall mutually assist each other
" with a body of 60,000 men, to reconquer Silesia,
" &c."

The

The reader will at once perceive the unjuſt tendency of this article; and theſe were the titles, by which the court of Vienna propoſed to avail itſelf of, for the recovery of Sileſia. Every war that could ariſe between the king of Pruſſia and Ruſſia, or the republic of Poland, is to be looked upon as a manifeſt infraction of the peace of Dreſden, and a revival of the rights of the houſe of Auſtria to Sileſia; though neither Ruſſia nor the republic of Poland were at all concerned in the treaty of Dreſden; and though the latter, with which Pruſſia otherwiſe lived in the moſt intimate friendſhip, was not then even in alliance with the court of Vienna. From this it ſeems very manifeſt, that the 4th ſecret article of the treaty of Peterſburg, is ſo far from being a defenſive alliance, that it contains a plan of an offenſive alliance, tending to wreſt Sileſia from the king of Pruſſia.

From this article it ſeems obvious, that the court of Vienna had prepared three pretences for the recovery of Sileſia; and by comparing it with her conduct from that time, it is very viſible that ſhe thought to attain her end, either by provoking the king of Pruſſia to commence a war againſt her, or by kindling one between his majeſty and Ruſſia or Poland, by her ſecret intrigues or machinations; conſidering which, it is not a matter of any wonder, that this treaty of Peterſburg ſhould have been the hinge upon which all the auſtrian politics have turned, from the peace of Dreſden to this time; and that the negotiations of the court of Vienna have been principally directed to ſtrengthen this alliance, by the acceſſion of other powers.

The court of Saxony was the firſt that was invited to this acceſſion, in the beginning of the year, 1746. They eagerly accepted the invitation, as ſoon as made; furniſhed their miniſters at Peterſburg, count de Vicedom, and the ſieur Pezold, with the neceſſary full powers for that purpoſe; and ordered them to

declare,

declare, that their court was not only ready to accede to the treaty itself; but also to the secret article against Prussia: and also, that if, upon any fresh attack from the king of Prussia, the empress queen should, by their assistance, happen not only to reconquer Silesia, and the county of Glatz, but also to reduce him within narrower bounds; the king of Poland, as elector of Saxony, would stand to the partition stipulated between his polish majesty and the empress queen, by the convention signed at Leipsick, the 18th of may, 1745. Count Loss, the saxon minister at Vienna, was charged, at the same time, to open a private negotiation, for settling an eventual partition of the conquests, which should be made on Prussia, by laying down, as the basis of it, the partition treaty of Leipsick, of the 18th of may, 1745.

Throughout this unaccountable negotiation, it was affectedly supposed, that the king of Prussia would be the aggressor against the court of Vienna. But what right could the king of Poland draw from thence, to make conquests upon the king of Prussia? Or, if his polish majesty, in the quality of an auxiliary, would also become a belligerent party; it could not be taken amiss, that his prussian majesty should treat him accordingly, and regulate his conduct by that of the court of Saxony. This is a truth that was acknowledged, even by the king of Poland's own privy council; for being consulted upon their master's accession to the treaty of Petersburg, they were of opinion, that the 4th secret article went beyond common rules; and that his prussian majesty might look upon the accession to it as a violation of the peace of Dresden.

Count Brühl, prime minister to the king of Poland, being, without doubt, thoroughly convinced himself of this truth, did all in his power to conceal the existence of the secret articles of the treaty of Petersburg. For, at the time that he was eagerly negotiating in Russia, upon his court's accession to it, and to its secret

cret articles, he caused a solemn declaration to be made at Paris, " That the treaty of Petersburg, to which " his polish majesty had been invited to accede, did " not contain any thing more than what was in the " german copy," as appears from the count de Brühl's letter to count Loss of the 18th of june, 1747; and by a memorial, which count Loss delivered in consequence of it.

It is true, that the court of Saxony did yet defer, from one time to another, their acceding in form to the treaty of Petersburg; but they did not fail to let their allies know, again, and again, that they were ready to accede to it, without restriction, as soon as it could be done without too evident risk, and their share of the advantages to be gained should be secured to them. This principal is clearly expressed, in the instructions given the 19th of february, 1750, to general d'Arnim, when he was going to Petersburg, as minister from Saxony. This court being invited afresh, in the year, 1751, to accede to the treaty of Petersburg, declared its readiness to do it, in a memorial delivered to the russian minister at Dresden, and even sent full powers, and other necessary papers for that purpose, to the sieur Funck, their minister at Petersburg; but required at the same time, that the king of England, as elector of Hanover, should previously accede to the secret articles of the treaty of Petersburg;—And as his britannic majesty would never be concerned in this mistery of iniquity, count Brühl found himself obliged to wait the issue of the project, which had been formed, to make another alliance, of so innocent a nature as to be producible; the courts of Vienna and Saxony thought it necessary to put on these outward appearances of moderation, that they might not wound the delicacy of such of their allies, as were staggered at the secret views of the alliance of Petersburg; but for their part, they never lost sight of their darling plan, to divide the spoils of the king of Prussia beforehand, in keeping constantly

constantly to the fourth article of that treaty as their basis.

The reader will clearly perceive, from all the proofs that have now been produced, that the court of Saxony, without having acceded to the treaty of Petersburg, in form, was not less an accomplice in the dangerous designs, which the court of Vienna had grounded upon this treaty; and that, having been dispenced with by their allies, from a formal concurrence, they had only waited for the moment when they might, without running too great a risk, concur in effect, and share the spoils of their neighbour.

In expectation of this period, the austrian and saxon ministers laboured in concert, and underhand, with the more ardour to prepare the means of bringing the case of the secret alliance of Petersburg to exist. In this treaty it was laid down as a principle, that any war whatever between the king of Prussia and Russia, would authorise the empress queen to retake Silesia. There was nothing more, then, to be done, but to raise such a war. In order to bring this about, no means were found more proper, than to embroil the king of Prussia irreconcileably with her majesty, the empress of Russia, and to provoke that princess, by all sorts of false insinuations, impostures, and the most atrocious calumnies, in laying to the king of Prussia's charge, all sorts of designs against Russia, and even the empress's own person; and then upon Poland with regard to Sweden.

The instructions which the court of Saxony gave, in 1750, to general d'Arnim, when he was going to Petersburg, as their minister plenipotentiary, contains one express article, by which he is charged to keep up dexterously the distrust and jealousy of Russia with regard to Prussia, and to applaud every arrangement that might be taken against the latter. But no body executed these orders better than the sieur de Funck, the saxon minister at Petersburg, who was the life and soul of the whole party. This minister never let an opportunity

opportunity efcape him, of infinuating, that the king of Pruffia was forming defigns upon Courland, Polifh Pruffia, and the city of Dantzick; that the courts of France, Pruffia, and Sweden, were hatching vaft projects, in cafe of a vacancy of the throne of Poland; and numberlefs other falfities of the fame kind; which his pruffian majefty has fufficiently contradicted by his fubfequent conduct, which he has followed to the republic of Poland, and by the caution he has ufed never to intrude himfelf into the domeftic affairs of Poland and Courland, notwithftanding the example other powers had fet him.

It would be tedious to mention all the infinuations of this nature, which occur in the correfpondence of the faxon minifters. But more particularly in their difpatches of the 6th of december, 1753; 6th and 13th of february; 28th of july, and 1ft of december, 1754; wherein, among other infinuations, are mentioned, the commercial arrangements, the erection of mints, and of armaments in Pruffia; and in one of the difpatches is faid, that the king of Pruffia's views of aggrandifement upon polifh Pruffia, and his project to ruin the commerce of Dantzick, were well known. Thefe minifters even gave out in a private manner, that France and Pruffia had been bufied a long time at the Ottoman Porte, in raifing up a war againft Ruffia; and that, if they fucceeded therein, the king of Pruffia would not fail to execute his defign upon Courland. They next infinuated, that the king of Pruffia had found a channel in Courland by which he came at all the fecrets of the court of Ruffia.

By the concurrence of fo many calumnies and impoftures, they at length fucceeded, in enfnaring the emprefs of Ruffia's good faith and equity, and in prejudicing her againft the king of Pruffia, to fuch a degree, that by the refult of the affemblies of the fenate of Ruffia, held on the 14th and 15th of may, 1753, it was laid down for a fundamental maxim of the empire, to oppofe every further aggrandifment of

that

that monarch, and to crush him by a superior force, as soon as a favourable opportunity should occur, of reducing the house of Brandenburg to its primitive state of mediocrity. This resolution was renewed in a great council, held in the month of october, 1755, and was extended so far, that it was resolved, "With-
"out any father discussion, whether that prince should
"happen to attack any of the allies of the court of
"Russia, or one of the allies of that court should
"begin with him *".

In order to form an idea of the joy, which count Brühl conceived upon this resolution of the court of Russia, and how well he was disposed to bring his own to concur it; I shall produce the following passages. In the dispatch of the 11th of november, 1755. He answers the sieur Funck; that, "The
"deliberations of the grand council are so much the
"more glorious to Russia, in that there can be no-
"thing more beneficial to the common cause, than
"previously to settle the effectual means of destroy-
"ing the overgrown power of Prussia, and the un-
"bounded ambition of that court."

The convention of a neutrality in Germany, signed at London the 16th of january, having silenced all count Brühl's calumnies, and shaken his iniquitous system; he redoubled his efforts in Russia, in order to prevent the re-establishment of a good understanding between the king of Prussia and the court of Petersburg. In his letter of the 23d of june, 1756, he explained himself upon this subject in the following terms:

* In the same letter is the following passage, "To this end the
"court of Russia will erect magazines for 100,000 men at Riga,
"Mittau, Liebau, and Windau; and they have found for this
"service a fund of two millions and a half of rubles, and another
"annual fund of a million and an half, to maintain these arrange-
"ments."
Extracted from a letter from the sieur Funck, to count de Brühl.
Petersburg, october 20, 1755.

"A

" A reconciliation between the courts of Berlin and
" Peterſburg, would be the moſt critical and the
" moſt dangerous event that could happen. It is
" to be hoped, that Ruſſia will not hearken to ſuch
" odious propoſals; and that the court of Vienna
" will be able to thwart ſo fatal a union."

The court of Vienna having perfectly ſucceeded in this reſpect; and imagining, after the new connections they entered into this year, that they had caught the opportunity of recovering Sileſia without obſtruction; they loſt no time in taking their meaſures accordingly, all Europe ſaw with ſurpriſe, the armaments the court of Ruſſia made in the ſpring, both by ſea and land, without any apparent object; they gave out that theſe preparations were made in conſequence of the treaty concluded with the court of Enggland, in 1755; but it was very plain, that this declaration was a mere pretence, ſince England had made no requiſition for ſuccours. Soon after this, Bohemia and Moravia were crowded with troops; magazines formed; and all the preparations made for an immediate war. The deſigns of the king of Pruſſia's enemies were vaſt and unbounded. The diſpatches of count Fleming, which his pruſſian majeſty afterwards publiſhed, with other important papers of the ſame nature, are filled with a great number of curious paſſages. Amongſt others, he relates, that count Kayſerling had received orders to ſpare neither pains nor money, in order to get an exact knowledge of the ſtate of the revenues of the court of Vienna; and he aſſures, that this court had remitted a million of florins to Peterſburg. He very often expreſſes his own perſuaſion of an eſtabliſhed concert between the two courts of Vienna and Ruſſia;—that the latter, in order the better to diſguiſe the true reaſons of their armaments, made them under the apparent pretence of being thereby in a condition to fulfil the engagements they had contracted with England;
—And that when all the preparations ſhould be finiſhed,

they were to fall unexpectedly on the king of Pruffia. This perfuafion runs through all his difpatches; and it is reafonable to give credit to a minifter fo intelligent, fo well informed, and fo much in the way of being fo.

Upon combining thefe circumftances together, viz. —That treaty of Peterfburg, which authorifes the the court of Vienna to recover Silefia, as foon as a war breaks out between Pruffia and Ruffia;—The refolution folemnly taken in Ruffia, to attack the king of Pruffia upon the firft opportunity, whether he fhould be the aggreffor or be attacked;—The armaments of the two imperial courts, at a time, when neither of them had any enemy to fear, but when the conjunctures feemed to favour the views of the court of Vienna upon Silefia;—The ruffian minifters formally owning, that thofe armaments were defigned againft the king;—Count Kaunitz's tacit avowal;— The pains which the ruffian minifters took to make out a pretence for accufing the king of Pruffia, of having endeavoured to ftir up a rebellion in Ukraine: —From the combination of all thefe circumftances, I fay, there refults a kind of demonftration, of a fecret concert entered into againft his pruffian majefty.

That wife monarch could not fhut his eyes againft meafures of fuch a tendency as thefe, which were likely to become fo fatal to himfelf, as his majefty had been fo long informed of all thefe particulars, from good quarters. The immenfe preparations of the court of Vienna, at leaft obliged him to order M. Klinggrafe, his plenipotentiary minifter at the imperial court, to demand of the emprefs queen, whether all thofe great preparations of war, which were making on the frontiers of Silefia, were defigned againft the king, or what were the intentions of her imperial majefty? To this equitable demand, the emprefs queen anfwered in exprefs terms, " That in the pre-
" fent juncture, fhe had found it neceffary to make
" armaments,

"armaments, as well for her own defence, as for that of her allies, and which did not tend to the prejudice of any body."

So vague an anfwer at fo critical a time, required a more precife explanation. Wherefore M. Klinggrafe received frefh orders, and reprefented to the emprefs, that after the king, his mafter, had diffembled as long as he thought confiftent with his fafety and glory, the bad defigns which were imputed to the emprefs, would not fuffer him longer to difguife any thing; that he had orders to inform her, that the king was acquainted with the offenfive projects, which the two courts had formed at Peterfburg; that he knew, they had engaged to attack him together unexpectedly; the emprefs queen with 80,000, and the emprefs of ruffia with 120,000 men; that this defign, which was to have been put in execution in the fpring of this year, was deferred till next fummer, on account of the ruffian troops wanting recruits; their fleet mariners; and Livonia, corn to fupport them; that the king made the emprefs arbiter of peace or war; that if fhe defired peace, he required of her a clear and formal declaration, confifting of a pofitive affurance, that fhe had no intention to attack the king either this year or the next; but that he fhould look on any ambiguous anfwer as a declaration of war; and that he called heaven to witnefs, that the emprefs alone would be guilty of the innocent blood that fhould be fpilt, and of the unhappy confequences of war.

To fo juft and reafonable a demand was given an anfwer ftill more haughty, and lefs fatisfactory than the former, the purport whereof will be fufficient to convince the public of the ill intentions of the court of Vienna.

This anfwer conveys, in fo many words,—" That his majefty the king of Pruffia had already been employed for fome time, in all kinds of the moft confiderable preparations for war, and the moft difquieting,

" difquieting, with regard to the public tranquility;
" when on the 26th of laft month, that prince had
" thought fit to order explanations to be demanded
" of her majefty, the emprefs queen, upon the mili-
" tary difpofitions that were making in her domi-
" nions, and which had not been refolved upon, till
" after all the preparations which his pruffian majefty
" had already made.

" That thefe were facts known to all Europe.

" That her majefty the emprefs queen, might there-
" fore have declined giving explanations upon ob-
" jects which did not require them; that however fhe
" had been pleafed to do it, and to declare with her
" own mouth to M. Klinggrafe, in the audience fhe
" granted him on the 26th of july,

" That the critical ftate of public affairs made her
" look upon the meafures which fhe was taking, as
" neceffary for her fafety, and that of her allies; and
" that in other refpects they did not tend to the pre-
" judice of any one.

" That her majefty the emprefs queen had un-
" doubtedly a right to form what judgments fhe
" pleafed on the circumftances of the times; and that
" it belonged likewife to none but herfelf to eftimate
" her dangers.

" That befides her declaration was fo clear, that
" fhe never could have imagined it could be thought
" otherwife.

" That being accuftomed to receive as well as to
" practife, the attentions that fovereigns owe to each
" other, fhe could not hear, without aftonifhment
" and the jufteft fenfibility, the contents of the me-
" morial prefented by M. Klinggrafe the 20th in-
" ftant, an account of which had been laid before
" her.

" That this memorial was fuch, both as to the
" matter, and the expreffions, that her majefty the
" emprefs queen, would find herfelf under a neceffity
" of tranfgreffing the bounds of that moderation,
" which

"which she had prescribed to herself, were she to answer the whole of its contents."

But yet in answer to it, she was pleased that M. Klinggrafe should be further acquainted,

" That the informations which had been given to
" his prussian majesty, of an offensive alliance, against
" him, between her majesty the empress queen, and
" her majesty the empress of Russia; as also, all the
" circumstances and pretended stipulations of the said
" alliance, were absolutely false and invented; and
" that no such treaty against his prussian majesty did
" exist, or ever had existed.

" That this declaration would enable all Europe
" to judge of what weight and quality the dreadful
" events are, which M. Klinggrafe's memorial an-
" nounces; and let them see, that, in all events, they
" can never be imputed to her majesty the empress
" queen."

Such was the answer of the court of Vienna, to the king of Prussia, as incongruous as it was insufficient; and as to the matters of fact, which relate to his prussian majesty's measures, nothing is so far from truth as what the empress queen advances. Those facts which that court would have to be looked upon, as known to all Europe, are so different from what it declares them to be, that it will be necessary, for the reader's instruction, to set that affair in a clear light. Upon the russian armament in the month of june, the king of Prussia caused four regiments to pass out of his electorate into Pomerania; and gave orders that his fortresses should be put into a state of defence; this, and a few other very trifling movements is what gave so great umbrage to the court of Vienna, that an army of above 80,000 men was ordered to assemble in Bohemia and Moravia. If the empress had detached troops out of Bohemia into Tuscany, would the king of Prussia have had room for apprehensions for Silesia, and for assembling a numerous army there? From this it is plain, that the march of the four regiments to Pomerania, only served the court of Vienna as a pretext to palliate her ill intentions.

On his prussian majesty's hearing of the great military preparations carrying on in Bohemia, he ordered three regiments of foot, which had been in quarters in Westphalia, towards Halberstadt; but did not send a single regiment into Silesia; the troops remained quiet in their garrisons, without even horses, and the other necessaries for an army which is to encamp, or which has designs of invasion. During this time the court of Vienna continuing, on one hand, to hold the language of peace, and, on the other, to take the most serious measures for war; not content with these demonstrations, caused another camp to be marked out, near a town, named Hotzenplotz, situated on a spot, belonging indeed to them, but which lies directly between the fortresses of Neisse and Cosel; and prepared a great army in Bohemia to occupy the camp of Jaromers, within four miles of Silesia. These motions of the court of Vienna obliged the king of Prussia to consider his own safety, especially, as it was reasonable to suspect the designs of that court, who he knew was not altogether very well intentioned towards him: wherefore he thought it high time to make the dispositions which his safety and dignity required; he gave orders for his army to provide themselves with horses, and to be in readiness to march.

Had his prussian majesty formed any design in prejudice to the empress queen, every one who is at all acquainted with the formidable power of that monarch, must be sensible, that he would have had it in his power to execute them many months before the time in question, and not having staid for her assembling such formidable forces for her defence. But that monarch was negotiating whilst his enemies were arming. Such is the manifest weakness of the principal foundation, whereon all the arguments of the austrian court, are founded.

But

But this is not the only passage of the emprefs queen's anfwer that shows such a formed defign of equivocating in her negotiations,—she mentions her fo clear declaration to M. Klinggrafe. This declaration, though called fo clear, is certainly on the whole, unintelligible, who are the allies of the emprefs, that were threatened with war? Was it the court of France? Or that of Ruffia? One muft be ftrangely blinded, to attribute to his pruffian majefty a defign of attacking either of thefe two courts, and fuch an enterprize, would furely require fomewhat more than four regiments being fent into Pomerania. The court of Vienna, in this memorial, fay, they did not intend to attack any body; might not they as eafily have faid, that they would not attack the king of Pruffia by name?

But the article in this memorial, on which the court of Vienna infifted moft, in her anfwer, was, her alliance with Ruffia, the ftipulations of which, as they faid, were abfolutely falfe and invented. To be fure it was very eafy for the auftrian minifters to deny this convention; but befides the facts which were publifhed about it, there were circumftances which feemed fufficiently to indicate, at leaft a concert. In the beginning of june, the ruffian troops approached the frontiers of Pruffia. An army of 70,000 men was formed in Livonia, at the fame time that they were preparing at Vienna to affemble a ftrong army in Bohemia, which was to appear there under the name of an army of obfervation. Thefe inftances, befides many more that might be produced, was it neceffary, are fufficient to fhow in the cleareft light, the defigns of the court of Vienna.

In fhort, it plainly appears, that count Kaunitz propofed to fhut the door againft all means of explaining and conciliating matters; and, at the fame time, to purfue the preparations of his dangerous defigns, in the expectation that the king of Pruffia, would be fo far provoked, as to take fome ftep, which might serve to make him pafs for the aggreffor.

The conduct of the court of Drefden fquared exactly with that of Vienna; under the feigned character of a neutral power, count Brühl refolved, that his country fhould be equally forward with his allies, in their defigns againft his pruffian majefty. It is eafy to judge of this, by the counfel, which count Fleming gives count Brühl, in his difpatch of the 14th of july. " To grant the paffage to the pruffian troops; and afterwards to take fuch meafures as fhould be moft proper."

By a letter from count Fleming of the 18th of auguft, the emprefs queen explained herfelf to that minifter in the following terms:

" That fhe required nothing for the prefent, from the king of Poland, as fhe was very fenfible of his ticklifh fituation; that however, fhe hoped he would, in the mean while, put himfelf in a good pofture, in order to be prepared at all events; and that, in cafe any breach fhould happen between her majefty and the king of Pruffia, fhe would, in time, not be averfe to concur, in cafe of need, in the neceffary meafures for their mutual fecurity."

But not to detain the reader longer than is neceffary, on producing fuch a concatination of facts, to prove that his pruffian majefty was not the aggreffor in thofe troubles that enfued this train of dark and fecret negociations; it evidently appears, that the faxon court had a fhare in all the dangerous defigns which were formed againft that monarch;—their minifters were the authors, and chief promoters of them;—and though they did not formally accede to the treaty of Peterfburg, they had however agreed with their allies to fufpend their concurrence therein, till fuch time only, as the king's forces fhould be weakened and divided, and they might pull off the mafk without danger.

The king of Poland had adopted as a principle, that any war, between the king of Pruffia and one
of

of his polish majesty's allies, furnished him with a title to make conquests upon Prussia. And it was in consequence of this principle, that he thought he could, in time of peace, make a partition of the dominions of his neighbour.

Count Brühl entered very eagerly into the plot with the court of Vienna, by the injurious reports he undertook to propagate:—and I think I have made it appear very clearly, that there was a secret concert existing between the courts of Vienna and Saxony; in consequence of which, the latter did intend to let the king's army pass, in order to act afterwards, according to events, either in joining his enemies, or in making a diversion in his dominions, unprovided with troops.

Such were the designs of the secret enemies of his majesty the king of Prussia; and in such a cause, let any man put himself in that monarch's place, would he not have drawn upon himself an everlasting reproach, in the opinion of all equitable and impartial judges; would he not have rendered himself accountable to all his posterity; if he had not made use of every expedient, that divine and human laws had put in his power, to prevent, in good time, those designs, that tended to deprive him of the greatest part of his dominions, and to plunge him into absolute destruction.

For an instance of the bad designs of Saxony, we need but consider the warlike preparations made in that country, at the same time that her majesty the empress queen was doing the same in Bohemia and Moravia; large magazines were every where formed, and the king of Poland resolved to put himself at the head of his army, and post himself in the most advantageous manner for facilitating his junction with the austrian army in Bohemia: an immense road was cut through the mountains of Bohemia, and marked at certain distances with posts bearing this remarkable inscription THE MILITARY ROAD; all these are so many circumstances, that completely open the designs of the court of Saxony to a full view. This new MILITARY ROAD, in particular, could never surely have been made in order to facilitate the passage of the prussian army; and those posts, which actually remain to this day, are so many speaking proofs of the concert, which had long been forming between the courts of Vienna and Saxony, and were but too strong a justification of the reasons his prussian majesty had to prevent the effects of it.

Before I proceed to trace that monarch in the measures which he thought it necessary, in this conjuncture, to take; I shall, for the reader's assistance, in recollecting precisely all that train of negociation between the courts of Vienna, Dresden, and Petersburg, just cursorily recapitulate these affairs in as short a compass as possible; and then proceed in giving an account of the military affairs in this part of the world, which drew the attention of all Europe.

In the first place, he is to remember, that the emprefs queen having ceded Silesia to the king of Prussia, by the treaties of Breslau and Dresden, soon began to envy that monarch the possession of so valuable a part of her former dominions. The desire of repossessing herself of that country, and of revenging herself against the king of Prussia, induced her to attempt at any rate to gratify those two favourite desires; but fearful of the power and enterprising genius of the prussian monarch, she, although superior in her forces, sought for some ally to join with her, in these ambitious designs: she cast her eyes on the elector of Saxony, king of Poland, who answered her with all possible cordiality, and similitude of notions: these two powers formed a secret concert, and invited the empress of Russia to accede to the same design; that princess was more cautious, and as she had not at that time the least glimpse of dispute with the king of Prussia, was not so easily drawn into the scheme. The courts of Vienna and Dresden finding this difficulty, contrived and propagated a thousand calumnies

calumnies, tending to depreciate that monarch, and infused intimations to the empress of Russia of many bad designs formed by Prussia against her; and in time, by this means, and by gaining over several of the empress's ministers to their party, they persuaded her to come fully into their iniquitous schemes, which concluded in the treaty of Petersburg, between the court of Vienna and Petersburg: Saxony by reason of her situation so much in the power of Prussia, was excused from formally acceding to this treaty before matters were brought to such a crisis, as she might do it without any great danger to herself. By this treaty, the empress queen was entitled to retake possion of Silesia, in case his prussian majesty should attack her, or any one of her allies, or even the republic of Poland.

The plan for the part which Saxony was to take in the war, which was inevitably to follow; was, in case Prussia demanded at any time a passage for his troops through that electorate, in his way to the dominions of the empress queen, in such case to grant that demand; and, as soon as his prussian majesty should have his hands full in Bohemia, or elsewhere, to march with all the forces of the electorate, into the very heart of the prussian dominions, which would then be destitute of forces for their defence. The better to ensure success in these measures, the empress of Russia made immense preparations for the subsisting an army of 120,000 men, which, by the treaty of Petersburg, were to march against Prussia. The empress queen in Bohemia and Bavaria, on the frontiers of Silesia, formed camps of 80,000 men, and the whole face of those countries wore the appearance of an approaching war. The king of Poland, elector of Saxony, on his part assembled an army, in his electorate, of 30,000 men, and formed magazines for their subsistence; and cut an immense road through the mountains into Bohemia; and called it the MILITARY ROAD.

Such

Such were the preparations and meaſures of his pruſſian majeſty's enemies, when he thought it not ſafe to continue any longer without being certain that they were not deſigned againſt him. He accordingly ordered his miniſter plenipotentiary at the imperial court, to demand againſt whom theſe great preparations were making ; but receiving an equivocating anſwer, he again demanded a ſolemn promiſe of the empreſs that ſhe would not attack him in the courſe of this year, or the next ; but being alſo refuſed a catagorical anſwer, and having good intelligence of all the above particulars, and the bad deſigns of his enemies ; he very juſtly thought that it would be inexcuſable in him not to avert the blow, which hung in ſo formidable a manner over his head, by ſtriking at the boſom of his enemy, to diſable him from executing the bad deſigns he had formed. Such was the caſe of his pruſſian majeſty ; and all Europe muſt allow, that he was at liberty to attack any of the three powers in confederacy againſt him without violating in the leaſt degree, the laws of nations : and although, he began hoſtilities, yet his enemies were the aggreſſors * in the war.

---

* By aggreſſion, is underſtood every act, which is diametrically oppoſite to the ſenſe of a treaty of peace. An offenſive league ; —the ſtirring up of enemies, and prompting them to make war upon another power ;—deſigns of invading another prince's dominions ;—a ſudden irruption :—all theſe different circumſtances are ſo many aggreſſions ; although the laſt, only, can be properly called an hoſtility.
Whoever prevents theſe aggreſſions, may commit hoſtilities ; but is not the aggreſſor.— In the ſucceſſion war, when the troops of Savoy were in the french army in Lombardy, the duke of Savoy made a treaty with the emperor againſt France :—the french diſarmed theſe troops, and carried the war into Piedmont :—it was therefore the duke of Savoy, who was the aggreſſor ; and the french, who committed the firſt hoſtilities.—The league of Cambray was an aggreſſion :—if the Venetians had, then, prevented their enemies, they would have committed the firſt hoſtilities ; but they would not have been the aggreſſors.

CHAP.

## CHAP. IX.

*King of Pruſſia demands a paſſage for his troops through Saxony. King of Poland's anſwer. King of Pruſſia enters Saxony. Takes poſſeſſion of the electorate. Pruſſian army blockades the ſaxon camp at Pirna. Motions of the auſtrians. Marſhal Schwerin enters Bohemia. Marſhal Keith marches into Bohemia. Battle of Lowoſchutz. The ſaxon army capitulates. King of Poland ſets out for Warſaw. Pruſſian army retreats into Saxony. And goes into winter quarters. Sad ſtate of Saxony. Auſtrians go into winter quarters. Affairs in Ruſſia. Deſigns of France. Preparations of the king of Pruſſia. Reflections. Marſhal Keith.*

HIS majeſty the king of Pruſſia, clearly foreſeeing that a war was inevitable, and that a paſſage through Saxony was abſolutely neceſſary for his army, ordered M. de Malzahn, his miniſter at the court of Dreſden, to demand ſuch a paſſage. On the 29th of auguſt, he accordingly demanded a private audience of the king of Poland, and made the following verbal declaration to his majeſty, on the part of the king his maſter:

" His majeſty the king of Pruſſia finds himſelf obliged, by the behaviour of the empreſs queen to attack her, and to march through the territories of Saxony into Bohemia: he accordingly demands a paſſage through the electoral dominions of his poliſh majeſty, declaring, that he will cauſe his troops to obſerve the ſtricteſt diſcipline, and take all the care of the country that the circumſtances will permit. His poliſh majeſty, and his royal family, may at the ſame time depend upon being in perfect ſafety, and of having the greateſt reſpect paid them, on the part of his pruſſian majeſty. As to the reſt, after reflecting upon the events of the year 1744, there is no reaſon

reason to be surprised, that the king of Prussia should take such measures, as may prevent a return of what then happened. Moreover, he desires nothing so much as a speedy re-establishment of peace, in order to give him the happy opportunity, of restoring the king of Poland to the quiet possession of his dominions, against which he has not, in other respects, formed any dangerous designs."

M. de Malzahn added, " That the necessity which the king his master was under of acting in this manner, could only be imputed to the calamity of the times, and the behaviour of the court of Vienna."

The king of Poland, in the surprise which this declaration threw him into, answered M. de Malzahn, " That he should not have expected a requisition in the form that it had just been made to him; that being at peace with all the world, and under no engagement relative to the present object with any of the powers actually at war, or those about to enter into it, he could not conceive the end of making such a declaration; but that he should give answer upon this subject in writing, and hoped his prussian majesty, contenting himself with a quick passage, would neither forget the respect due to a sovereign, nor that which all the members of the germanic body reciprocally owe to each other."

Soon after this verbal answer, the king caused another to be delivered in writing to M. de Malzahn, which imported much the same as the other, but was more explicit.

Besides lord Stormont, the british minister, who went on the part of the king of Poland, to wait on the king of Prussia, his polish majesty likewise sent the count de Salmont, one of his ministers. His prussian majesty received them very politely, heard their proposals, and told them, " That he himself wished for nothing more than to find the king of Poland's sentiments acquiesce with his declarations: that the neutrality which his polish majesty seemed

desirous

desirous to observe, was exactly what he required of him; but that in order to render this neutrality more secure, and less liable to variation, it would be proper for his polish majesty to separate his army; and send the troops he had assembled at Pirna back into their quarters; that a step of this nature would be a full proof of a neutrality not to be doubted off; and that after this he should take a pleasure, in shewing by an equal condescention, his disposition to give real marks of his friendship for his polish majesty, and concert with him what measures might be proper to be taken, according to the situation of affairs."

But to comply with these terms was not the design of his polish majesty; he had raised an army of 30,000 men for other exploits, than to march back again into their quarters. As to his prussian majesty, foreseeing that war was become inevitable, and that the king of Poland, by his actions, was resolved to continue his military preparations; at last resolved to enter Saxony, and by striking so effectual a blow, dissenable his enemies from executing the formidable scheme they had projected.

This great monarch having prepared with the utmost diligence, a powerful army, found it ready for action by the end of august. His situation at this critical conjuncture was alarming; the power of the house of Austria, of itself an overmatch for him; he knew he had to cope with besides a vast army of russians, who were upon their march for Prussia; add to these, the king of Poland, at the head of 30,000 men; nor was his majesty without fears from the part which France might take, in the situation which her new ally the empress queen then was in.

But, being prepared for the worst that could happen, he resolved to begin hostilities by attacking Saxony; having first conferred the chief command in Prussia, on marshal Lehwald, an officer of the greatest courage and abilities; and that in Silesia, on marshal Schwerin, a soldier grown old in the prussian service, and

and a particular favourite of the king's, having taught his majesty the first rudiments of the art of war; reserving to himself that of the principal army, intended to act in Saxony and Bohemia.

The saxon general had made choice of the post of Pirna, for the rendezvous of their troops, as the most convenient, either for deceiving the prussian army, in case of its advancing into Bohemia, or for receiving succours from the austrians. Upon the first motion of the prussian troops, for marching into Pomerania, or, in case of necessity, for joining marshal Lehwald, the saxons abandoned all their garrisons bordering on Brandenburg, and took post between the Moldaw and the Elbe. They afterwards returned to their quarters; and, a second time, broke up and repaired to their respective cantonments. The motive on which they acted being known, proper measures were taken; and the king of Prussia, entering Saxony on the 29th of august, marched with his troops, divided into three columns, towards Pirna. The first set out from the duchy of Magdeburg, under the command of prince Ferdinand of Brunswic, directing their route to Leipsic, Borna, Kemnitz, Freyberg, Dippoldswalde, to Cotta. The second command by the king, and under him field marshal Kieth, marched through Pretsch, Torgau, Lonmatsch, Wilsdruff, Dresden, and Zehist. The third commanded by the prince of Brunswick Bevern, crossing Lusatia, took its route through Elsterwerde, Bautzen, Stolpe, to Lohmm. These three columns arrived the same day at the camp at Pirna, which they invested. The division commanded by the king, took possession of Dresden, and cut off all communication between that city and the saxon camp; and on the 8th his majesty took up his quarters at Wilsdruff. On the 10th, a great part of the prussian army marched in order towards the saxon camp, and the head quarters were placed at Seidlitz, not much above half a german mile distant

from

from Pirna. And the same day one regiment of cuirassiers, and three of dragoons, marched through Dresden into the camp at Wilsdruff, where a body of 16000 men were still left.

The division under prince Ferdinand of Brunswic, amounting to about 15000 men, entered Leipsic on the 20th. And so impenetrable are the councils of his prussian majesty, that even prince Ferdinand, when he set out upon his march, did not know what course he was to take further than Gros-Kugel, where, upon opening his instructions, he found the king's orders to advance to Leipsic, and take possession of it.

Notice was given the same evening to the deputies of the corporation of merchants, that they were to pay all taxes and customs only to the order of his prussian majesty; the deputies waited on prince Ferdinand of Brunswic, next morning at 11 o'clock, who received them very politely, and repeated to them, that from that day, all contributions were to be paid to the order of the king of Prussia, and not to his polish majesty; and assured them that they might depend upon his friendship, protection, and care to maintain good order. The same day the prince took possession of the custom-house and excise-office; and ordered the magazines of corn and meal to be opened for the use of his troops.

Whilst his highness prince Ferdinand transacted these affairs in so resolute a manner at Leipsic, his majesty the king of Prussia did the same at Dresden. The king of Poland, on the news of the irruption of the prussians, left his capital, the city of Dresden, attended by his two sons, prince Zavier, and prince Charles, on the 3d of september, and put himself at the head of his troops, encamped at Pirna, resolving to defend himself to the last. The queen, and the rest of the royal family, remained in the city, and were treated in the most polite manner by the king of Prussia, who took possession of it the 8th. That monarch established all the offices for the execution of

L  public

public bufinefs belonging to the pruffian army, at Torgau, which was the place where contributions and duties of all kinds were paid: and as the cafh and treafure of the army were kept here, 1500 peafants were fet at work to throw up entrenchments round the place, to prevent its being attacked or furprifed. The deputies from Leipfic were conducted hither, and detained as a fecurity for the obedience of the regency of that city, and the payment of its duties and contributions. A pruffian commiffary was left to take care of thefe payments, but what is extraordinary, not one foldier.

I have already obferved, that the three columns of the pruffian army met at Pirna the fame day. They were no fooner encamped round this poft, than it was perceived, that notwithftanding the inferiority of the faxon army, the advantageous fituation of the ground it poffeffed, was fo great, that it was not to be attacked without confiderable lofs. It was therefore determined to turn the attack into a blockade, and to treat the faxon army rather in the manner of a town befieged, than like a poft, which might be attacked according to the cuftom of war carried on in an open country.

The fituation of the faxon camp, which made it almoft impregnable, was as follows, viz. The plain between Pirna and Koenigftein, where the faxon camp was pitched, is a continued rock, with a diclivity down to the Elbe on one fide, and into a valley on the other. This declivity ends on one fide of Koenigftein, from whence begins a thick foreft, in which the faxons cut down trees, and barricaded themfelves. On this fide of Pirna is a narrow paffage, where, as well as in the town itfelf, they made intrenchments, and raifed in and about their camp, near 60 redoubts, which were well provided with a great number of cannon. But this advantageous fituation did not remedy the want of water, provifions, and forage; the faxon generals omitted nothing that might induce

* the

the prussians to proceed on their march for Bohemia, and leave them behind, without attacking them. But former experience had given the king of Prussia wisdom, with regard to future transactions. If, on the one hand, no direct attack was thought adviseable; so, on the other, no enemy was to be left behind. Besides strictly blockading the saxons, it was also resolved to form an army of observation, to prevent any succours being sent from the austrian army. In consequence of this resolution, the prussians took possession of the posts of Leopoldshain, Marckersdorf, Hellendorf, Cotta, Zehist, Sedlitz, as far as the Elbe, where, by their bridge, they had a communication with the posts of Lohmm, Welen, Obreswaden, and Schandau. In these different places were distributed thirty-eight battalions, and thirty squadrons. Seventy-nine battalions and seventy squadrons, were destined for Bohemia, which entered by detachments, moving to Peterswalde, Ausig, and Jonsdorf. This body was commanded by marshal Keith, by whose orders general Manstein made himself master of the castle of Ketschen, taking an hundred austrians prisoners. The marshal encamped at Jonsdorf, where he staid till the end of the month.

Hitherto marshal Brown had kept close in his camp at Kolin; which was almost completely formed by the 21st of august, most of the artillery for that purpose being arrived; but the troops were not all complete then; the marshal had under him prince Piccolomini, seven lieutenant field marshals, and sixteen major generals; besides this, the austrians were then assembling troops at Ollischau. The court of Vienna drew all the forces of her imperial majesty's immense dominions, into Bohemia: all the officers in the austrian Netherlands received orders to join their regiments directly, and hold themselves in readiness to march on the first notice, and were very soon detached into Bohemia; and orders arrived at Brussels,

Bruffels, to raife feveral independent companies of 100 men each : parties of 5 or 6000 croatians were continually marching through Vienna for their camps in Bohemia and Moravia.

Marfhal Schwerin, as I before obferved, was appointed by his pruffian majefty to command in Silefia; that general, after paffing through the county of Glatz, had advanced to Nachot, afterwards to the banks of the Mettaw, and laftly to Aujet, where he routed a detachment of huffars, and dragoons, commanded by general Bucof, and took 200 prifoners. Afterwards the marfhal took poffeffion of the camp of Aujeft, and foraged under the walls of Konigfgratz, where prince Piccolomini was encamped. Near Hoenmaut the pruffian huffars defeated 400 auftrian dragoons, and took many of them in their flight. This was all marfhal Schwerin could do. The camp at Koningfgratz was fituated at the conflux of the Adler into the Elbe : the enemy were entrenched, and this poft in its front too difficult to be attacked.

When his pruffian majefty took poffeffion of Drefden, he fent an officer to the queen to demand the keys of the cabinets, the archieves, and treafures of her hufband : her majefty unwillingly complied ; and when the pruffian officer received the keys of her, he requefted further, that her majefty would alfo put him in poffeffion of a certain cafket, containing fome particular papers, and defcribed it to her : the queen denied having any knowledge of fuch a cafket, and told the officer fhe knew not what he meant. Madam, replied he, (pointing to a cabinet) the cafket I am ordered by my mafter to demand, is in that cabinet.—The queen in fome confuffion affured him, he was miftaken, for the cabinet contained no fuch papers. But the pruffian officer infifted upon having it opened, and finding that the moft peremptory demands would not be complied with, by her polifh majefty, he broke it open himfelf in her prefence, presence, and took out the very casket he had demanded, and which contained all the original conventions, and letters which passed between the courts of Saxony, Vienna, and Petersburg.

His prussian majesty finding himself possessed of so invaluable a treasure, instantly published them, that all Europe might be convinced of the necessity there was for his beginning hostilities in his own defence.

Great efforts were only to be made in Saxony; the situation of the saxon camp, made it necessary for the austrians to advance to their relief, and the prussians found it necessary to keep these enemies off, as well as to continue the blockade of the saxon camp in the closest manner. The condition of the electorate was certainly at this time on the verge of destruction, the prussians had taken possession of all the towns and fortresses, and had demanded about a fortnight after their entrance, to be delivered in the space of three weeks at farthest, 1100 oxen, 2500 sheep, 200,000 measures of oats, 150,000 quintals of hay, and 20,000 trusses of straw; the value of them all was supposed to amount to 625,000 crowns.

In the mean time the empress queen, found herself obliged in honour, to relieve her ally the king of Poland; accordingly she ordered marshal Brown to disengage the saxons. His army was encamped at Budin, near the conflux of the Egra with the Elbe; and for the executing these orders, he had the choice of three ways; one by attacking and defeating marshal Keith's army, which was no easy task: the second, by marching to the left, through Belin, and Teoplitz, to enter Saxony, which laid him under the necessity of exposing his flank to the prussian army, and even of being deprived of his magazines at Budin and Welsern: the third, by sending a detachment through Leutmeritz, and proceeding to the saxons by the way of Böhmisch, Leipe and Schandau. This last measure could not produce any thing decisive; the ground in the neighbourhood of Schandau, and

Ober-Raden, being so difficult, that a small body of troops may stop an entire army. But his prussian majesty, in so critical a time, judged his presence was necessary in Bohemia. Accordingly, he left the camp at Setlitz, on the 28th of september, and the same day reached marshal Keith's camp at Jonsdorf. On the 29th, the army in Bohemia was ordered to march: the king going before with eight battalions and twenty squadrons, encamped at Jirmitz, where the scouts of the army brought advice, that marshal Brown was, the next day, to pass the Egra. His majesty now judged, that the best way was to draw near the enemy; in order to observe all their motions. On the 30th, all the troops followed the king in two colums, the one by the way of Proscobot, and the other by the way of Jirmitz. From Jirmitz he marched with his van, towards Welmina, where he arrived that evening, an hour before sunset. There he saw the austrian army, with its right wing at Lowoschutz, and its left towards the Egra. That evening the king, himself, occupied, with six battalions, a hollow, and some rising grounds, which commanded Lowoschutz, and which he resolved to make use of, the next day, in order to march out against the austrians. The army arrived, at night, at Welmina, where the king only formed his battalions behind one another, and the squadrons in the same manner, which remained all night in this position; the king himself sitting up all night, and having no other covering but his cloak, before a little fire, at the head of his troops. On the first of october, at break of day, he took with him his principal general officers, and shewed them the ground he intended to occupy with his army; viz. the infantry forming the first line, to occupy two high hills, and the bottom betwixt them; some battalions to form the second line; and the third to be composed of the whole cavalry. The ground where the prussians formed themselves in order of battle, contained only the six battalions of the van, the

ground

ground continuing to widen towards the left. The declivity of thefe mountains was covered with vineyards, divided into a great many inclofures, by ftone walls, three feet high, as belonging to different perfons. In thefe vineyards, marfhal Browne pofted his pandours to ftop them, fo that, as every battalion of the left entered the line, it was obliged to engage the enemy. But their fire being faint and unfteady, it confirmed his pruffian majefty in his opinion, that marfhal Browne was retreated, and that the pandours and bodies of cavalry feen in the plain were his rear. This opinion appeared the more plaufible, from the impoffibility of feeing any appearance of an army; a thick fog hiding every thing, and did not difperfe till paft eleven. His majefty ordered his artillery to play on the cavalry in the plain, upon which it feveral times altered its form. Sometimes it appeared numerous; fometimes drawn up chequer-ways; fometimes drawn up in three contiguous lines; fometimes five or fix troops filed off to the left, and difappeared. After the king had found that the battalions were poffeffed of the hollow, in the manner he had ordered it, he thought, that the firft thing to be done, was to drive back the enemy's cavalry, which ftood in the front. Accordingly he ordered twenty fquadrons of horfe to charge them; who, having formed themfelves at the foot of the eminence, where the pruffian infantry was pofted, charged and broke the auftrian horfe. But, as the auftrians had placed behind their cavalry in hollow places and ditches, a great body of infantry, with feveral pieces of cannon, the pruffian cavalry, through the brifknefs of their attack, found themfelves expofed to the fire of this cannon and infantry: which obliged them to return and form again, under the protection of their own infantry and cannon, and this without being purfued by the auftrian cavalry. It was not till now, apprehended, by his pruffian majefty, that the auftrians were facing him with their whole army. The king at that time was for placing his cavalry behind in a second line; but before this order could be brought, his horse, prompted by their natural impetuosity, and a desire of distinguishing themselves, charged a second time, bore down all opposition, passed through the same flank fire, as at the first charge, pursued the enemy above 300 paces; and, in the excess of ardour, crossed a ditch 10 feet wide. Beyond this ditch, at the distance of 300 paces was another; behind which appeared the austrian infantry, drawn up in order of battle. Immediately 60 pieces of cannon played upon the prussian horse, which therefore repassed the ditch, and returned to their infantry, at the foot of the mountain, without being followed. The king then ordered his cavalry to post themselves behind the infantry. About this time, the fire on the left wing began to increase. Marshal Brown had successively brought on 20 battalions, who, passing by Lowoschutz, lined the banks of the Elbe, to support the pandours in the vineyards; and the enemy used all possible efforts to flank the left of the prussian infantry, the king perceived the necessity of supporting it, and ordered the battalions of the first line to turn to the left; the battalions of the second line filled up the intervals, which had been occasioned by this motion; so that the cavalry formed the second line, which supported the infantry. At the same time the whole left of the infantry, marching on gradually, wheeled about, and attacked the town of Lowoschutz in flank, in spite of the prodigious fire of the enemy: the prussian grenadiers fired in through the doors and windows, and roofs of the houses, in the burning of which, the battalion of Kleist and Bornstadt chiefly distinguished themselves. In this action, though only the attack of a post, every prussian soldier of the left wing fired ninety shot. They had no more powder nor ammunition for their cannon; notwithstanding which, the regiment of Itzenblitz and Manteufel entered Lowoschutz, with

their

their bayonets fixed, and drove before them nine fresh austrian battalions, which marshal Brown had just posted there. The battle concluded with a disorderly flight of the austrians. What hindered the prussian cavalry from taking advantage of it was, first, the broad ditch mentioned in describing the second gallant attack made by them; and secondly, the masterly disposition of marshal Brown, in taking all the left of his infantry, which had not been attacked, to cover his broken troops which were flying in the utmost confusion. In this order marshal Brown waited the approach of night to retreat. At an hour after midnight he began his march towards his camp at Budin, breaking down all his bridges over the Egra. The next day, the prince of Bevern was detached by the king of Prussia, with a body of 8000 men to Schirkowitz, which was on their right; and from thence he sent out parties along the Egra, to reconnoitre the passes. The austrian army amounted to 60,000 before the battle, which lasted seven hours, during which, the cannonading was incessant on both sides. The loss of the austrians was computed at about 7000 men killed or wounded; 500 taken prisoners; amongst whom was prince Lobkowitz, four pieces of cannon, and three standards. The loss of the prussians did not exceed 6 or 7000, among whom was general Ludritz, an officer of great merit and experience. The prussian army encamped on the field of battle, where it continued without molestation, foraging within cannon-shot of the austrian army.

On the 6th, his prussian majesty received advice that marshal Brown had made a detachment, in which was his own regiment; and that these troops had moved to Raudnitz, and were advancing towards Bohmischleipe, in their way for Saxony, and consisted of about 6000 men. Although the weakness of this detachment could cause little apprehension, his majesty thought that his army in Saxony, consisting only of thirty squadrons, might want a reinforcement of horse;

especially

especially if the saxons should attempt to force the pass of the Hellendorf, where the cavalry might be usefully employed, particularly in the plains of Peterswalde. These considerations determined the king to go thither in person. Accordingly, setting out from Lowoschutz, on the 13th, with 15 squadrons of dragoons, he arrived at his other army, on the 14th at noon.

The reader may now perceive that the battle of Lowoschutz was not entirely decisive. For although his prussian majesty, in the account which he published of this campaign, pretends, that his army in Bohemia was intended merely to cover the blockade of the saxon camp; yet we may perceive that his intention, when he set out for Bohemia, was, in case he got a decisive victory, to march directly to Prague, to facilitate the conquest of all that kingdom: every impartial man, will, I believe, agree, that this monarch, had he gained such a victory as I am speaking of, would not have directly marched back to his army in Saxony; his business would in every respect have been more completely done, had he got possession of Prague and thereby been enabled to extend his winter-quarters into the very heart of Bohemia. But I would not be thought from hence to derogate from the real greatness of this victory, although disputed by the austrians, that his prussian majesty gained it; we may find by marshal Brown's inability to relieve the saxons, on which account he engaged the prussian army; and the advantage the victor's cause received from it, was very considerable; it was the first action of the war, and the soldiers looked on it as a good omen of future success. His prussian majesty in this victory found the happy effects of that exquisite discipline to which he had inured his soldiers; the fire of the prussian soldiers, as well as their artillery was so extremely heavy and unintermitting, that it was almost impossible for any troops to stand unbroken before it.

In

In the mean time great changes happened in the camp at Pirna, since the 10th of october. The saxons had that day attempted to throw a bridge over the river at Wilstead. The prussians had there a redoubt, from whence a captain with 50 grenadiers fired on the saxon's boats. He took seven or eight of them, and others he sunk with their cannon; so that the design of the saxons miscarried. They now altered their design, and, seeing the difficulty of transporting their boats on the Elbe, where they had the fire of three prussian redoubts to pass, they therefore loaded their pontoons on horses, and carried them thus by land to a place near Konigstein, opposite to the village of Halbstadtel. This outlet of their camp had excited the attention of the saxons, as being the most easy, on account of the succours they expected from the austrians. For the better understanding of this relation, it will be necessary to break here the thread of the narrative, in order to describe the nature of the ground, which is known to be the basis of military dispositions. The description which I before gave of the post of Pirna, has shewn its situation to be very strong; but with this defect, that it is as difficult to come out of it as to force it. According to the situation of the ground, the saxons could attempt to force a passage only by Hermsdorf and Hellendorf. This would certainly have been attended with great loss, though there was a probability of saving by this attempt a part, at least, of their men. It cannot but be thought, that they were entirely unacquainted with the situation of Halbstadt, Burgearsdorf Zeigenruck, Schandau, and with the disposition of the prussians in these posts. The prussian general Zeschwitz, with eleven battalions and fifteen squadrons, was posted between Schandau, and Wendischefere; and oppofite to him in the villages of Mitteldorf and Altendorf, encamped marshal Brown with his detachment. Leschwitz was much stronger than Brown. The impracticable situation of these rocks hindered the austrians from advancing to Bugersdorf. This could not be done without a body double their number, or filing off, two a-breast, in sight of general Leschwitz towards Alstadt. Where the saxons intended to pass, is a small plain, in the center of which stands Lilienstein, a steep mountain. On both sides of this rock, in the form of a cresent, five battalions of grenadiers guarded an impracticable barricade of felled trees. Behind them at the distance of 500 paces, two brigades of foot were placed in the defile of Burgersdorf, supported by five squadrons of dragoons; and behind this defile is Ziegenruck, a perpendicular rock, 60 feet high, and which forms a semi-circle round these difficult posts, joining the Elbe, at its two extremities. From this inconvenient place, however, it was, that on the 11th the saxons began to form their bridge. The prussian officers, instead of disturbing them, suffered them to finish it. The descent from Tirmsdorf, towards the Elbe, is tollerable practicable; but, after they had finished their bridge, the great difficuty remained of climbing up the rock, from whence they could go only by one foot-path to Alstadtel. It was on the 12th, in the evening, that they began their march. Two battalions of grenadiers, after infinite difficulty, got on the other side. On the 13th, this road was intirely destroyed by the continual rains; so that there was no possibility of getting their cannon from their entrenchments; and accordingly they left them behind. This day their cavalry, their baggage, and their rear found themselves confusedly embarrassed, one being stopped by another. The difficulty of the passage hindered the march of their troops, the van could only file off one by one, whilst the main body and the rear were obliged to remain motionless on the same place. On the 13th, very early in the morning, prince Maurice of Anhalt received the first advice of the retreat of the saxons. The prussion troops without delay, marched in

seven

seven columns. It was with great labour they climbed those rocks, during which, however, they met with no opposition. Upon gaining the height, they formed; the prussian hussars fell upon four saxon squadrons, which composed their rear-guard, and drove them to their infantry, near Tirmsdorf. The prussian companies of hunters, lodging themselves in a wood, on the flank of these troops, extremely galled them with their fire. At the same time, prince Maurice ordered the foot regiment of Prussia to advance on an eminence, to the right of the saxons; and two pieces of cannon being brought to play on their rear guard, a general flight ensued. The hussars threw themselves on the baggage of the army, and plundered it; and the hunters conveyed themselves into the woods, near the Elbe; from whence they galled the rear guard in its retreat. The saxons now lost all presence of mind, and cut down their bridge, which was carried away by the current to the post of Raden, where it was stopped. The prussian army encamped on the eminence of Stuppen, its left joining to the Elbe, and the right extending along a large hollow way, terminating near Hennersdorf. Such were the situations of the prussian, austrian and saxon troops, when the king of Prussia arrived on the 14th, with his dragoons, at the camp at Struppen.

Marshal Brown had arrived on the 11th, at Lichtensdorf, near Schandau, and immediately acquainted the saxons with his arrival, letting them know, that he would stay there all the next day, but no longer; and, in the mean time, waited for the notice of a certain signal, to begin the attack on the prussian posts, which signal was not given. The saxons were in a cul de sac, or place, through which there was no passage, where it was impossible for them to act, and they laboured under unsurmountable difficulties; so that, though the king of Poland, who was at Konigstein, was ardent, for making an attack, his generals convinced him of the utter impossibility of it.

Marshal

Marshal Brown perceiving all the danger of the situation he was then in, retreated on the 14th towards Bohemia. Whereupon, a prussian officer, with a body of hussars fell upon the rear of the austrians, consisting of 300 hussars, and 200 pandours; and, routing them, the hungarian infantry was put to the sword. This affair, which gave rise to so many debates and reproaches among the austrian and saxon generals, is very easily decided; the case was, that neither party had a sufficient knowledge of the ground which the saxons had pitched upon for their retreat, and to which alone was owing the surrender of the saxon army. The king of Poland, who was yet in the castle of Konigstein, seeing his army in such a situation, that it could not force a passage by the sword, and without all hopes of provisions or succours, permitted his troops to surrender themselves prisoners of war. Count Rutowski was appointed to draw up the capitulation *. The king of Prussia made no difficulty of restoring the colours, standards, and kettledrums, which were carried to the king of Poland at Konigstein. According to the capitulation the saxons marched out of their camp. On the 16th, in the morning, bread was sent to the soldiers, as soon as the capitulation was agreed to. On the 17th they passed the Elbe, preceded by their general officers, at a place called Raden, where the prussians had a bridge of boats; from thence they marched into a plain in the neighbourhood, and after passing be-

---

* His prussian majesty's answer to the 5th article of capitulation, is conceived in those spirited terms, which the prince was so wont to use. Rutowski demanded that the life and grenadier guards should be excepted in the capitulation; to which his majesty answered, " There is no exception to be made, because it is known
" that the king of Poland did give orders for that part of his troops
" which is in the said kingdom to join the russians, and to march
" for this purpose to the frontiers of Silesia; and a man must be a
" fool to let troops go which he holds fast, to see them make head
" against him a second time, and to be obliged to take them priso-
" ners again."

tween

tween two battalions of pruffian guards, they were received by two battalions of the prince of Pruffia's regiment, drawn up on the right and left; they there formed a hollow fquare, and had the articles of war read, and the military oath adminiftered to them. As there was but one bridge laid over the river, and the roads from the faxon camp were extremely bad; and as every regiment took the oath feparately, this ceremony lafted all that day and the next. The foldiers were all armed, and moft of them entered into the fervice of his pruffian majefty, and the officers were permitted on their parole, to go to their places of refidence.

The whole faxon army confifted of 16,000 men, 3000 of which were horfe and dragoons. The foldiers were extremely well looking, robuft young men, and had not fuffered for want of provifions during the blockade of five weeks. But the cavalry was almoft ruined.

On the 18th, the king of Poland fet out for Warfaw. The troops of Pruffia were withdrawn from all the places in this road; and the fame regard fhewn to his perfon, as crowned heads reciprocally obferve towards each other, in the moft profound peace. The queen of Poland, together with the royal family, continued in their capital; and had the fame honours paid them from their enemies that furrounded them, as they were accuftomed to receive from their own fubjects.

It was expected by many, that the king of Pruffia, after gaining fuch an acceffion of ftrength, as the faxon army, would again march into Bohemia, and face marfhal Brown on a more equal footing than before. But that wife monarch, weighing the difadvantages that might accrue to his army by hazarding a winter's campaign, in a country, where the feverity of the weather is generally more deftructive than the moft defperate battle; againft the advantages that might be gained by a fecond victory, at a feafon when

it

it was impossible to improve it, prudently resolved to withdraw his army into quarters of cantonment, and there to wait the motions of the enemy. Accordingly, marshal Keith was ordered to send off the baggage of his corps on the 21st of October, the horse and heavy artillery on the 22d; which was accordingly executed.

His prussian majesty left Struppen the 20th, accompanied with 10 battalions, to cover the retreat of his bohemian army, and lay that night at Peterswalde, and the next at Lenai; on the 22d, in the morning (leaving his battalions at Lenai) went to Lowoschutz, but returned that night to Lenai. On the 23d, early in the morning, the camp at Lowoschutz broke up; they formed into two columns, the first commanded by marshal Keith, the second by the prince of Prussia. Marshal Keith detached four battalions by the banks of the Elbe, to guard the right of the army, and, at the same time, to pick up the detachments placed along the river: they joined the army at Lenai. The prince of Bevern commanded the rear guard, which consisted of eight battalions, five squadrons of dragoons, and five of hussars. On the left of the rear of the army, but at some distance, was posted part of the regiment of leithen hussars, to prevent the austrian irregulars from acting; they lay that night at Lenai, the 23d, where they rested the 24th and 25th.

In the mean time, marshal Brown could not well penetrate into the designs of his prussian majesty; but thinking it probable, that he was making his dispositions for retreating, he sent a detachment of 3000 men, under general Haddick, with a design to harrass the rear of the prussian army; but he found his prussian majesty had made so masterly a disposition, that it was in vain to attack him. He accordingly retired.

That monarch had occupied with his ten battalions all the high grounds about Lenai, and his army continued

tinued to retire in perfect safety, his battalions still marching on, and keeping possession of the heights. The army advanced on the 26th to Teutsch Neudorff, encamped there, and the next day to Schoenwalde, and re-entered Saxony on the 30th, where it was cantoned between Pirna and the frontier along the Elbe. General Zastrow, with his brigade, was posted at Gishübel and Gottleube, where he was attacked by the austrian pandours; but they were repulsed with loss, and pursued beyond Peterswalde; after which, disheartened by the warm reception they always met with, they no longer disturbed the advanced posts of the prussian army.

At the same time the army at Lowoschutz was quitting Bohemia, marshal Schwerin was ordered to return into Silesia. He had passed the Elbe at Jaromitz: and, after procuring all the forage possible, he marched towards Schalitz; to which place some thousands of hungarians followed him, a body of his troops attacked them, and drove them as far as Smirsitz; after which, he continued his march unmolested. On the 2d of november, he entered the county of Glatz, and put his army into places of cantonment.

His majesty the king of Prussia, entered Dresden in triumph, on the 21st of november, accompanied by the princes of his house, and several general officers, on horseback, followed by his regiment of life-guards, and took his residence at count Brühl's magnificent palace. He rode every day, and immediately on his coming, examined the fortifications of the city, as well as the provision and ammunition, with which it was stored: ten thousand of his troops were quartered in the city and the neighbouring villages. The number of mouths this occasioned to be at Dresden, enhanced the price of corn so much, that a bushel of wheat cost five crowns. And what enhanced this scarcity was, a monopoly, one single man having farmed all the mills in Saxony,

M and

and the bakers were all obliged to have their corn ground at thefe mills; and although three memorials were prefented to his polifh majefty, requefting a remedy to fo great a grievance; yet, fuch was the inattention of that court to the good of its fubjects, that they rejected them, and the mills continued farmed.

The king of Pruffia, during his ftay at Drefden, in order to keep off the enemy's irregular troops from making incurfions into Saxony, ordered ditches to be made ten ells broad, and five deep; and by laying trees acrofs, made a fort of barricade. His majefty alfo ordered the fortifications of Drefden to be confiderably repaired and formed a very confiderable magazine in Germany; ufe of his troops. That monarch of his pruffian majefty difcovered the unjuft defigns of his enemies, and did as much as the greateft king could have done, to prevent their execution. He drove his enemy, the king of Poland, out of his hereditary dominions, and took poffeffion of them himfelf, making his whole army prifoners of war. He carried the war into countries belonging to the emprefs queen, and gained a victory over her troops. In the paper war which was carried on between his, and his enemies minifters, at moft of the courts in Europe, he was equally victorious. In fhort, his pruffian majefty appeared every where, and conqueft always for his attendant.

I fhall conclude this chapter with fome account of field marfhal Keith, fo often mentioned in it. This great man was a native of Scotland, that country having the honour of giving him birth in 1696. He is defcended from one of its moft antient and noble families. He was drawn into the rebellion againft his majefty king George the Ift, in 1715, and behaved with great refolution and bravery, at the battle of Sherriffmuir. At the fuppreffion of the rebellion, he went into France, where he ftudied mathematics under the celebrated
M. de

land and her family still resided; and though a paper war continued at the Hague, and several other courts, between the kings of Poland and Prussia, yet nothing was to be seen at Dresden, but the greatest politeness and complaisance. The king of Prussia admiring a very fine set of pictures in the royal palace; her polish majesty being informed of it, ordered them to be immediately carried to that monarch. On the other hand, nothing was wanting to alleviate the disagreeableness of her present situation. The prussian officers were always present at the operas and balls, in the brigade, the which paved the way to several marriages between them and her polish majesty's maids of honour. The czarian majesty, whenever any birth-day happened, always sent marshal Keith a commission of brigadier general in his name. Finding that he this winter. In this quality he served under count Munich against the turks, commanding a body of 8000 men, at the siege of Oczakow, with great reputation, and receiving a wound in the thigh, for the cure of which he made a journey from Petersburgh to Paris; as soon as he recovered he came over to London, and was very well received by his britannic majesty, who knew that he was forced into the rebellion, by a bigotted mother. On his return into Russia, peace reigned for some time through that empire; but a war breaking out between the russians and swedes, they came to the battle of Wilmanstrand, wherein the former got the victory, owing to the good conduct of marshal Lacy and general Keith. He afterwards commanded an army of 30,000 men near Petersburg, when the amazing revolution in the russian empire was brought about, which placed the empress Elizabeth, daughter of Peter the great, on the throne of Russia. He also commanded an army against the swedes, in the war which took place soon after the revolution. On the conclusion of the peace with Sweden, the empress sent him ambassador to Stock-

that quarter. The french alfo gave out, all over Europe, that they intended marching a formidable army to the affiftance of their ally the emprefs queen; and the preparations they made on the frontiers of France, indicated fome great defign in hand.

To defend himfelf againft fo formidable a confederacy, this great monarch was obliged to let his own prepartions for war keep pace with thofe of his enemies. He made levies all over his dominions, that his troops might bear fome equality in number to thofe of his antagonifts. In fhort, he fhowed, that his refources encreafed in proportion, as his dangers multiplied.

Such was the end of the firft campaign in Germany; glorioufly finifhed on the part of his pruffian majefty. He had difcovered the unjuft defigns of his enemies, and he did as much as the greateft king could have done, to prevent their execution. He drove his enemy, the king of Poland, out of his hereditary dominions, and took poffeffion of them himfelf, making his whole army prifoners of war. He carried the war into countries belonging to the emprefs queen, and gained a victory over her troops. In the paper war which was carried on between his, and his enemies minifters, at moft of the courts in Europe, he was equally victorious. In fhort, his pruffian majefty appeared every where, and conqueft always for his attendant.

I fhall conclude this chapter with fome account of field marfhal Keith, fo often mentioned in it. This great man was a native of Scotland, that country having the honour of giving him birth in 1696. He is defcended from one of its moft antient and noble families. He was drawn into the rebellion againft his majefty king George the Ift, in 1715, and behaved with great refolution and bravery, at the battle of Sherriffmuir. At the fuppreffion of the rebellion, he went into France, where he ftudied mathematics under the celebrated

M. de

M. de Maupertius; he also made himself perfect master of the military part of geometry. From Paris he set out on his travels into Italy, Spain, Portugal, and Switferland, On his return to that city, the czar of Muscovy, who was then at Paris, invited him to enter into his service, which Mr. Keith then refused. He was a volunteer in the french army at the storming the harbour of Vigo, in the year 1719, when he received a dangerous wound. From Paris he went to the court of Madrid, where, by the interest of the duke of Liria, he obtained a commission in the irish brigade, then commanded by the duke of Ormond: He accompanied the duke of Liria, in his embassy from the court of Spain, to Muscovy, which introduced him into the service of the czarina, who gave him a commission of brigadier general, and soon after, that of lieutenant general, and was invested with the order of the black eagle. In this quality he served under count Munich against the turks, commanding a body of 8000 men, at the siege of Oczakow, with great reputation, and receiving a wound in the thigh, for the cure of which he made a journey from Petersburgh to Paris; as soon as he recovered he came over to London, and was very well received by his britannic majesty, who knew that he was forced into the rebellion, by a bigotted mother. On his return into Russia, peace reigned for some time through that empire; but a war breaking out between the russians and swedes, they came to the battle of Wilmanstrand, wherein the former got the victory, owing to the good conduct of marshal Lacy and general Keith. He afterwards commanded an army of 30,000 men near Petersburg, when the amazing revolution in the russian empire was brought about, which placed the empress Elizabeth, daughter of Peter the great, on the throne of Russia. He also commanded an army against the swedes, in the war which took place soon after the revolution. On the conclusion of the peace with Sweden, the empress sent him ambassador to Stock-

Stockholm; and foon after created him field marfhal in the ruffian armies. But taking fome difguft to the ruffian fervice, whofe pay is very fmall, he entered into the fervice of his pruffian majefty, who received him in the moft gracious manner, made him governor of Berlin, and a field marfhal in the pruffian armies; enjoying a large revenue, and the moft gracious treatment from the king of Pruffia. The firft occafion for a difplay of his abilities, in the fervice of his new mafter, was the invafion of Saxony by that monarch: and of which I have juft been endeavouring to prefent the reader with a clear and diftinct view. His genius in the art of war, will appear more fully in the fubfequent tranfactions.

CHAP.

CHAP. X.

*Affairs in England and France. Recapitulation of the affairs of France. Rise and progress of french power. Changes in the english ministry. Parliament meets. King's speech, and addresses. Board of enquiry on Stuart, Cornwallis, and Effingham. French king stabbed. Message to the house of commons. Naval transactions. Affairs in the East-Indies. Court martial on Admiral Byng. Its resolutions and sentence. The members of it examined by the house of lords. The admiral executed. Reflections.*

NO part of history is so extremely difficult to write, as that which presents us with an account of the transactions performed in our own time. It is almost impossible entirely to dispel the cloud of obscurity which cover the motives, and secret springs that occasion many remarkable events. An historian ought to be in the cabinet of princes, and at the head of their armies; yet, even with these advantages, the prejudices of religion, and partiality towards his own country, will be apt to taint the truth of his narrations. In short, so many great and noble qualities are requisite to adorn the mind of a complete historian, that very few since the creation of the world have advanced near to the highest pitch of historic excellence. But in the latter ages of the world, we have never found that any one, who ventured into that part of history I just mentioned, ever gained a great reputation; owing to the difficulty of judging clearly on the actions of our cotemporaries. The reader must pardon this short digression. To return.

Hitherto the british nation had been engaged in an unsuccessful war against France. The advantages which

which the enemy had gained, were not of very great consequence in themselves; but as they brought a reputation on their arms; and yet more, as they sunk and depressed the spirits of their adversaries. The english pined with discontent, on their not being victorious in a just and necessary war. The only consolation they received, was from the eclat of the king of Prussia's success; and the hopes of a change in the english ministry, and, consequently, of one in the measures of the nation. The discontents of the people ran very high throughout the kingdom: they could not forget Minorca: one may perceive how imbittered their minds were, by reading the addresses which were presented to the king on that occasion, from most of the boroughs and corporations in England.

Bad success, in the beginning of a war, under such a government as subsists in England, is the necessary consequence of a war. France, from the nature of her government, constantly keeps up a great force both by land and sea; so that, no sooner has she resolved on a war with any of her neighbours, than her forces are ready to march against her enemies. In England the case is quite different: let a war be ever so necessary, a king of England can take no steps to prosecute it, before its necessity and consequences are debated in parliament; and, even when they are approved of, the forces to carry on such a war are all to be raised, (a very few excepted) and disciplined; it is always some time before such troops as those can be brought to a clear knowledge of their manual exercise; without which, every one knows, they can be of but little use; and when they have acquired a competent dexterity in that part of the art of war, they are not then, by any means, on an equality with veteran troops.

From these reasons it is very evident, that France must, almost in the nature of things, have a great advantage

advantage over England, in the beginning of every war : not only reason, but the remembrance of past events will teach us this piece of political knowledge. But it is necessary for the clearer understanding of this work to take a view of the state of France at this period.

The reader must not here expect to find this potent kingdom considered in the same light, as it was during the reign of her late monarch Lewis XIV, who approached almost as near to universal monarchy, as the emperor Charles V did in Germany and Spain. It was a general concatination of events that rendered France so extremely formidable.

That monarch succeeded Lewis XIII in the throne, in 1643, at a time when France was neither in a very flourishing nor a very feeble state. Ann of Austria obtained the sole regency of the kingdom ; and made cardinal Mazarine, her chief minister, master of France and of herself. He had obtained that power over her, which an artful man will acquire over a woman, born without strength sufficient to govern, yet, with constancy enough to persist in her choice *.

This minister, who governed France with variety of success, for 18 years, was formerly a mere adventurer, without any great pretences to family, credit or fortune ; by birth a gentleman of Rome : his first patron was cardinal Sachetti ; then he became a captain of horse ; but being taken notice of by cardinal Antonio Barberrini, he laid aside the military, and assumed the ecclesiastical habit. He was agent for the french, at the peace of Casal, and behaving with courage and dexterity, recommended himself to cardinal Richelieu, who took him entirely into his confidence, and procured him a hat from Rome. He

* Vide Voltaire's Works.

had

had a fine person, an easy and insinuating address, was possessed of all genteel accomplishments, had an air of courtesy, and kindness, spoke sensibly of affairs of importance, agreeably and pleasantly on all other topicks. In short, he was an able statesman, and a finished courtier; but as for religion, virtue, honour, probity or regard for the people, they were (to speak without envy or prejudice) things out of his way; he did not either pretend to them himself, nor was he suspected of having any acquaintance with them by others.

On his death the administration of affairs fell into the hands of Tellier, Colbert, and de Lionne, who had address enough, by flattering their master, to keep their posts for a considerable time. Colbert was comptroller general of the finances; a man of great parts, and most extensive genius: the war which preceded the treaty of Aix la Chapelle, concluded in 1668, was carried successfully through the abilities and advice of this minister; who always kept the revenues of France in most excellent order: by that treaty France gained several important towns in Flanders. But the greatness of Colbert's genius is best seen in the great encouragement he gave to trade and manufactures; it was through his management, that France became a maritime power. It was really astonishing to behold the sea-ports, which before were deserted and in ruins, now surrounded by works which were at once both their ornament and their defence; covered also with ships and mariners, and containing already near sixty large men of war. New colonies under the protection of the french flag, were sent from all parts into America, the East-Indies, and the coasts of Africa. These were the great effects of that able minister's administration, more for the advantage and glory of France than all the sounding conquests of Lewis XIV.

But

But the affairs of that nation took a very fatal change, in the war that monarch went into to support his grandson on the throne of Spain. His able ministers, who had formerly conducted his affairs with so much glory, were now all dead, and in their room none were placed but youths of no experience: Condé, Luxemburg, and Turenne, no longer commanded the armies of France; military discipline, the very soul of armies, was utterly neglected; the marine was ruined, and all trade was at a stand. The peace of Utrecht saved the nation from entire destruction.

During the regency of the duke of Orleans, France recovered herself considerably; that prince's administration was certainly the best calculated for the interest of the kingdom, of any he could possibly pursue; and his plan for foreign affairs was the best laid, and best conducted, that the french had ever seen. He found the kingdom burdened with an immense national debt, by some calculated to be near three hundred millions sterling: every one knows the rise and progress of the famous Missisippi scheme, by which the nation annihilated so many millions. As destructive as such a scheme might be to individuals, yet the nation in general gained considerably by it; and from that period, we find France continually regaining her credit, commerce, and power. At the beginning of the war of 1741, she was again much too powerful for the repose of Europe; by sea indeed, that power was not so formidable as it was by land; since it is very certain, at the beginning of it, the whole naval power of France did not consist of quite forty ships of war of all sizes, which, though it be very short of what it was at the opening of the present century, yet is much superior to any force the french had of that nature, before the reign of Lewis XIV. And the commerce of France, though it was much inferior to what it had been, was yet certainly

very

very confiderable; for France loft by that war, in its trade, two hundred millions of their money, which makes above nine millions three hundred thoufand pounds of ours: by which we may perceive, that their trade was arrived at a furprifing height; but then we alfo find that it was reduced by that war to nothing.

After the conclufion of the peace, the french miniftry continued to load the kingdom with exorbitant taxes, to pay thofe debts they had contracted during the war; but the miferable condition of the nation at that time, was fuch, that they could not afford fo large a part of their property, as was neceffary to difcharge them; fo that France at the commencement of the late war was burdened with very near the fame debts, as fhe was at the conclufion of the preceding one.

With England the cafe was different. This nation indeed, was burthened with a very heavy national debt; but then fhe enjoyed a more extenfive and flourifhing commerce than France, and her naval power infinitely exceeded that of her enemy. Yet thefe advantages we find were ballanced at the beginning of the war, by the advantages which the government of France has over a limited one in military proceedings. This was the cafe in the war of which I am fpeaking; hitherto, very indifferent fuccefs had crowned the attempts of the britifh nation; Europe, Afia, and America, were equally the unfuccefsful theatres of our military affairs.

This bad fuccefs, although it depended in part on the natural confequences of the war, yet the miniftry then at the helm of affairs in this kingdom, certainly did not fhew thofe abilities, and refolution, that were neceffary to carry on fo great an undertaking as a war with France. In England a minifter always makes a very bad figure at the eve of a war. It is the nature of our conftitution, to have an oppofition to every

minifter's

minister's measures, carried on in parliament: this ran extremely high at the beginning of this war; ever since the loss of Minorca, which reflected so much disgrace on the british nation, the kingdom in general wished ardently for a change, both of ministers and measures.

The effects of this general discontent were soon perceived; for we find, that in the beginning of november, his majesty was pleased to make the following alterations in the ministry; the duke of Devonshire was made first lord commissioner of the treasury, in the room of the duke of Newcastle, who was created a duke of Great Britain by the title of the duke of Newcastle under Lyne, in the county of Stafford. The other commissioners were, the right hon. Henry Legge, Robert Nugent, esq. the lord viscount Duncannon, and the hon. James Grenville. The right hon. Henry Legge, was also appointed chancellor and under treasurer of the Exchequer. The right hon. the earl of Ilchester, and James Cressert, esq. were made comptrollers of the accounts of his majesty's army. The new commissioners of the admiralty were Richard earl of Temple, the hon. Edward Boscawen, Temple West, and John Pitt, esqrs. George Hay, L.L.D. Thomas Orby Hunter, and Gilbert Elliot, esqrs. The right hon. George Grenville, was made treasurer of his majesty's navy. Earl Temple, lord Mansfield, John viscount Bateman (treasurer of his majesty's houshold) and Richard Edgecombe, esq. (comptroller of his majesty's houshold) were sworn of the privy council. ' - ' lord Berkeley was made captain of his majesty' d of pensioners. The right hon. Wills Hill, earl of Hillsborough, in Ireland, was created a baron of Great Britain, by the title of lord Harwich. Sir George Lyttleton was created Baron Lyttleton. The 4th of december following, his majesty appointed the right hon. William Pitt, to be one of his majesty's principal secretaries

cretaries of ftate, in the room of the right hon. Henry Fox, who refigned. This principal, amongft the party who were now pufhed out of the miniftry, finding the current run fo ftrong againft him, thought it prudent to refign, with hopes that he might have an opportunity to regain his power, and eftablifh himfelf more firmly in his loft feat.

Private adventurers by fea, met with more general fuccefs in their undertakings than the royal fquadrons. That of the antigallican privateer in particular; it was fitted out by the fociety of antigallicans; it was formerly the Flamborough man of war, then a merchant's veffel, and afterwards the antigallican privateer; fhe mounted 28 guns, and carried 208 men; was commanded by captain William Fofter. She failed from Deptford the 17th of feptember. About 100 leagues weft of Lifbon, fhe met with the Maria Therefa, a french fhip from the Weft-Indies, mounting 14 carriage guns, and carrying 30 men; after a brifk engagement for a quarter of an hour fhe ftruck, and was valued at upwards of 20,000 l. A little further fouth, the antigallican took a fnow, of 180 tons, from Bourdeaux, laden with wine, bale goods, pitch, and diftilled waters, valued at near 15,000 l. A little north eaft of Madeira, fhe was chafed by two french men of war, but efcaped by means of a calm.

They next cruifed off the coaft of Galicia in Spain; and on the 26th of december in the morning, difcovered a fail; they gave chace under fpanifh colours; at 12 got within gun-fhot, when fhe fired a gun, upon which the antigallican took down fpanifh and hung up englifh colours, on which the enemy gave them a broad-fide, and killed three men, but had no return till the englifh captain was clofe along-fide, where he engaged till three, when fhe ftruck. She proved to be the duke de Penthievre Eaft-India man, bound laft from Madagafcar, and commanded by
captain

captain Villeneuf, was upwards of 1000 tons burthen, mounting 50 guns; the french captain and 12 men were killed, the second captain shot through the shoulder, and 27 more were wounded. Capt. Foster lost 12 men and 26 wounded. The captain proceeded for Cadiz, where he met with very disagreeable treatment, for the spaniards in the french interest, together with the french consuls insisted that the duke de Penthievre was taken within gun-shot of the coast of Spain; the truth of this did not appear altogether so clear; but if it was so, the behaviour of the spaniards in the affair was unprecedented, and contrary to the laws of nations: a rupture with Spain at that time, would have been of very bad consequence; so the restitution of the prize was agreed to by the english ministry.

Such was the issue of an affair which made much noise, and occasioned very just observations on the partiality of the spaniards to our enemies the french; which some were pleased to attribute to the dishonour which the nation sustained in the loss of Minorca; and that certainly with some reason; for the spaniards were the first nation who exposed their surprise at so strange an affair as the conquest of Minorca: It appeared very strange in their eyes, that the most powerful maritime nation in the world, should suffer so ignominious a loss. Even at this day, it is not clearly proved, whether the indiaman was a lawful prize or not; but thus far we may affirm with certainty, that the irregularity with which the spaniards conducted, or rather obscured the transactions in this affair, was illegal, and fully proved how partially they acted towards the french.

But it is now time to give the reader some account of the proceedings in parliament, for we must look into them to perceive the important springs that move the great machine of the british power. That august assembly met on the 2d of december, when his majesty

majesty came with the usual state, and made a most gracious speech to both houses; and received as dutiful and affectionate addresses.

His majesty mentioned his having sent the hanoverian troops home, and in the lords address he was thanked for bringing them over; but it occasioned a warm debate in the house; however, as his majesty had sent for them at the request of his parliament, the thanks were at last agreed to by the majority of the house. But in the address of the commons, no such paragraph of thanks appeared.

In pursuance of what was mentioned concerning them, in his majesty's speech, we find that the hanoverians were sent home; and in that manner ended part of a measure which reflected so much dishonour on the nation; and will always be remembered in the annals of Britain with regret. But it was not yet thought seasonable to part with the hessians. They were ordered into winter quarters.

Indeed there was nothing in England at this time but wore a gloomy appearance. It is a very great presumption, that the affairs of a nation does not go well, when there are many court martials and boards of enquiry; this was the case in the beginning of this war in England. His majesty by a warrant dated november the 22d, directed sir John Ligonier, general Huske, and general Cholmondeley to enquire into the conduct of major general Stuart, and the colonels Cornwallis, and the earl of Effingham. The charge against them, was their not joining their respective commands in the island of Minorca. The board met december the 8th, and were also to enquire, whether they had used their utmost endeavour to throw themselves into fort St. Philip's; and why, being only passengers, they assisted at the sea council of war, which advised Mr. Byng to return immediately to Gibraltar.

The

The three officers made much the same defence; they proved that it was not in their power to be at Minorca before Mr. Byng's fleet, and that they could not throw themselves into that island; that as to their assisting at the council of war, they supposed themselves under the command of the admiral; and assisted, as they thought they were bound to co-operate with the sea officers, to the utmost of their power, for the advancement of his majesty's service. General Cornwallis added verbally, " May I be permitted " to say, that I have been now upwards of 26 " years in his majesty's service, and employed in " more service, and greater variety, perhaps, than " any officer of my years and standing in the army; " that it has been my good fortune, during the " course of my service, never to have had a repri- " mand, or even a rebuke, from any superior officer; " and, that I have had the honour to serve under " the several general officers appointed for this en- " quiry; I flatter myself they will bear testimony of " my zeal for, and forwardness in, the king's service " upon all occasions." On the whole, the board humbly submitted it to his majesty, as their unanimous opinion, that the conduct of the said major general and colonels was clear from any suspicion of disobedience of orders, or neglect of duty.

In France, the winter was spent in the usual preparations for war; but every thing was suddenly stopped on the 6th of january, by one of the most desperate attempts recorded in history. As the king was going from Trianon to Versailles, to visit madam de Victoire; about six in the evening, as his majesty was just stepping into his coach, to return to Trianon, a man, who had concealed himself between the hind wheels, rushed forward, with his hat on, made his way to the king's person through the guards (one of whom he shoved against the dauphin) and struck his majesty on the right side, of which however,

ever, he only complained, by saying, "That man has given me a violent blow, he must be either mad or drunk." But having perceived that his hand which he clapped to his side, was bloody, he said, "I am wounded; seize that fellow but don't kill him. His majesty was immediately carried to his apartment. The wound, (which from the first was not thought dangerous) was given with a sharp pointed knife, which glanced upwards between the fourth and fifth rib, but was not of any considerable depth; and at the first dressing, it was even judged that the cure would be speedy. That night the king slept an hour and a quarter, and every day recovered more and more. The day after the king received the wound, the dauphin was charged with the administration of the kingdom, and presided in the council of state during the king's illness. The next day, all the presidents and counsellors of the parliament, assembled, and deliberated on the event; and in the evening they carried to Versailles the deliberation.

The wretch, Robert Francis Damien (for that was his name) was born in 1714, at Arras; in 1738 he married, and had a daughter by that marriage. His brother was immediately taken into custody. His father was still living, in the 85th year of his age. The process against him was begun at Versailles, and the conclusion of it was, that his father, wife and daughter, should quit the kingdom for ever; but as for himself,——humanity won't permit me to recite the barbarous shocking cruelties which were made use of at his execution, to torture a poor wretch, who plainly appeared, by his trial, to be mad.

The preparations which were making by France, convinced the british ministry, that the war England was engaged in, would prove a continental one. The french were drawing their troops together from all parts, into two camps on the frontiers of Flanders, which seemed, by their situation, to contain armies destined ftined to act in Germany. Indeed it was believed, in all the courts of Europe, that France would, early in the spring, march an army into the electorate of Hanover, to involve an innocent people into the horrors of a bloody war, because their sovereign was king of England. In fact, this design of the french was so much regarded in England as to occasion the following message being sent by his majesty, by Mr. secretary Pitt, to the house of commons, the 17th of february, 1757, viz.

"George R.

It is always with reluctance that his majesty asks any extraordinary supplies of his people; but as the united councils and formidable preparations of France, and her allies, threaten, with the most alarming consequences, Europe in general; and as these most unjust and vindictive designs are particularly and immediately bent against his majesty's electoral dominions, and those of his good ally the king of Prussia; his majesty confides in the experienced zeal and affection of his faithful commons, that they will chearfully assist him, in forming and maintaining an army of observation, for the just and necessary defence and preservation thereof; and enable his majesty to fulfil his engagements with the king of Prussia, for the security of the empire, against the irruption of foreign armies, and for the support of the common cause.

G. R."

This message was referred to the committee of supply; and on the 21st it was resolved to grant his majesty 200,000 l. for the purposes therein mentioned in it. Let us for a moment enquire into the utility of this measure; and we shall find, for all what some pretended politicians are pleased to tell us to the contrary, that it was a necessary one; we might be very sure,

sure, when first the british ministry seized the ships of France, that that nation would revenge itself by attacking Hanover, and it certainly was confonant with laws, human and divine, to resolve to defend it, considering the unhappy hanoverians were forced into a destructive war, on our account, without having more to do with the troubles then in Europe than the inhabitants of Lapland; and, as the measure was just and necessary, it was also necessary to form an army of observation, for that purpose. His royal highness the duke of Cumberland was appointed by his majesty for that command; he embarked at Harwich the 9th of april, in his way to Hanover, where he arrived safe: and where I shall leave him till I come to give an account of the operations of the troops under his command.

The naval affairs of England at this period, were not of great eclat. The french were extremely busy in fitting out two great fleets at Brest, and port l'Orient; the english ministry had taken care to have a superior one lying off Brest harbour, under the command of sir Edward Hawke, who, in that station, succeeded Mr. Boscawen, and had dispatched admiral West with 11 sail of the line on a cruise to the westward: But all these precautions did not hinder a french squadron getting out of Brest, and the other likewise from port l'Orient. The one convoyed troops for the west, and the other set sail for the East-Indies. The former was under the command of M. de Beaufremont, and consisted of sixteen sail of the line, and five frigates, carrying between 5 and 6000 men on board. Another french squadron, under the command of M. de Revest, a french admiral, also sailed from Toulon for America; admiral Saunders was then at Gibraltar, with an english one, and was informed that the french appeared off Malaga, upon which he went, with five ships, in pursuit of them; the 5th of april he saw the french, and, being to leeward, formed a

line,

line, as did the enemy, and some of the ships began to engage at a distance; but before the rest got up, they lost sight of the french, and could meet with them no more: what was peculiarly unfortunate was, Mr. Saunders's not being able to prevent Revest passing the Streights, which he did, in his way to America. The english West-India fleet, under admiral Townshend, at this time, consisted of four ships of the line and three frigates: it was very surprising that the british ministry had not sent a greater force to that station, espcially as there were so many french squadrons ready to sail.

In the East-Indies a much brighter success attended the british arms. Mr. Watson, the english admiral, who commanded in the East-Indies, sailed from Madrass, on the 16th of october, with three sail of the line and some frigates, for Bengal, and after a tedious voyage arrived, december the 5th, at the port of Balasore, in the kingdom of Bengal, where strengthening his force with what recruits he could draw together, he entered the Ganges, and after a short resistence, on the 30th of january, made himself master of Busbudgia, having landed colonel Clive to attack it by land: the conquest of this fort opened a passage to Calcutta, the late principal settlement of the company in Bengal, and the scene of the deplorable sufferings of so many of our unfortunate countrymen. The troops and sailors, at the very sight of the place, were animated with revenge, and attacked it with so much bravery, that they became masters of it the very day it was approached, and found in it four mortars, 91 guns of different sizes, and a considerable quantity of all kinds of ammunition. In a few days afterwards, they burnt and destroyed the city of Hughley, together with the granaries and store-houses of salt, situated on the banks of each side the river, which was of great prejudice to the nabob's army.

The nabob, in the mean time, finding how victorious the englifh arms were, when oppofed only by garrifons of indians, marched down, on the 2d of february, 1757, with his whole army, confifting of 10,000 horfe and 12,000 foot, with a defign to drive the englifh from their late conquefts. Col. Clive immediately demanded of the admiral a detachment of failors, to come to the affiftance of the land forces; accordingly the admiral detached capt. Warwick with a party. On receiving this reinforcemet, the colonel determined to attack the nabob in his camp, although he was fo much fuperior to him in numbers. On the 5th, he put this bold defign in execution; the victory was complete, the nabob being obliged to quit the field of battle, fince none of his troops could ftand againft the defperate bravery of their enemies.

The confequence of this battle was, that the nabob made propofals of peace to col. Clive, which were agreed to. By this treaty the englifh Eaft-India company were re-eftablifhed in the poffeffion of all its fettlements and privileges, an immunity from all taxes was granted, and a reftitution promifed of all that the company had fuffered at the taking of Calcutta.

The war with the indians being thus for a while concluded, the admiral thought he could not better employ his forces than by attacking the fettlement of the french at Chandernagore, fituated feveral miles higher up the river than Calcutta, being a place of confiderable ftrength and importance, and one of the greateft which the french had in that part of the Eaft-Indies. Col. Clive, for this expedition, put himfelf at the head of 700 europeans, and 1700 blacks, and the admirals Watfon and Pocock commanded the fleet, which was to fecond the operations of the land forces. To prevent an attack from fhipping, the french funk feveral large veffels in the river; but this intended precaution was of no fervice, for Mr. Watfon

Watson having diligently sounded the river, found a safe passage, without weighing up any of the ships; so that on the 24th he sailed up, and fired so briskly on the place, the same being done from col. Clive's batteries on the shore, that it capitulated in three hours. They had in the fort 1200 men, 500 of which were europeans, and 700 blacks; 183 pieces of cannon, from 24 pounders and downwards; three small mortars, and a considerable quantity of ammunition.

This great success paved the way for more considerable operations. The english had found that the nabob, although he had signed a peace with them, was not to be trusted; and would break it on the first good opportunity. Mr. Watson and col Clive having reestablished the East-India company in their possessions, and things being quiet, consulted the most considerable of their body which were the wisest measures to be put in execution against the nabob, so as to ensure themselves in safety. That prince had shewn his bad intentions, by not executing the late treaty, on frivolous pretences. It was resolved, that the most expedient manner of bringing him to reason, was by force of arms; accordingly they prepared to attack him, a scheme full of the most dangerous difficulties; but these were in great part removed, by a most fortunate incident, which they had not the least reason to expect, when they took the resolution to attack him.

The nabob, as I have more fully said before, was one of the most horrid tyrants that ever afflicted any nation; his subjects, as well as his enemies, had experienced the violence and perfidy of his temper; they were all discontented with his government, particularly the most considerable officers in his army, who had entered into a conspiracy against him, at the head of which was Jaffier Ali Cawn, a man of great power and interest. No sooner were their designs ripe for execution, than they communicated them to the english government in Calcutta, desiring their assistance. Nothing could better agree with their designs; they were too weak to encounter alone, although the spirit of their leaders had overlooked the numbers of their enemies; but being aided by this conspiracy, they did not doubt of punishing the nabob, in such a manner as his perfidy deserved. They did not hesitate a moment, but entered into a treaty with Jaffier Ali Cawn, and the rest of the conspirators; and in consequence of that action, the english troops marched under colonel Clive. That none of the landmen might be kept at home, the admiral garrisoned Chandernagore with his sailors, and moreover detached 50 of them to join the army, to serve as gunners. All these steps being taken, in order to ensure success in their attempt, they advanced up the river, with design to bring the nabob's army to a battle; they effected this in a few days, and the victory was decided in favour of the english, being fought on the the 22d of june. A considerable part of the nabob's army, under the command of Jaffier, remained inactive during the engagement; and the nabob finding himself deserted by his own officers, fled with the few that remained faithful to him, leaving the field of battle to his enemies. The battle was no sooner over, than Jaffier Ali Cawn openly declared himself, and entered Muxadavat, the capital of the kingdom, with an army of his friends, and victorious allies. By the assistance of col. Clive, he placed himself in the ancient seat of the nabob's, and received the homage of all ranks of people, as suba of Bengal, Bahar and Orixa: he soon after put to death the deposed nabob.

By the alliance which colonel Clive concluded with Jaffier, and by the reduction of Chandernagore, the french were entirely driven out of Bengal, and all its dependencies, this being one of the articles of the treaty. By the rest a perpetual alliance,

ance, offensive and defensive, was made between the parties, the territories of the company were enlarged, and upwards of 2,000,000 sterling was stipulated to be paid, as an indemnification to the East-India company, and the sufferers in the taking of Calcutta. The new nabob, through gratitude to those who had placed him in his throne, gave, besides the above large sums, about 600,000 l. as a gratuity to the sea squadron and troops.

In this wonderful manner was the english successful in the East-Indies. In thirteen days they effected so great a revolution, with such an inconsiderable number of troops, giving away a kingdom near as big as France, a kingdom more fertile, more populous, and infinitely more rich. All this was the result of that prudence, conduct, and courage, with which the admiral and colonel, seconded by the intrepidity of their men, formed and executed such noble and daring projects. Indeed, the joy of the nation, on hearing these signal successes, was much damped by the death of admiral Watson, who lost his life by the unwholesomeness of the climate, having gained a great and lasting reputation.

In England, the face of affairs had not such a bright aspect. The nation, at this time, was entirely held in suspence, about the fate of Mr. Byng. By his majesty's command, signified to the commissioners of the admiralty, that unfortunate admiral was brought before a court martial, which met on the 28th of december, 1756, on board the St. George ship in Portsmouth harbour, and consisted of the following members:

Thomas Smith, esq. vice-admiral of the red,
Francis Holbourne, esq. rear-admiral of the red,
Harry Norris, esq. rear-admiral of the white,
Thomas Broderick, esq. rear-admiral of the blue.

Captain

Captain Charles Holmes,
Captain William Boys,
Captain John Simcoe,
Captain John Bentley,
Captain Peter Denis,
Captain Francis Geary,
Captain John Moore,
Captain James Douglas,
Hon. Augustus Keppel.

The admiral's instructions, letters, and other necessary papers being read to the court, they proceeded to examine their witnesses. These examinations would be tedious to the reader; and besides, every paragraph so abounds with naval terms, understood only by sea officers, that not one man in twenty would be able to understand a syllable of it; for which reason, I shall only give the substance of the resolutions of the court martial, and make such remarks upon them, in particular, and on the sentence in general, as will enable the reader to form some judgment on an affair, concerning which, opinions are at this day divided.

The 26th of january it was found, that the court had come on the three preceding days to the following resolutions, viz.

1. It does not appear the admiral made any unnecessary delay in his way from St. Hellens to Minorca.

2. It appears, that on the fleet's getting sight of Minorca, on the 19th of may, the admiral detached capt. Harvey with three frigates, to endeavour to land a letter for general Blakeney; and to reconnitre the enemies batteries.

3. It appears, that those frigates were got near to Mahon, endeavouring to execute the orders, till they were called off by signal from the admiral.

4. It appears that the fleet stood towards the enemy the remaining part of the day.

5. The court are of opinion, that the admiral proceeded properly, upon discovery of the french fleet, to stand towards them.

6. It appears, that major general Stuart, lord Effingham, and col. Cornwallis, and 200 men, with their officers, belonging to the garrison, were on board the squadron.

7. The court are of opinion, that as so great a number of officers were on board the fleet, the admiral ought to have put them on board one of the abovementioned frigates, to have landed them, if found practicable; and if not landed before he saw the french fleet, to have left the frigates to have effected it notwithstanding.

8. It appears, that from the morning of the 19th, when the admiral first saw the french fleet, till the 20th at noon, the admiral took proper measures to gain and keep the wind of the enemy, and to form and close the line of battle.

13. It appears, that the admiral made the signal for battle about 20 minutes after two o'clock.

14. It appears, at the time the signal was made for battle, our van was considerably nearer to their van, than our rear was to their rear.

15. It appears, that upon signal being made for battle, the ships of our van division bore down properly, for the ships opposed to them, in the enemy's line, and engaged them, till the five headmost ships of the enemy went away out of gun-shot.

16. It appears, that the Intrepid having engaged 10 minutes, or a quarter of an hour, lost her foretopmast.

19. It is the opinion of the court, that the admiral, in the Ramillies, after the signal was made for battle, separated the rear from the van division, and retarded

the

the rear division of the british fleet from closing with, and engaging the enemy, by his shortening sail.

20. It is the opinion of the court, that instead of shortening sail, the admiral ought to have made the Trident and the Princess Louisa signals to make more sail; and he ought also to have set so much sail himself, as would have enabled the Culloden to have kept her station, in order to have got down with as much expedition as possible to the enemy, and thereby have properly supported the van division.

23. It appears, that when the firing had been continued a little while in the Ramillies, an alarm was given, of a ship being close under her lee-bow, which proved to be the Trident; upon which the admiral shortened sail, and ordered his men to cease firing till they should see french colours.

24. It appears, that the Princess Louisa was also seen about the same time, upon the weather-bow of the Ramillies.

25. The court are of opinion, that while the Ramillies was firing, in going down, the Trident, and ships immediately a-head of the Ramillies, proved an impediment to the Ramillies continuing to go down.

26. The court are of opinion, that the admiral acted wrong, in directing the fire of the Ramillies to be continued, before he had placed her at a proper distance from the enemy; as he thereby not only threw away shot uselessly, but occasioned a smoke, which prevented his seeing the motions of the enemy, and the position of the ships immediately a-head of the Ramillies.

32. The court are of opinion, that after the ships, which had received damage in the action, were as much refitted, as circumstances would permit, the admiral ought to have returned with the squadron off St. Philip's, and have endeavoured to have opened a communication with that castle; and to have used
every

every means in his power, for its relief, before he returned to Gibraltar.

33. The court are of opinion, that admiral Byng did not do his utmost to relieve St. Philip's castle, in the island of Minorca, then besieged by the forces of the french king.

34. The court are of opinion, that admiral Byng, during the engagement, did not do his utmost to take, seize, and destroy the ships of the french king, which it was his duty to have engaged; and to assist such of his majesty's ships as were engaged in fight with the french ships, which it was his duty to have assisted.

35. It appears, by the evidence of lord Robert Bertie, lieutenant colonel Smith, captain Gardiner, and by other officers of the ship, who were near the person of the admiral, that they did not perceive any backwardness in the admiral, during the action, or any marks of fear or confusion, either from his countenance or behaviour; but, that he seemed to give his orders cooly and distinctly, and did not seem wanting in personal courage.

36. Resolved, that the admiral appears to fall under the following part of the 12th article of war, to wit, " or shall not do his utmost to take or destroy every ship, which it shall be his duty to engage; and to assist and relieve all and every of his majesty's ships, which it shall be his duty to assist and relieve."

37. Resolved, as that article possitively prescribes death, without any alternative left to the discretion of the court, under any variation of circumstances, that he be adjudged to be shot to death, at such time, and on board such ship, as the lords commissioners of the admiralty shall direct. But as it appears by the evidence of lord Robert Bertie, lieutenant colonel Smith, captain Gardiner, and other officers of the ship, who were near the person of the admiral, that they did not perceive any backwardness in him during the

the action, or any marks of fear or confusion, either from his countenance or behaviour, but that he seemed to give his orders cooly and distinctly, and did not seem wanting in personal courage, and from other circumstances; the court do not believe, that his misconduct arose either from cowardice or disaffection; and do therefore unanimously think it their duty most earnestly to recommend him as a proper object of mercy.

At the same time that these resolutions were transmitted to the lords of the admiralty, the members of the court drew up a representation to that board, which, as it is a very remarkable paper, I shall present the reader with it at full length.

"We the underwritten, the president and members of the court martial, assembled for the trial of admiral Byng, believe it unnecessary to inform your lordships, that in the whole course of this long trial, we have done our utmost endeavours to come at truths, and do the strictest justice to our country and the prisoner; but we cannot help laying the distresses of our minds before your lordships, on this occasion, in finding ourselves under a necessity of condemning a man to death, from a great severity of the 12th article of war, part of which he falls under, and which admits of no mitigation, even if the crime should be committed by an error in judgment only; and therefore, for our consciences sakes, as well as in justice to the prisoner, we pray your lordships, in the most earnest manner, to recommend him to his majesty's clemency. We are, &c. Dated jan. 27, 1757.

Such were the resolutions of this court martial; and such their representation to the admiralty. The reader, no doubt, in his perusal of them, has been much surprised to find the admiral's judges condemn him to death, for his falling under part of the 12th article of war, and most earnestly recommending him to his

majesty,

majesty, as a proper object for mercy; and their reason for this sentence is, the severity of that article of war. But here I must warn the reader, not to expect certainty or demonstration in what I shall advance on this subject; I shall only make a few remarks, such as naturally arise from a due confideration of the whole affair.

The 12th article of war runs,—" Every person in the fleet, who, through cowardice, negligence, or disaffection, shall, in time of action, &c. &c.—and being convicted thereof, by the sentence of a court martial, shall suffer death." On this, Mr. Byng, (in his defence, which is penned with great art and judgment) justly observes, that, in order to bring any person within the peril of this article, he must be convicted of cowardice, negligence, or disaffection; for though he should fail to engage or assist, &c. unless this failure apparently proceeds from one of these causes, he is not guilty.—Negligence cannot be taken in so large a sense, as to mean every sort of neglect or omission; but such gross negligence only, as evidently indicates cowardice or disaffection.

Let me in the next place observe, that the court martial, in their 37th resolution, acquits him from cowardice or disaffection, in these words, " The court do not believe, that his misconduct arose either from cowardice or disaffection." Consequently they could then condemn him only for his negligence; that word equally means the negligence occasioned by cowardice or disaffection, and that occasioned by error in judgment; the former of these, the court acquits him of; and, as to the latter, they formed a very just opinion of it, when they represented to the admiralty the great severity of the 12th article of war, which admits of no mitigation, even if the crime should be committed by any error in judgment only.

In

In the 7th refolution of the court martial, they are of opinion, that the admiral ought to have put the officers on board one of the frigates he fent a-head to be landed. But it ought here to be remembered, that when the fleet arrived off Minorca, feveral of the fhips were difperfed; and the officers belonging to the garrifon were diftributed throughout the different fhips of the fleet; and could not have been put on board one of the frigates at that time, without fome hours delay; when, at the fame time, the fleet was advancing with a frefh gale of wind, and fair for the harbour. Would it not have been very injudicious in the admiral, when the enemy's fleet appeared fteering towards ours, and was known to be fuperior to it, to weaken his own force*; efpecially as his fleet was badly manned, and fickly; for the men belonging to the frigates were neceffary, and were actuaally diftributed to reinforce the line of battle fhips: the enemy were at that time mafters of the harbour, and it might have been regarded as an imprudent ftep to hazard fo many officers in a fingle frigate, under that circumftance.

In the 37th refolution of this court martial, they are of opinion, that the admiral ought to have returned, after the action off St. Philip's, and have endeavoured to open a communication with the caftle, before he returned to Gibraltar. I muft, on this refolution, remark, that after the action, the enemy's fleet was feen feveral times lying between the englifh fleet and the harbour, fo that it was impoffible to attempt it, without coming to a fecond battle. The french fleet had not, to appearance, fuffered any di-

---

* Mr. Weft, in his evidence, fays, that the garrifon of St. Philip's was to look on the englifh fleet at that time as its protection, as far as it might be fuppofed able to protect it; therefore, the weakening the force of the fleet would have been highly inexcufable, under the circumftance of feeing the enemy's fleet, as well as by expofing the englifh fleet to that of the enemy, who was at that time, in my opinion, fuperior to it.

minution

minution in its force; whereas four of our ships were rendered incapable of action, the Intrepid was obliged to be towed with jury masts to Gibraltar, and when the Portland arrived there, it could not be hoved down; and was reported unfit for service: further, the admiral called, on the 23th of may, a general council of war, of all the sea and land officers, who were unanimously of opinion, that it was for his majesty's service to proceed directly to Gibraltar. And what is very remarkable, this council of war was taken no notice of in the resolutions of court martial *.

As

* I shall here beg leave to give a few short extracts from the trial.
Admiral West was asked,
Quest. Do you apprehend, if it had been practicable, and the land forces had been thrown in to reinforce the garrison, that the ships would have been fit for action, to engage the enemy's fleet?
Answ. No, I think not.
Quest. Do you apprehend that the throwing in such an inconsiderable reinforcement, as one hundred officers and recruits, had there been a probability of effecting it, would have been a sufficient reason for loosing time, and delaying to attack the enemy's fleet, when in sight?
Answ. I have said of how little use it appears to me, these officers and soldiers would have been to the garrison; and though, even they might have been of more use than I imagine, the men were at that time very necessary to the service of the fleet, and therefore not to be parted with, independent even of the delay which it might have occasioned.
Quest. Do you apprehend it would have been proper for the admiral to have left any of the frigates, and by that means to have lessened his force, and deprived the fleet of the use of any of the ships or men, when upon the brink of coming to an action?
Answ. As some ships of the fleet, from sickness, or being short of complement, wanted men to supply the deficiency, I do apprehend, that the leaving any frigates behind, would have been improper, as their men would have been taken away from supplying such deficiency in part, for which they were necessary.
Captain Gardiner was asked,
Quest. Had you any men killed in the action!
Answ. No; nor do I look upon her to have been engaged as the admiral could have wished, and expressed his inclination to do, having several times said in our going down, while the shot were

flying

As soon as the sentence was known, the lords of the admiralty received a petition from the lord visc. Torrington, nephew to the admiral, importing, that himself, and the rest of his afflicted family, being advised that many material things might be offered to their lordships, to shew, that the sentence of the court martial ought not to be executed; prayed the permission to lay before them by council, to be appointed on behalf of the admiral, such reasons as might be offered for not executing the sentence. In answer to which petition, the lords of the admiralty appointed the next day to receive the reasons in writing, mentioned in the petition.

It being towards the close of the term, the council applied to could not, by reason of their indispensible attendance on the several courts of law and equity, be prepared so soon to advise and assist his lordship and family; accordingly they presented a second petition, praying an indulgence of a few days longer. But on the 9th of february, the lords of the admi-

flying over us, and hitting us, that he did not intend to throw his shot away, till he came near the enemy.

Lord Robert Bertie was asked,

Quest. Was you near to the admiral's person before, and during the time of the action, and did you observe his behaviour?

Answ. I was near him the whole day of the action in general.

Quest. Did you perceive any backwardness in the admiral during the action, or any marks of fear or confusion, either from his countenance or behaviour?

Answ. No; he seemed to give his orders cooly and distinctly, and I do not apprehend, that he was in the least wanting in personal courage.

Quest. Did the admiral appear sollicitous to engage the enemy, and to assist his majesty's ships, that were engaged with the enemy?

Answ. Yes.

Quest. Did your lordship on, or after the day of action, hear any murmuring or discontent among the officers or men, upon any supposition, that the admiral had not done his duty?

Answ. I never heard any one of the Ramillies speak the least disrespectfully of the admiral, or ever hint that the admiral had not done his duty.

ralty

ralty prefented a memorial to his majefty, of which the following is an extract:

"The proceedings of the court martial on admiral Byng, have been reported to us, and we have taken them into our moſt ſerious and deliberate confideration, and doubts having arifen, with regard to the legality of the fentence, particularly, whether the crime of negligence, which is not expreffed in any part of the proceedings, can, in this cafe, be fupplied by implication, we find ourfelves obliged moſt humbly to befeech your majefty, that the opinion of the judges may be taken, whether the faid fentence is legal."

In confequence of this memorial, his majefty laid the fentence before the judges; who gave their opinion, that it was a legal fentence; which opinion being tranfmitted to the commiffioners of the admiralty, they figned a warrant the 16th of february, directed to vice-admiral Bofcawen, at Portfmouth, directing him to have the admiral fhot, on board what fhip he thought proper, on the 28th, by a platoon of marines.

But he was refpited for fome time; for on the 26th his majefty fent a meffage to the houfe of commons, from which I have made the following extract:

"Being informed, that a member of the houfe of commons, who was a member of the court martial, has, in his place, applied to the houfe, in behalf of himfelf, and feveral other members of the faid court, praying the aid of parliament, to be releafed from the oath of fecrecy impofed on courts martial, in order to difclofe the grounds, whereon fentence of death paffed on the faid admiral; the refult of which difcovery may fhew the fentence to be improper; his majefty has thought fit to refpite the execution of the fame, in order that there may be an opportunity of knowing, by the feparate examination of the members of the said court, upon oath, what grounds there is for the above suggestion."

In consequence of this message, a motion was made for bringing in a bill, to release from the obligation of the oath of secrecy, the members of the court martial, pursuant to the exception contained in the said oath; and accordingly the bill was prepared, presented, read, amended, and ordered to be engrossed all in one day. The 28th, it was read the third time and passed, and carried up to the lords for their concurrence; but that house examined the members of the court martial on oath: the principal questions asked them were,

1. Whether you know any matter that passed, previous to the sentence pronounced upon admiral Byng, which may shew that sentence to have been unjust?

Unanimously answered in the negative.

2. Whether you know any matter that passed, previous to the sentence, which may shew that sentence to have been given through any undue practice or motive?

Unanimously answered in the negative.

3. Whether you are desirous, that the bill now under the consideration of the house, for dispensing with the oath of secrecy, should pass into a law?

This and the next question were answered in the negative, by admirals Smith, Holbourn, and Broderick; captains Holmes, Geary, Boys, Simcoe, Douglass, Bentley, and Denis. But admiral Norris, and the captains Moore, and Keppel, answered this question in the affirmative.

4. Whether you are of opinion, that you have any particulars to reveal, relative to the case of, and the sentence passed upon, admiral Byng, which you judge necessary for his majesty's information, and which you think likely to incline his majesty to mercy?

Admiral Norris's answer to this question was, at the time I said I was desirous the act should take place,
I un-

I underſtood that we ſhould have an opportunity of delivering our particular reaſons, for ſigning the ſentence, and letter of recommendation. Capt. Moore's was, I do not think myſelf at liberty, while I am under this oath to anſwer that queſtion. Capt. Keppel's was, I think that I cannot anſwer that queſtion without particulariſing the reaſons for my vote and opinion.

The houſe as ſoon as this examination was finiſhed, unanimouſly rejected the bill: and the ſentence was executed on the admiral the 14th.

On this unfortunate affair, concerning which, opinions are ſo much divided, I ſhall only obſerve, that many quote paſſages in the trial of the admiral which ſhew, that admiral Weſt, and ſeveral of the captains in the van, knew no reaſon why, Mr. Byng in the rear, ſhould not come to a cloſer engagement; but this proves only that the admiral was faulty; but does it from thence appear, that this fault proceeded from cowardice or diſaffection, might it not as well be attributed to an error in judgment. I have made this remark only in anſwer to a ſet of abſurd people, who will produce a few anſwers in the trial to ſtrengthen their argument; but as to regarding the reſolutions of the court martial, they will pretend that no confidence is to be placed in them.

It ſhould alſo be remembered, that Mr. Byng's fleet was ſent out to protect or relieve Minorca: Now let it be aſked, did thoſe who ſent him apprehend, that Minorca could be invaded before his arrival, and the deſcent covered by a ſuperior ſquadron, when they ſent him out with an inferior one—If they did, their conduct is unjuſtifiable—If they did not, their ignorance is inexcuſable.

It is very plain, from the conduct of the britiſh miniſtry, that they never expected Mr. Byng could meet with the french ſquadron; his inſtructions the leaſt intended fighting of any ſervice. But indeed he was poſitively aſſured, before his departure from England,

land, by the highest naval authority, that the enemy could not fit out more than six or seven ships of the line at the most. We need only read the admiral's instructions to be convinced, that this was the real opinion of the admiralty; for he is ordered—If on his arrival at Gibraltar, he should hear that a french squadron had passed the Streights, to difpatch admiral West with a fuperior fquadron after them to north America, and repair with the remainder himfelf to Minorca. By this it is very evident, that the miniftry in England did not know the french force; or elfe, how was Byng to difpatch a fuperior fleet after them, when the whole fleet he commanded was inferior to them. What epithet fhall we beftow on an adminiftration, no better informed of the enemy's motions than this conduct evinces?

But if we confider the whole affair with that attention it deferves, fhall we not evidently perceive, that the admiral fell a facrifice to cover the guilt of others, who were more powerful than himfelf. Let me afk againft whom the fury of the populace would have directed itfelf, if contrary winds had kept Mr. Byng a week or a fortnight longer at Spithead, or at Gibraltar; and if, at the fame time, the french had had a fkilful general at their head (for then Blakeney, inftead of holding out eight or ten weeks, would not have been able to defend himfelf three) under thofe circumftances, it would have been impoffible for Mr. Byng, even to have endeavoured any thing; for it would have been taken before he got there. Had this been the cafe, I fay, who would have been the objects of the public rage? Mr. Byng, or thofe who fent him? It was neceffary to throw duft in the eyes of the people; or elfe, why was the Gazette (a paper fuppofed to be publifhed by authority) proftituted to fpread a falfe lift of the ftrength of both fleets among the people, not only by undervaluing the enemy's force, of which it is poffible the writer

might

might be ignorant, but by overating Mr. Byng's, in which it is impossible he should be innocent. Why was the admiral's letter mangled and curtailed in the manner it appeared in that paper?

To say more on this subject will, I fear, be tedious to the reader. But thus much every honest man will allow, that it was a fatal severity to execute an admiral of a noble family, whose ancestors had rendered such services to the crown, under such an infamous charge, when the very court martial that condemned him, declared him innocent, either of cowardice or disaffection; and for the sake of their own conscience recommended him in the most earnest manner as a fit object for his majesty's clemency.

# CHAP. XI.

*Changes in the ministry. Naval transactions. Affairs in north America. Earl of Loudon appointed generalissimo. He prepares to attack Louisburg. Affairs in Germany. Situation of the belligerent powers. Motions of the prussian and austrian armies. King of Prussia enters Bohemia. Battle of Richenberg. Battle of Prague. Prague invested. Marshal Daun takes the command of the austrian army. Battle of Collin. King of Prussia retires into Saxony.*

NOTHING can be of such great consequence to the welfare of any nation, as to have one settled plan of action (especially in time of war) to direct the steps of those who sit at the helm of affairs. Let great genius's form fine plans of operations; yet if they are not in power long enough to direct their execution, all their schemes will most probably prove abortive. The state of Great-Britain at this conjuncture, was really deplorable; the ministry which had so lately been established, and which the greatest part of the nation wished to see firmly seated in power, could no longer hold their seats. On the 5th of april, Mr. Pitt, by his majesty's command, resigned the office of secretary of state, and Mr. Legge was moved from being chancellor and under-treasurer of the Exchequer; a new commission for the admiralty appeared, with the earl of Winchelsea at their head. The party of the duke of Newcastle, and Mr. Fox, who had been so lately obliged to quit their places, now resumed them. This faction, which was now uppermost, differed very much in their plan of action, from that of the late ministry; their chief characteristic was the great fear they were constantly in, of the overgrown power of France; they thought

it

it eligible to bridle this at any rate, but principally by maintaining the ballance of power, which they proposed to effect, by raising up enemies to France, on the continent, with british subsidies, and even by sending over british troops to join the belligerent powers in their alliance. The late ministry's scheme when they were in power was different; they were equally of opinion, that the power of France was to be curbed, but thought the means of doing this, was more natural by our naval power; a conduct which the insular situation of their country dictated to them. It is surprising to find how great a degree of popularity this party possessed in the nation; no sooner were they out of power, than they had the freedoms of almost all the corporations in the kingdom presented to them, in gold boxes, which shewed how much the nation regretted their disgrace at court.

The naval affairs of the two nations were at this period, of but little consequence; the latter end of march and beginning of april, several squadrons were equipping at Portsmouth and Plymouth; one under admiral West, designed for Ireland, in its way to America, consisting of 11 sail of the line, one frigate, a bomb, and a convoy of 50 transports, sailed from St. Hellen's the 16th of april; we had a small squadron at this time in the Downs, and another to the westward, cruising; and admirals West and Broderick had been cruising some time in the bay; but with little success. The french were hard at work in their ports, but sent no squadron to sea.

In north America our affairs had for some time wore the same dismal appearance as they had done from the beginning of the war; but the earl of Loudon, having in the latter end of the year 1756, laid before the ministry a plan for carrying on the war in that country, and which being approved of, his lordship was named by his majesty to command there in chief; better success was expected for the future,
especially

especially as a large body of troops was sent over to reinforce the army there. The plan his lordship was desirous to have executed, was the conquest of Cape Breton, and after that to proceed towards bringing all Canada under subjection, by the conquest of Quebec. To facilitate the undertaking this scheme, the transports with troops from England, arrived at New York, in january 1757. Lord Loudon finding the men much fatigued with the hardships of a long voyage billetted them, by reason of their number, indiscriminately on public and private houses; this occasioned a great heat between the magistrates and his lordship, who asked them, if they thought that men who had suffered a long winter's voyage, to come to their defence, were to perish in the streets for want of proper accommodations; and also, whether they thought that the indians would stand upon rights and privileges, if these men were ordered back, and they were to come in their room. After some ferment the billetting took place, as it certainly was a necessary measure.

As soon as his lordship heard that the transports were arrived, he assembled the governors of the several neighbouring colonies, to consult with them on the means of protecting their frontiers, during his absence on the expedition; nothing was required of them, but to remain on the defensive: and accordingly the plan was settled with the number of troops which each colony was to furnish, and their destination fixed. Having dismissed them, his excellency left Philadelphia the 27th of march, having stayed there ten days. But before I proceed, it is necessary to take notice of a general embargo which lord Loudon laid on all outward bound ships: his lordship thought this was the most likely way to hinder the enemy from getting any intelligence of his designs; and also, that the transports would then the more easily find men to navigate them. The embargo

bargo might certainly be productive of those good consequences; but as it was detrimental to the interests of many private people, particularly the merchants, it occasioned a great clamour; for at that time corn was excessively scarce in England, owing in part to a bad crop the last year, and the infamous villainy of the farmers, many of whom kept up large quantities in expectation of a higher price, when the poor were starving round about them; the merchants in England wrote over to those in America, to ship off large quantities for them, as there was plenty in the colonies, they accordingly did; but before the vessels could sail, the embargo took place: it occasioned so much disgust in England and the plantations, that an express was afterwards sent to put it out of the power of the commanders to embargo vessels for Great Britain or Ireland. Although the embargo was of some use, yet, as lord Loudon must know how pressing the wants of England were for corn, it has been thought by many, a bad step, although he had the full authority to do it.

During the month of april, his lordship was employed in preparing the transports at Boston, New York, and Philadelphia, those for the two former amounting to 90 sail. On the 5th of may, being all met at New York, they received orders to be in readiness to embark the forces; and sir Charles Hardy, governor of the place, having received his majesty's commission as rear admiral of the blue, hoisted his flag on board the Nightingale. It was now about the time, when they expected admiral Holbourn's fleet at Hallifax; but the commander in chief was very impatient that the men might embark, at last he ordered that service to be performed, which was done between the 22d and 25th, and then sailed down to Sandy Hook, where they came to an anchor. On the 5th of June, his excellency embarked on bord the Sutherland, but determined not to sail without

out further intelligence, becaufe he had learned before he left New York, from the prifoners of fome french prizes, that they were part of a french merchant fleet, under a convoy of five fhips of the line, defigned for Louifburg. This intelligence was confirmed by an exprefs from Bofton, informing, that five french men of war and a frigate had been feen cruifing off Halifax. It was impoffible to proceed to that port with the tranfports, while fo confiderable a force was in their road, and yet to remain any longer at New York, would be lofing fo much time, that the expedition againft Louifburg would become very uncertain; his lordfhip therefore difpatched two men of war to view the coaft, and fee if they could hear any thing of the french fleet: they foon after returned, but had feen nothing; lord Loudon then finding that to wait any longer, would almoft put it out of his power to do any thing that campaign, ventured to fail from New York, with the tranfports. This was the critical time as it were, on which depended the fate of all our fchemes, for had the french fell in with the tranfports, the confequences would certainly have been dreadful; fo that all depended on admiral Holbourn's being arrived, and by that means having the coaft clear, or elfe lord Loudon's efcaping the enemy; however, he arrived fafe at Halifax the 30th, his lordfhip would never have run fo great a rifk, had had it not been for faving time, which became fo exceeding precious, on account of the fleet's not arriving from England, till fo late in the feafon. The forces were foon landed, and encamped at Halifax; but as the ground was rough and incumbered, they were employed in making a parade for exercifes and reviews; and a large garden for furnifhing vegetables for the fick and wounded that might happen to be fent home from the fiege, in cafe the intended expedition fhould take place: parties of rangers were alfo fent to patrole in the woods, and feveral prime fail-

ing

ing vessels were dispatched to look into the harbour of Louisburg, and to make what discoveries they were able; in short, the general took all possible methods in his power at this interval, to keep the troops properly employed, and to gain the necessary intelligence of the strength of the enemy. At last admiral Holbourn, with the fleet and forces from England, arrived at Halifax in the second week in july, having been waited for with the utmost impatience by lord Loudon; and where I shall leave them for the present, and return to lay before the reader what had been transacting in Europe.

The war in America, and by sea, was at this time of but little eclat; it was in Germany only, where those great actions which surprise mankind were performed: at the close of the preceding campaign, the king of Prussia had made the saxon army prisoners, and took up his winter quarters in the heart of Saxony. That monarch was threatened with the immense number of enemies which he expected would attack him this campaign; nor were his expectations groundless, for the queen of Hungary having found by the battle of Lowoschutz, that she had to deal with an enemy truly formidable, resolved to have more powerful forces against him this campaign; she accordingly assembled an army of 100,000 men, in Bohemia, under the command of prince Charles of Lorrain, assisted by marshal Brown; nor did the empress trust entirely to her own preparations; during the preceding winter the process in the emperor's aulic council was continued against the king of Prussia; and also in the diet of the empire. We may easily conceive with how much impartiality and justice the proceedings in this court were carried on, when those who feared the king of Prussia were glad of an opportunity to humble him, and when the greatest number of them were awed by the power of the house of Austria. His prussian majesty was condemned for his pretended

tended obstinacy; and the fiscal had orders to notify to him, that he was put under the ban of the empire, and adjudged fallen from all the dignities and possessions which he held under it. The circles of the empire were ordered to furnish their contingents of men and money, to put this sentence in execution; but these were collected very slowly, the troops were badly composed, and most probably they would never have been able to act, if it had not been for the assistance they received from France. The inveteracy of her hungarian majesty did not stop here, she made requisitions to her allies for the assistance they were obliged by treaty to furnish her with. The czarina had prepared a great army of 60,000 men, under the command of marshal Apraxin, who had began their march in the winter through Lithuania, to attack ducal Prussia, and equipped a strong fleet in the Baltic, to co-operate with her land forces. The french resolving to convince the empress queen how advantageous to her, her connection with the house of Bourbon would be; formed two great armies, which had been drawing together for a considerable time; the first was composed of 80,000 troops, under the command of marshal de Estrees, which was designed against the king of Prussia's Westphalian dominions, in quality of allies to the empress queen, and guardians of the liberties of Germany, and to no other intent, as they pretended; but it was really designed to reduce Hanover also. The other french army was commanded by the prince de Soubise, consisting of about 25,000 men; and was designed to strengthen the army of the empire. These were not the only enemies of the king of Prussia: the king of Sweden, though allied both in blood and inclination to his prussian majesty, was yet obliged by the senate to send troops against him; they were inspired with the hopes of recovering their ancient possessions in Germany, and what made them

push

push the design of making war against that monarch the more briskly, was the subsidies of french gold which circulated amongst them plentifully. The duke of Mecklenburg also declared, that he would join the swedish army with 6000 men; for which conduct he has since paid very severely.

This was the state of the enemies of the king of Prussia, a mighty confederacy, consisting of five of the most powerful kingdoms in Europe; let us next see the measures which that monarch took to save himself from being crushed with their numerous forces.

The russians had brought no forage with them, trusting to what they should find in their march through Poland; but his prussian majesty, who was informed of the condition of his enemy, bought up all the corn and forage in their march towards Prussia, which put them to inconceivable difficulties, and retarded their march extremely; it certainly was a fine stroke of the king of Prussia to distress them. His majesty appointed general Lehwald to command an army of 30,000 men against Apraxin. But it was against the austrians that the greatest efforts were to be made; his prussian majesty commanded one army himself, in Saxony; the prince of Bevern another in Lusatia; and marshal Schwerin, a third in Silesia.

But before his majesty made the grand attack upon Bohemia, he took the wisest measures in Saxony, in case of bad success in his expedition against the austrians. New works were added to the old ones at Dresden, and the greatest diligence used to put it in a respectable posture of defence; all the burghers were disarmed, and their arms deposited in the arsenal. The austrian detachments began in april to appear on the frontiers of Saxony, to observe the motions of the prussians, but many of them were taken prisoners; these trifling matters did not take off the attention of the prussians; every thing was preparing
with

with the greatest expedition to begin the campaign, and troops were in motion throughout Saxony, Voigtland, and Lusatia.

About the middle of april, three great bodies of his prussian majesty's troops entered Bohemia by different routs. Marshal Schwerin penetrated into it from Silesia, through the county of Glatz, on the 18th, at the head of 50,000 men. His highness the duke of Bevern did the same, from Zittau in Lusatia the 20th, entering Bohemia at Graenstein, taking the rout of Reichenberg. His majesty himself, at the head of a third army, marched towards Egra. The austrians imagined, that his prussian majesty had some distinct plan of action, independent of his other armies, and accordingly prince Charles detatched 20,000 men, under the command of the duke d'Aremberg, to watch his motions.

The march of the prince of Bevern soon brought on an action; in his march towards Reichenberg, he drove away the enemy from all their posts. The same morning, a party of his hussars defeated some hundred of austrians, commanded by prince Lichtenstein, who were posted before Kohlig. The 21st at break of day, the prussians marched in two columns by Habendoff, towards the austrian army, posted near Reichenberg, 28,000 strong, and commanded by count Konigseg; as soon as the prussian lines were formed, they marched towards their enemy's cavalry, which was ranged in three lines, of about 30 squadrons, their two wings were sustained by the infantry, which was posted among felled trees and entrenchments. The prussians immediately cannonaded the austrian cavalry, who received it bravely, having on their right a village, and on their left a wood, where they had entrenched themselves with felled trees and pits. But the prince of Bevern having caused 15 squadrons of dragoons of his second line to advance, and ordered the wood on his right to be attacked by

some

some battalions of grenadiers, entirely routed the enemy's cavalry: the generals Norman, Katt, and the prince of Wurtemberg signalizing themselves extremely. The prussian hussars distinguished themselves by the warm reception they gave the austrian horse grenadiers; notwithstanding their artillery took them in flank. Lieut. gen. Lestewitz, at the same time attacked with the prussian left wing, the enemy's redoubts, which covered Reichenberg; though there were many defiles and rising grounds to pass, which were all occupied by the enemy; yet the regiment of Darmstadt forced the redoubt, and put to flight, and pursued the austrians, after some discharges of their artillery and small arms, from one eminence to another, for the distance of a mile, as far as Rochlitz and Dorffel. In short, the prussians gained a complete victory; the battle began at six o'clock in the morning, and continued till eleven. His highness the duke of Bevern, shewed great courage and military skill. The loss of the austrians was considerable; three standards were taken, and all their cannon and ammunition waggons.

Nor was marshal Schwerin less successful. He entered Bohemia with his troops in five columns, driving the austrians before him, as he passed the defiles, marching with incredible celerity, he reached Konigshoff on the Elbe, the 20th. At Trautenau, two austrian generals, and the princes Xavier and Charles of Saxony narrowly escaped falling into his hands. He made himself master of the circle of Buntlau without opposition, seizing a great magazine of corn and meal, belonging to the austrian army. He soon after joined his body of troops to those of the prince of Bevern, who, after the battle of Reichenberg, had advanced towards Prague, by the king's orders.

I left his majesty himself near Egra, opposed by the duke of Aremberg, with 20,000 men; by a masterly stroke of generalship, he made a movement to the left, which cut off all communication between d'Aremberg's detachment, and the main army of the auſtrians; and puſhing his advantage, he advanced with prodigious expedition towards Prague, where he joined marſhal Schwerin, and the prince of Bevern.

Prince Charles of Lorrain's army confiſted of about 95,000 men, being joined by an army from Moravia, the remains of that corps which was beat by the prince of Bevern, and by ſeveral regiments of the garriſon of Prague. It had taken poſt on the banks of the Moldau, near that city, in a camp almoſt inacceſſible, with his left wing inclining to the mountain of Ziſcha, and his right towards Sterboholi, where he waited on the hill the approach of the pruſſian army. But the king, who had paſſed the Moldau, with deſign to attack them, reſolved to turn the enemy's camp; for which purpoſe, his army defiled by Potſchernitz, towards the left, which count Brown perceiving, defiled by his right, to avoid being taken in flank. The pruſſians marched beyond Bichowitz, traverſing defiles and moraſſes, which ſeparated their infantry a little: this infantry having made its attack too precipitately, was the firſt time repulſed; but they made a freſh attack, and forced the enemy on the right. The pruſſian cavalry on the left, after three charges obliged the auſtrian cavalry on the right of their army to fly. The pruſſian centre routed the infantry, and puſhed quite through the auſtrian camp. The left of the pruſſian army then marched directly towards Michelly, where it was joined by the cavalry and cut off the auſtrian army, whoſe right was running away towards Saſzawa. The right of the pruſſians immediately attacked the left of general Brown, and ſucceſſively ſeized on three batteries on different eminences. From every advantage of ſituation the ardour of the pruſſians in this battle drove the enemy, encouraged by the preſence of their ſovereign, and filled with a noble enthuſiaſm of bravery, which generally enſures ſucceſs. The ſileſian army, which

was

was lead to action by marshal Schwerin, had a very rude shock to sustain; having morasses to pass, precipices to climb, and batteries to face, nothing but the presence of the king could have animated his troops in general to have performed such prodigies of valour. Some regiments of prussian horse, in the beginning of the action, suffered severely. The foot had still greater difficulties to surmount than the horse; many generals followed the example of the first field marshal, by dismounting, and leading their regiments sword in hand, through marshes, over precipices, and and across 1000 fires. It was here that the brave marshal Schwerin was killed, at the head of his regiment, with the colonel's standard in his hand: The loss of so experienced a soldier, was almost a balance to a victory; yet the enemy also suffered a great loss, in the death of marshal Brown, who was wounded, but not mortally, had not his regret made his wound fatal. Never was victory more complete than this of Prague; 40,000 of the enemy threw themselves into that city, and the rest fled towards Benneschau; a vast number was slain, and near 10,000 taken prisoners; the camp, military chest, 250 cannon, and all the trophies of the completest victory fell into the hands of the conquerors. This famous battle was fought the 6th of may.

His prussian majesty having gained so decisive a victory, convinced the world that he knew how to improve it: he instantly invested Prague, and an army within its walls: the king divided his forces into two bodies, marshal Keith commanded one, which invested the little town on this side the Moldau; and the king in person with the other, blocked up the old city, on the other side the river. As it was defended by a complete army, it was impossible to take it by assault; yet the immense garrison made it probable, that famine would oblige them to surrender; but the king of Prussia resolved not to trust

trust solely even to this, but made great preparations to bombard the city; the redoubts and batteries being in good forwardness by the 23d of may, the austrians made a well conducted and desperate sally with 10,000 men: they attacked a battery which was not finished, but were repulsed several times, the action lasting three hours; but at day break they retired into the city, in some confusion, not being able to make any impression on the prussian posts; their design was, also to have burnt the bridges of communication on the Moldau. His highness the prince of Bevern commanded, during the siege, an army of 20,000 men to cover it. On the 29th of may, at night, after a most dreadful storm of rain and thunder, on the signal of a rocket, four batteries, which discharged every 24 hours, 288 bombs, besides a vast multitude of red hot cannon balls, began to pour destruction on that unfortunate city, which was soon in flames in every part; we may conceive the horrors that reigned in Prague, from this bombardment, when 12,000 horses without forage were ranged in the streets and squares. This terrible bombardment continued without intermission: on the 10th of june, a red hot cannon ball set the city on fire near the Moldau, burnt five hours, and entirely consumed the second quarter of the new city. In the evening the fire broke out again, and the wind blowing hard, spread very fast, levelling every thing for several hundred yards. The bombardment continued incessantly night and day, so that the fire was no sooner quenched in one part, than it broke out in another; the besiegers often seeing it burning in seven or eight places at once. The principal magistrates, burghers, and clergy, seeing their city on the point of being reduced to an heap of rubbish, made the most moving supplications to the commander to listen to terms. But he was deaf to their prayers, and hanged up two of their senators, who were more importunate than

than the reſt. On the 6th of june, 12,000 uſeleſs mouths were driven out of the city; and the pruſſians forced them in again. The fury of the bombardment continued, and it was thought that the city could not hold out much longer. Let us here for a moment conſider the ſituation of the affairs of the empreſs queen. By gaining two battles, her enemy was in poſſeſſion of half Bohemia; a whole army, and the capital of that kingdom was on the point of ſurrendering to him; to conclude all, her remaining troops were terrified with former defeats. Such was the ſtate of her affairs, when a general, till then unknown, began to turn the fortune of the war.

This was Leopold count Daun, who never had commanded in chief before. One thing remarkable concerning him, was, that although he was of a very noble family, yet his riſe in the imperial ſervice was owing merely to his merit, without being obliged to any court favour for his promotions. He had gained experience in various parts of Europe, under the greateſt generals, and in the moſt illuſtrious ſcenes of action.

This commander had for ſome time been collecting the ſcattered remains of the auſtrian army; and brought them within a few miles of Prague, always taking care to encamp on ſuch inacceſſible eminences, that it was impoſſible to attack him; at the ſame time, he made ſeveral falſe attacks on the outward poſts of the pruſſians, with his huſſars, which were oppoſed by detachments from the prince of Bevern's army. At laſt marſhal Daun drew into the important camp at Colin, with deſign to embarraſs the pruſſians. The king knowing how much that ſituation would accompliſh Daun's deſigns, fearing that he would cut off the prince of Bevern's communication with the army round Prague, and hearing that he was actually near 60,000 ſtrong, reſolved to diſlodge him; with

this

this intention, he left the camp before Prague, the 13th of June, to take the command of that corps, in his road he was joined by several detachments, so that the whole number of his army was about 32,000 men. On the 18th, about three in the afternoon, his majesty attacked the austrians, so much superior in numbers to his own troops, and entrenched in one of the most advantageous situations that could be chosen, defended by an immense artillery. Let it be sufficient to say, that the king of Prussia did every thing on this occasion, that the most impetuous and best regulated courage, assisted by that noble emulation, inspired by the remembrance of so many victories, could suggest. The prussians returned to the attack seven times, and never fought with greater bravery. Both the king's brothers were in the field, and did every thing that could be expected from them. At last his majesty, at the head of his cavalry, made one furious and concluding charge; but all was unsuccessful. In short, his majesty was obliged to draw off his troops; having suffered very severely in the action, but more so from desertions, and all the ill consequences of a defeat. We must attribute the loss of this battle to the want of infantry and artillery, and fighting on a ground, where the foot could not be sustained by the horse; besides these, the advantageous situation of the enemy, so much more numerous than the prussians, their vast artillery, the great bravery they shewed in the action, and the courage and skill of marshal Daun, all conspired to render the great efforts of the prussians useless\*.

---

\* Soon after this battle, his prussian majesty wrote the following billet to one of his generals:

"I have no reason to complain of the bravery of my troops, or the experience of my officers. I alone was in the fault, and I hope to repair it." This noble and candid manner of owning his faults, raised the king's character as an hero more than ever.

Although

Although the king of Pruffia was defeated, yet his troops retired in excellent order and unpurfued. His majefty was obliged to raife the fiege of Prague directly; marfhal Keith decamped from his fide the 20th, and the whole army prepared with expedition to retire into Saxony. By the 16th of july the pruffian army was encamped at Leitmaritz, and the head quarters of the auftrians at Nifmes; the pruffian army were mafters of the Elbe. On the 21ft he quitted this camp, croffed the Elbe, and encamped at Lowofitz; in its way to Linai; the 24th, he took poft at Nollendorf, leaving marfhal Keith at the head of 25,000 men, to guard the paffes that lead from Bohemia to Saxony. During the retreat of the pruffian army, their rear and out parties were continually infefted with the auftrians; but fuffered little from them. The 26th, the king and his brother prince Henry arrived with the army in the neighbourhood of Pirna, where they encamped. The prince of Pruffia had retreated into Lufatia with another part of the army. The auftrians followed him, and the latter end of july, laid the town of Zittau in afhes, by a dreadful bombardment; obliging the garrifon to furrender. The prince of Pruffia was then in danger of being furrounded by the enemy, who were increafing in Lufatia every day; but to prevent this, his pruffian majefty left the camp near Pirna, the beginning of auguft, croffed the Elbe, and marched with part of his army to his affiftance, leaving the remainder under marfhal Keith, to guard the paffes of the mountains of Bohemia. By making this forced march, the prince's army was relieved, and the auftrians obliged to retire to their pofts on the right: here I fhall leave his majefty for the prefent.

The battle of Colin was fought at a moft critical moment. The king, who before that expected to be mafter of Prague, and all Bohemia, in a few days, was

was obliged to raife the fiege with lofs, and was driven out of that kingdom, which, a little time before he expected to conquer. Had his majefty only continued the fiege with vigor, and let the prince of Bevern have watched Daun; or, had he but taken a more numerous army to fight him, how different a face would this campaign have wore.

# CHAP. XII.

*Motions of the French. Their army pass the Rhine and Weser. Army of observation marches. Battle of Hastenbeck. Convention of Closter-seven. Russians enter Prussia. Battle of Norkitten. King of Prussia marches into Lusatia. Offers the austrians battle. Marches into Saxony. Austrians attack general Winterfeldt. Swedes enter Pomerania. General Haddick lays Berlin under contribution. Russians retire. Swedes retire. Schweidnitz taken. Battle of Breslau. Breslau taken. Bad state of the king of Prussia's affairs.*

I Observed before, that the french court had resolved to send two armies into Germany, in quality of allies to the empress queen. The principal one was really designed against the electorate of Hanover, consisting of 80,000 of the choicest troops of France, commanded by marshal de Estrees, having under him M. de Contades, Mr. Chevert, and the count de St. Germain, officers of reputation; Munster was fixed upon for the head quarters, and the army was in full march in the latter end of april, when it crossed the Rhine. The other body of french troops was commanded by the prince de Soubise, which, as I before said, was designed to strengthen the army of the empire. But before it passed the Rhine, it made itself master of Cleves, Meurs, and Guelders, belonging to the king of Prussia, laying the country under heavy contributions. In the mean time, the army under marshal de Estrees continued its rout by slow marches towards the electorate of Hanover; and to oppose him, the army of observation, which his britannic majesty raised, commanded by his royal highness the duke of Cumberland, was assembled by the beginning of may, and consisted of about 40,000

hanoverians,

hanoverians, and heffians; the part of Weftphalia between the Rhine and the Wefer is rough and barren, and very difficult to fubfift an army in, efpecially fuch a one as d'Eftrees's, which was encumbered with a vaft quantity of baggage, and a multitude of ufelefs mouths. The duke of Cumberland threw all the obftacles in his way that was poffible, but they were overcome by the abilities of the french general; who, by his fuperiority of numbers, obliged the duke to pafs the Wefer, and paffed it after him the beginning of july. D'Eftrees was no fooner on the other fide of the Wefer, than he laid all the neighbouring ftates and country under exceffive contributions: the landgraviate of Heffe Caffel was the firft that fuffered. Minden on the Wefer, and Gottingen on the Leine, received french garrifons, without oppofition. The french general, from his camp at Stadt-Oldendorf, fent to the regency of Hanover a requifition, dated the 21ft of july, demanding, that deputies fhould be fent to their head quarters, to treat about contributions, &c. About this time, the duke of Cumberland, who was encamped near Hamelen, marched from thence by Vorenburg, and Haftenbeck towards Halle; and the better to obferve the motions of the enemy, and if poffible, to ftop their progrefs; his royal highnefs, on the 19th of july, detached lieut. general Zaftrow, with 12,000 men, to feize the important pafs of Stadt-Oldendorf; but he came too late, the french being already in poffeffion of it: Zaftrow then by a forced march rejoined the duke's army, at Latford, on the Wefer. On the 20th, d'Eftrees advanced with his whole army into the fine plain at Stadt-Oldeldorf; and the next day encamped at Halle; on the 24th, the french drove the hanoverian parties from the village of Latford; and the duke perceiving it was the intention of the enemy to attack him, drew up his army on the height between the Wefer and the woods, with his right towards that river, and his left clofe to

the

the wood, the village of. Haftenbeck being in his front. In the evening he withdrew all his out pofts, and the army laid on their arms all night. The 25th in the morning, the enemy appeared, marching in columns, as if they intended to attack the hanoverians, and cannonaded them very feverely the whole day, with an artillery much fuperior to the duke's: that night the army alfo laid on their arms. At five the next morning, the cannonade began again, with great fury, upon a hanoverian battery, fupported by the heffian infantry and cavalry, who ftood the brunt of the fire with incredible bravery, and fteadinefs. At feven in the evening, the firing of fmall arms began on the hanoverian left; the cannonading continuing for 6 hours, all the while without intermiffion. The duke had placed fome grenadiers in the wood, who finding that great numbers of the enemies troops were marching about them, retired and joined the left of the army, on which the french poffeffed themfelves of the hanoverian battery on the left, without oppofition. It was here that the hereditary prince of Brunfwic diftinguifhed himfelf, by attacking and repulfing a fuperior force of the enemy, and retaking the battery. The french being in poffeffion of a height that flanked both the duke's lines of infantry, he ordered the army to retreat, which was done in good order, to Hamelen. It was confidently faid, that his royal highnefs had won the battle, but did not know it; thus far is certain, that the french who marched into the woods of Lauenftein, were feized with a pannic, fuppofing they were ready to be attacked by the hanoverians, and fired on one another; and if their confternation had been known, and a well regulated attack had been made on that part of their army, it would probably have been defeated. It was afferted pofitively, that de Eftrees had word brought him from all quarters, that the enemy appeared on the right and left, and were

going

going to flank him, which determined him to alter his difpofition.

The duke of Cumberland, from Hamelen, retreated to Hoya, where he encamped; but moved to Verden, on the 12th of auguft. On the 6th of that month, marſhal d' Eſtrees refigned his command, to marſhal duke de Richelieu, who fuperfeded him, by means of madam de Pompadour's intereſt with the king of France. Richelieu advanced faſt upon the hanoverians; the duke of Cumberland retreated towards Stade: and Bremen opened its gates to the conqueror. By the beginning of feptember, the duke was encamped under the cannon of Stade.

By his royal highnefs's retreating after the battle of Haftenbeck, into the dutchy of Bremen, he was cooped up without a poffibility of efcaping from the french, unlefs there had been a fleet of ſhips ready at Stade, to have embarked his army for England, where they would have done no good; but if the duke had retired towards Magdeburg, his army would have been of great fervice to the caufe, by joining the troops of the king of Pruffia, and once more oppofing the french; for it was to be expected, that they would not content themfelves with the poffeffion of Hanover, but would march againſt the king of Pruffia, as foon as poffible. The plan which his royal highnefs followed, had very different confequences. Under the mediation of the king of Denmark, the remarkable convention of Clofter-Seven was figned, the 8th of feptember, by which 38,000 hanoverians laid down their arms, and had quarters affigned them by the french general, in, and round about Stade, out of which they were not to move. The troops of Heffe, Brunfwic\*, and Saxe-Gotha, were fent back to their refpective countries, and difpofed of as it was agreed between their fovereigns, and the king of France.

\* Vide appendix.

Hiftory,

Hiftory, I believe, can hardly produce a cafe parallel to this. That an army of above 40,000 fhould, by a convention, and without fighting, lay down their arms, and become prifoners of war, (only under a different name) is really to me aftonifhing. All the remarks I fhall add on this unaccountable affair are, that the king of Pruffia this campaign, with 32,000 men attacked marfhal Daun with 60,000 and fought that defperate battle I have before fpoke of: with 25,000 the fame monarch afterwards gained the battle of Rofbach, againft 50,000 french, &c. and laftly, the battle of Minden was gained by 40,000 men againft 95,000 french. So much depends on the commander of an army! But to quote more inftances of this nature would be tedious; his royal highnefs the duke's abilities have before been difplayed in the plains of Fontenoy, more confpicuoufly than it is in my power to paint them.

The french army having thus glorioufly ended the campaign in Hanover. Marfhal Richelieu marched his troops towards the dominions of the king of Pruffia. I before obferved, that befides this army, the french fent another into Germany, under the prince de Soubife; which joined the troops of the empire, and were in full march to attack the king of Pruffia. I fhall leave the operations of thefe two armies for the prefent, and turn towards another quarter, where we fhall find new enemies advancing againft his pruffian majefty.

The ruffian army of 80,000 men, had been advancing by dilatory marches for fome time, under the field marfhal Apraxin. They had got no further than Wilna, by the 6th of june, in their way towards Kowno, the general rendezvous. And at the fame time, fome ruffian cruifers blocked up the ports of Konigfberg, and Memel. However, in the begining of july, the ruffians made themfelves mafters of Memel; they then divided their forces, one body being

ing commanded by Apraxin himself, and the other by general Fermor. Marshal Lehwald, at the head of about 30,000 prussians, commanded in Prussia; the 14th of July he quitted his camp at Insterburg, and encamped in the neighbourhood of Welaw, with design to cover Konigsberg. The russian general sent numerous detachments over most parts of Prussia, burning and destroying the country with the most horrid barbarity. Lehwald finding himself not strong enough to cover the country, and protect it from the savage enemy, resolved to attack their main army, in its entrenchments; which he did on the 30th of august. The russian army amounting to 80,000 regulars, was entrenched in a most advantageous camp, near Norkitten. It was composed of four lines, each of which was defended by an entrenchment, with a numerous artillery, and batteries placed on all the eminences. Lehwald's army hardly consisted of 30,000 men. The attack began at 5 in the morning, and was carried on with so much vigor, that the prussians entirely broke the whole first line of the enemy, and forced all their batteries. The russian cavalry was routed, and a regiment of grenadiers cut in pieces. But when marshal Lehwald came up to the second entrenchment, seeing that he could not attempt to carry it without exposing his whole army, took the resolution to retire, which he did in excellent order, without the enemy's ever stirring out of their entrenchments to pursue him. The loss of the prussians did not exceed 3000 men; but it was very evident, that the russians must have lost four times as many, although conquerors; the prussians lost 11 pieces of cannon. Lehwald, after the battle, returned to his camp at Welaw; but in a few days changed its position, encamping at Peterswalde. That great general, though defeated, was more formidable, after the battle, to the russians, than they were to him; he maintained his posts, and kept them from advancing.

In

In the mean time the king of Prussia was very hard pushed himself. I left him just retired into Saxony, after the unfortuaate battle of Collin. Finding that the austrian army made the greatest efforts towards Lusatia; the prince of Prussia, at the head of his army, had posted himself near Waltersdorf, to cover the country; but, as marshal Daun advanced very briskly towards him, he was in danger of being surrounded: upon which, the king, who was near Dresden with his army, crossed the Elbe, the latter end of july, and advanced to the assistance of the prince his brother, whose army, with this reinforcement, then amounted to 45,000 men; leaving 25,000 men under marshal Keith, at Lenai, on the other side of the Elbe. The king marched to Bautzen, where he joined the prince. By his majesty's orders, marshal Keith marched from Lenai through Dresden, with 20 battalions and 40 squadrons, crossed the Elbe, and joined him at Bautzen, leaving prince Maurice of Anhalt Dessau, with 12 battalions and 10 squadrons encamped at Pirna, to check the incursions of the austrian regulars. The king's army, after the junction with Keith, consisted of 60,000 men, he marched the 30th of july from Bautzen, towards Gorlitz, upon which, the austrians retired from Labau, encamping between Gorlitz and Zittau. The king having made several motions, took post on the 15th of august at Budin. It was here that he had continual advices of the approach of the army of the empire, and the french under Soubise, towards Saxony; as they advanced very fast, he resolved to leave Lusatia, and march his army against them; but as he wanted extremely first to fight the austrians, he endeavoured by all possible means to bring them to a battle; on the 16th, he drew up his army within sight of the austrians. The next day he reconnoitred their situation; and, to leave nothing undone that might bring on an action, he sent general Winterfeldt, with 16,000 men,

men, on the other side of the Neisse, to try to take them in flank. Finding it impossible to draw them to a battle, he suddenly decamped, leaving the prince of Bevern, prince Ferdinand, and general Winterfeldt, with 30,000 men near Gorlitz, to observe the austrians. His majesty took the road to Dresden, where he arrived the 29th, in his way towards Erfurth, with design to fight the french and imperialists.

No sooner was his majesty gone, but the austrians came out of their camp, and began to shew themselves every where. On the 17th of september, 15,000 austrians attacked two battalions of Winterfeldt's army, which they cut in pieces; and, as the general was marching to their assistance, he received a wound of which he soon after died. The loss of so brave a general, was the greatest which the prussians sustained on this occasion. Indeed, the king of Prussia was at this time very hard pressed by his enemies; in the beginning of this month, 22,000 swedes penetrated into prussian Pomerania, and laid the neighbouring country under contribution. Berlin itself was also in danger, from another quarter. General Haddick with a large detachment of troops from the austrian army at Gorlitz, by forced marches pierced through Lusatia, part of Brandenburg, and presented himself before Berlin, on the 16th of october; the next day, the city paid him a contribution of 200,000 crowns, on which he retired precipitately, on hearing that prince Maurice was advancing against him. The prince set out from Torgau the 15th, and arrived at Berlin on the 18th, only one day too late.

The russians, in the mean time, after exercising such barbarities, as would shock humanity to relate them, made a most precipitate retreat out of Prussia; they began their march the 13th of september, leaving their sick and wounded to the amount of near 10,000 men; they gained three marches on Lehwald, so that, although he dispatched prince George of Holstein, with 10,000 men to pursue them, they were got too far. They took their rout through Lithuania, towards Russia. This retreat enabled marshal Lehwald to turn his arms against the swedes; he not only recovered that part of prussian Pomerania which the enemy had conquered; but also, all swedish Pomerania, except the town of Stralsund; leaving their ally, the duke of Mecklenburg, to feel the weight of the prussian arms. This nation did nothing to make them worthy of their warlike ancestors, who had so often been the terror of Germany.

His prussian majesty's affairs wore a more melancholy face in Silesia. The king was no sooner gone into Saxony, than the austrians poured into that province, from all quarters. One body of them had opened the trenches before Schweidnitz the 27th of october; and it did not capitulate before the 11th of november. The prince of Bevern was encamped near Breslau, to watch the motions of prince Charles, with the main army, who was near him. On the taking of Schweidnitz (with a garrison of 4000 men) the army which besieged it, joined prince Charles and marshal Daun, near Breslau, when it was determined to attack the prince of Bevern in his intrenchments, under the walls of that city, which was executed the 22d of november, with a treble superiority of numbers. The prussians sustained their attack with amazing intrepidity. The austrians lost near 20,000 men. A great part of their army had retired from the field of battle, and the rest were preparing to retire; when all at once the prussian generals took the same resolutions. A part of their army had suffered a great deal in the engagement. They became apprehensive of a total defeat, in case their intrenchments should be forced in any part. Accordingly they retired behind the Oder. Soon after the austrians returned, and with amazement saw themselves masters of the field

field of battle, which they had but juft been obliged to relinquifh. There certainly was fomething very ambiguous in the conduct of the pruffian generals in Silefia; the king found the want of old marfhal Schwerin more than ever. One thing, to appearance, was very remarkable, and gave rife to a thoufand conjectures; the prince of Bevern, two days after the battle, as he was reconnoitring without efcort, and attended only by a groom, was taken by an advanced party of croats, a fmall body of whom had paffed the Oder. The auftrians immediately improved their victory; their advantage, though very dearly bought, was followed by many others; Breflau capitulated the 24th; and here they found, as at Schweidnitz, vaft quantities of provifion, ammunition, and money. Almoft all Silefia was on the point of falling into their hands. Indeed, the fituation of his pruffian majefty at this time, was terrible. Part of Pruffia laid wafte by the brutal ferocity of the ruffians; part of Pomerania by the fwedes: all his weftphalian dominions, together with Halberftadt, and part of Magdeburg, in the poffeffion of the french, who were making incurfions even into Brandenburg: Berlin itfelf laid under contributions; Silefia conquered by the auftrians; and laftly, Saxony and Lufatia partly eat up by the auftrians, and the army of the empire, joined with the french. Such was the ftate of this monarch's dominions. For the prefent we muft leave him, marching to defend Saxony, againft the prince of Soubife.

CHAP.

## CHAP. XIII.

*Affairs in England. Parliamentary affairs. Transactions at sea. Secret expedition against Rochfort. Miscarries. Court Martial. Affairs in north America. Troops embark for Louisburg. The Expedition laid aside. Holbourn's fleet shattered in a storm. Fort William Henry taken. Affairs in Germany. Battle of Rosbach. King of Prussia marches into Silesia. Battle of Lissau. Breslau taken. Schweidnitz blockaded. Silesia conquered. Prussian and austrian armies go into winter quarters. Violent excesses of the french in Hanover. Hanoverian army resumes its arms. Siege of Harbourg. They go into winter quarters. Recapitulation of the events of the year* 1757.

IN the mean time, the english were pluming themselves with the victories of their illustrious ally; they won none themselves. The ministry was disliked, and their administration weak and confused; in short, we must not rank the year 1757 as glorious in the annals of Britain. Several fleets had been ordered out to cruise, in expectation of meeting with french ships; but they were generally unsuccessful: Admiral Boscawen in june, commanded one, which cruised at cape St. Vincent; admiral Townshend arrived from Jamaica, where he had been very successful against the small craft of the french. But these actions are not of any great eclat, nor of any great consequence in themselves. The transactions in the british parliament, were indeed, of more importance. In consequence of several speeches and messages from his majesty, they had at different times, between january and may, granted his majefty, for the year 1757, upwards of 8,350,000 l.*.

In the month of june, there happened an unexpected change in the englifh miniftry, which will juftly be reckoned a remarkable æra, in the englifh hiftory. A coalition of parties was hardly hoped for; but yet it was brought about. Mr. Pitt was again reftored to the office of fecretary of ftate; the duke of Newcaftle was placed at the head of the treafury, and Mr. Fox was appointed pay-mafter of the forces. This arrangement gave very general fatisfaction: the nation were fanguine in their hopes of better fuccefs in the war, now the violence of parties were extinguifhed, and the new miniftry formed a fcheme to gratify this eager defire. It is now time to give fome account of it.

As one captain Clerk was returning from Gibraltar, in his way to England, in 1754; he came along the weftern coaft of France. And by the politenefs of the governor of Rochefort, was fhewn the dock, fortifications, and every thing elfe in that city. In july, 1757, he was ordered to communicate, to fir John Ligonier, what obfervations he had made there; he accordingly wrote him an account of the fortifications, reprefenting them fo bad, that the miniftry refolved to undertake an expedition againft it; and were determined in this refolution, on feeing an authentic account of the military force of France, which they alfo received in july, By this it appeared, that the french army, in the beginning of the war, confifted only of 157,347 men, including militia. In auguft,

| | |
|---|---|
| * For the navy | 3,503,940 l. |
| For the army | 2,398,197 |
| For the heffians | 300,572 |
| For the hanoverians | 74,478 |
| Sundrys | 2,072,813 |
| | 8,350,000 |

1755,

1755, an augmentation was made of 29,000 foot, and 2500 dragoons. In december following, 5500 horſe were further raiſed. It alſo appeared by this memorial, that, in july 1757, the whole french army (without reckoning the militia and invalids, which were about 67,000) was under 200,000 men. The iſlands of Minorca, Corſica, with America, and the Weſt-Indies, took up 30,000 men. Maſhal d'Eſtree's army, if the regiments were complete, would amount to 92,000; Richelieu's to 32,000; a body of 6 or 7000 in garriſon at Toulon, Marſeilles, &c. By which it appears, that there were 160,000 regular troops employed, 40,000 then remained for garriſons, from Sedan to the frontiers of Switzerland, without ſpeaking of Flanders, and the coaſt, 20,000 from St. Vallery to Bergue, and 10,000 more from St. Vallery to Bourdeaux.

From this memorial, it appeared to the miniſtry, that the particular ports on the weſtern coaſt of France muſt be very weakly garriſoned. A conſiderable inducement to undertake the expedition. Sir Edward Hawke received his orders in the beginning of auguſt, and in conſequence repaired to Spithead, to collect the ſhipping together. In the ſecret inſtructions to him, and ſir John Mordaunt, the general of the land forces, they were directed to make their attack upon Rochfort; and in caſe it ſucceeded, or failed, Port l'Orient, or Bourdeaux were next to be conſidered, as the moſt important objects of their arms. A camp had been formed in the iſle of Wight, ever ſince the beginning of auguſt, conſiſting of the old buffs, the king's, Kingſley's, Hume's, Hodſon's, Brudenel's, Loudon's, Cornwallis's, Amhurſt's, and Bentinck's regiments of foot, containing 700 men each complete, which in all was 7000, with two battalions of marines, and one troop of light horſe. Theſe forces were embarked on board 45 tranſports, convoyed

convoyed by a grand fleet * of men of war. This noble armament failed the 8th of september. On the 20th, they made the ifle of Oleron, in the bay of Bifcay, over againft Rochfort. The 23d, they came in fight of the little ifland of Aix, which lies in the mouth of the river, leading up to Rochfort. Capt. Howe, by order of the admiral, in the Magnanime, attacked the fort on this ifland. Lord B――― m, who went a volunteer †, in another fhip of the fquadron, has fince told me, that although the object of Mr. Howe's attack was but inconfiderable, yet his conduct in it was admirable. The french, when he came within gun-fhot, fired ineffectually at him ; he received their fire, and continued to bear down with the greateft compofure, till he dropt his anchors clofe under the walls of the fort, and then began fo terrible and inceffant a fire, that his fhip feemed to be one continued flame ; in about an hour, the governor ftruck his flag, when the fmoak cleared up, and difcovered not a fort, but a heap of rubbifh.

On the 25th, a council of war was called, by defire of general Mordaunt, to confider of the expedi-

* Confifting of the following fhips ;

| | Guns. | | Guns. |
|---|---|---|---|
| Royal George | 100 | Intrepid | 64 |
| Ramilies | 90 | Medway | 64 |
| Neptune | 90 | Dunkirk | 60 |
| Namure | 90 | Achilles | 60 |
| Princefs Amelia | 80 | America | 60 |
| Barfleur | 80 | 6 Frigates | |
| Royal William | 84 | 2 Bombketches | |
| Magnanime | 80 | 2 Fire fhips | |
| Torbay | 74 | 2 Hofpital fhips | |
| Dublin | 74 | 6 Cutters. | |
| Burford | 74 | | |

† This amiable young nobleman, has fince attended the army under prince Ferdinand of Brunfwick, as a volunteer, in two campaigns. He was taken very ill at the latter end of the firft, at Caffel, fo that lord Granby defired him not to rifk his health by venturing on a fecond campaign; but his lordfhip's great bravery, and eager inclination to ferve his country, rendered him deaf to all intreaties.

ency

ency of landing to attack Rochfort, in which it was granted by every body, that landing could be effected; but that the place could not be taken by escalade. The general then desired another, which was held on the 28th, and wherein it was also unanimously agreed, that it was adviseable to land the troops with all possible dispatch. Immediately the disposition was made for the landing, under admiral Broderick, and all the captains; part of the troops were in the boats; when on the 30th, the admiral received a letter from Mr. Broderick, importing, that the generals were come to a resolution not to land that night, but to wait till next morning. Sir Edward Hawke then sent to know of sir John Mordaunt, whether the general officers had any further military operations to propose; that if they had not, he intended to proceed to England with the squadron without loss of time: in answer to which, sir John informed him, that having TALKED IT OVER with the general officers, they all agreed in returning directly to England; and accordingly, this most formidable armada arrived at St. Hellen's the 6th of october.

Never did there appear so general a discontent, as spread throughout the nation, on the failure of this expedition; it was equalled by nothing, but the ardent expectations of success before the fleet sailed. One party threw all the blame on the ministers, who planned the scheme. The other laid all the fault on the commanders, who ought to have executed it. But his majesty, by his warrant of the 1st of november, appointed a board of general officers, to enquire into the causes of the failure of the expedition; they met the 12th, and by their report, assigned several reasons, why the expedition failed; which reasons were so many absolute censures on the conduct of the commander. The general officers were, the duke of Marlborough, lord George Sackville, and gen. Waldgrave.

This determination of the board of enquiry, was far from being satisfactory to his majesty; by another warrant, dated the 3d of december, a general court marshal * was appointed to sit upon the trial of sir John Mordaunt, which met the 14th, and continued sitting till the 20th; when they all unanimously were of opinion, that sir John Mordaunt was not guilty of the charge exhibited against him, and did therefore acquit him.

To determine where the fault of the expedition's failing, really laid, is a matter very difficult. We found, that a board of officers censured the commander, on account of his behaviour, and a court martial acquitted him; the greater number of the publications, (many of them very stupid ones) we read on this affair, the more we shall be perplexed. Thus much, I think seems pretty plain; that the scheme of making a diversion on France, with design to assist the king of Prussia, by drawing the french troops

* And consisted of the following members.
   Lieut. general Lord Tyrawley, president.
     Lieut. general Charles lord Cadogan,
     Lieut. general John Guise,
     Lieut. general Richard Onslow,
     Lieut. general Henry Pulteney,
     Lieut. general sir Charles Howard,
     Lieut. general John Huske,
     Lieut. general John lord Delawar,
     Lieut. general James Cholmondeley.
     Major general Maurice Bockland,
     Major general William earl of Panmure,
     Major general William earl of Ancram,
     Major general William earl of Harrington,
     Major general George earl of Albemarle,
     Major general Henry Holmes,
     Major general Alexander Drury,
     Major general John Moystyn,
     Major general Edward Carr.
     Colonel William Kingsley,
     Colonel Alexander Duroure,
     Colonel Bennet Noel.
   Charles Gould, deputy judge advocate general.

out of Germany, was a good one; provided there were not troops enough in every part of that coast, to defend itself. It did not appear that this was not the case at Rochfort; I should also suppose, that the month of september was too late for such an expedition, especially in the boisterous bay of Biscay. In short, the design was not planned in a perfect manner, by the ministry: and we must say the same of the execution; there were some mistakes, which joined to the former, rendered it ineffectual. But the ministry certainly deserved praise in one particular (although in some others, the plan might be defective) in forming a design to employ with advantage our naval force, in an expedition, which, had it succeeded, would have been of great consequence, if not by assisting the king of Prussia, at least in destroying the source of the naval power of France.

The operations of the british arms in north America were not more brilliant. I left admiral Holbourn just arrived at Hallifax, in the beginning of july, from England with a grand fleet *, and lord

\* Consisting of the following ships, including those which were in north America, viz. one ship of the line, and 12 frigates.

| Ships. | Men. | Guns. | Ships. | Men. | Guns. |
|---|---|---|---|---|---|
| Newark | 700 | 80 | Port Mahon | 150 | 22 |
| Invincible | 700 | 74 | Nightingale | 150 | 22 |
| Grafton | 590 | 68 | Kennington | 150 | 20 |
| Terrible | 630 | 74 | Elphingham | 150 | 20 |
| Northumberland | 520 | 68 | Ferrit sloop | 120 | 16 |
| Captain | 580 | 68 | Furnace bomb | 100 | 16 |
| Orford | 520 | 68 | —— ditto | 100 | 16 |
| Bedford | 480 | 64 | Vulture sloop | 100 | 14 |
| Nassau | 480 | 64 | Hunter | 100 | 14 |
| Sunderland | 400 | 64 | Speedwell | 90 | 12 |
| Defiance | 400 | 64 | Hawke | 100 | 12 |
| Tilbury | 400 | 64 | Gibraltar's prize | 80 | 12 |
| Kingston | 400 | 60 | Jamaica | 100 | 14 |
| Windsor | 350 | 54 | Lightning fire ship | 50 | |
| Sutherland | 306 | 50 | | | |
| Winchelsea | 160 | 24 | | 10,200 | 1350 |
| Success | 150 | 22 | | | |

Loudon

Loudon waiting there for him with great impatience. The armament confisted of 17 ships of the line, 14 frigates and sloops, two bombs, one fire ship, with 179 transports, making 18,000 tons english ships, and 15,616 north american; 100 pieces of brass cannon, in 10 large ships, horses, steers, &c. in four others, and several more loaded with facines, gabions, &c. The army consisted of 15 regiments, 500 men of the train, 500 rangers, and 100 carpenters, making all 11,000 effective land forces. The first thing which the commander did, was to dispatch some vessels for intelligence of the enemy's situation and strength. And in the mean time, the troops were exercised in attacking a sham fort, according to the rules of war, lord Loudon very rightly judging, that this was a proper employment for them till he failed *.

When the vessels returned, they brought advice of a fleet's being arrived at Louisburgh; and, on the 4th of august, a french prize was brought into Halifax, by whose papers it appeared, that there were then in the harbour, 17 sail of the line, 12 frigates, 4000 regulars, besides 3000 belonging to the garrison. This news immediately suspended the preparations which had been made to embark. Councils of war were held one after another. The result of the whole was that as the place was so well reinforced, the french fleet superior to ours, and the season so far advanced, it was most prudent to defer the enterprize till a more favourable opportunity. I do not see any great reason to find fault with this determination, considering the circumstances abovementioned, although it was much found fault with in England. Lord Loudon returned to New York, and the admiral set sail for Louisburg,

---

* It was on this account, that lord Charles Hay condemned lord Loudon's conduct, as " Keeping the courage of his majesty's sol- " diers at bay, and expending the nation's wealth, in making sham " fights, and planting cabbages." For which he was, with the advice of a council of war, ordered under arrest.

in hopes to bring the french fleet to a battle; but with what reason, he should suppose, that they would hazard one, I know not, as their only business was to protect the town. The english squadron stayed off the harbour, till the 25th of september, when they were shattered in a most terrible storm, in which one of our ships was lost, eleven dismasted, and the rest returned to England in a very bad condition.

This was the end of the expedition against Louisburg; in which so great a force was so ineffectually used: we attribute the bad success to the long delay of Holbourn's fleet in England, it ought certainly to have been ready to sail sooner, and then so much would not have depended upon the wind and weather. Lord Loudon's conduct has been very much blamed, with what reason, I confess, I cannot see.

The reader may remember, that before general Johnson's victory over the french, there was built a fort, called William Henry, on the south edge of lake George, in order to command that lake, and cover our frontiers. The fort was strong at present, garrisoned by 2500 men; and general Webb with 4000 men was posted at no great distance. The french, when they were informed that lord Loudon was gone on the Louisburg expedition, made great preparations to attack this fort; the marquis de Montcalm brought against it 8000 regulars and indians, with a very good artillery to besiege it in form. It is here necessary to enquire, whether Montcalm could do all this so near Crown Point, without general Webb's knowing it. If he was not informed of it, where were his scouts, so necessary in that country: if he was informed of it, which is the common opinion, why did he not collect the neighbouring militia, and put the fort in the best posture of defence, he would have been of equal, perhaps superior force to the french; but this not being done, the consequences were, that the french after a six days siege, took the fort the 9th of august;

guft; it furrendering by the advice of general Webb. The garrifon marched out with their arms, and engaged not to ferve during 18 months ; the french favages paid no regard to the capitulation ; but committed a thoufand outrageous barbarities. And all was fuffered by 2000 men, with arms in their hands, againft a diforderly crew of barbarians. The enemy having demolifhed the fort, carried off every thing with the veffels on the lake, departing without making any further attempts. There is fuch an intricate darknefs in this affair, that were it cleared up, I fear a ftain would fomewhere be difcovered. This was the end of our third campaign in north America, we had actually near 20,000 regular troops, and a navy of upwards of 20 fhips of the line, and yet our forts were taken from us, and our indian allies left defencelefs, to the mercy of the enemy ; and without our doing any one action, that could repay us for all this load of bad fuccefs and difhonour.

It is in Germany only we muft look for more brilliant and decifive actions. I left his pruffian majefty returning from Lufatia, in his way to Saxony, with defign to fight the imperialifts and french, who were advancing towards Mifnia. His majefty reached Erfurth, the 14th of feptember, by the rout of Pegau, Naumburg, Frankenau, Buttleftadt ; from Erfurth, the king detached prince Ferdinand of Brunfwick with feven battalions and ten fquadrons, and fome artillery, towards Halberftadt ; to watch the motions of marfhal Richelieu's army. The combined army left Erfurth the 11th, on the approach of the pruffians, and retired to Eifenach, where they were encamped during the king of Pruffia's ftay at Erfurth ; but being reinforced confiderably, they then advanced, and his majefty retired in his turn : the reafon of which was, he wanted to fight them as near Mifna, and as deep in the winter as he could, becaufe, if he was victorious, a defeat at that feafon, would difenable his

enemy

enemy from acting any more, at least that year. On the contrary, if he failed, Saxony was at hand for him to retire into, and which the enemy could make make little impression on in winter. On the 28th, he marched back to Buttleſtadt; on which the combined army fixed their quarters at Gotha. His pruſſian majeſty finding that the enemy advanced with ſpeed, thought it time to fight them: he took that reſolution the 24th of october, when his army happened to be divided into ſeveral corps, ſome of them at the diſtance of 20 leagues aſunder. Marſhal Keith was in Leipſick with ſeven battalions, and his majeſty, on being informed that the enemy were marching directly towards that city, collected his whole army together, with ſuch expedition, that it was united by the 27th, remaining at Leipſick the 28th and 29th; it was then imagined, that the battle would be fought on the plains of Lutzen. On the 30th, the king drew nigh that place; and paſſed the Sala with his army at Weiſſenfels, Merſeburg, and Halle, and joined again the 3d, over againſt the enemy. On the 5th, intelligence was brought the king, that the combined army was in motion; in ſhort, the two armies met at the village of Roſbach. The latter was commanded by the prince of Saxe Hilburghauſen, and Soubiſe, and conſiſted of 50,000 men complete. The pruſſians did not amount to 25,000\*.

His

---

\* Juſt before the battle began, which was to decide the fate of ſo many nations, the king of Pruſſia addreſſed his troops in the following words:

"My dear friends, the hour is come, in which all that is, and all that ought to be dear to us, depends upon the ſwords which are now drawn for the battle. Time permits me to ſay but little: nor is there occaſion to ſay much. You know that there is no labour, no hunger, no cold, no watching, no danger, that I have not ſhared with you hitherto; and you now ſee me ready to lay down my life with you, and for you. All I aſk is the ſame pledge

of

His pruſſian majeſty had determined to make the attack with one wing only, and the diſpoſition of the enemy made it neceſſary, that it ſhould be the left wing. All the cavalry of his right, was marched to his left, and formed over againſt that of the enemy. Upon which the pruſſian cavalry moved on immediately, the french cavalry advanced to meet them, and the charge was very fierce, ſeveral regiments of the french coming on with great reſolution. The advantage however, was entirely on the ſide of the pruſſians. The french cavalry being routed, was purſued for a conſiderable time, with the greateſt ſpirit. But having afterwards gained an eminence, which gave them an opportunity of rallying, the pruſſian horſe fell on them afreſh, and gave them ſo thorough a defeat, that they betook themſelves to flight in the utmoſt diſorder, which happened at four in the afternoon. Whilſt the cavalry charged, the pruſſian infantry opened themſelves, enduring a very briſk cannonade from the enemy, which did ſome execution; and in about a quarter of an hour their fire began. The french could neither ſtand it nor reſiſt the valour of their enemies, who gallantly marched up to their batteries, which being carried one after another, they gave way in the greateſt confuſion. As the left wing of the pruſſians advanced, the right changed its poſition, and meeting with a ſmall riſing ground, they planted 16 pieces of heavy artillery, the fire of which taking the left wing of the enemy in front, galled them extremely. At five the victory was decided, the cannon ceaſed, and the french fled on all ſides. The king of Pruſſia ex-

---

of fidelity and affection, that I give. And let me add, not as an incitement to your courage, but as a teſtimony of my own gratitude, that from this hour, until you go into quarters, your pay ſhall be double. Acquit yourſelves like men, and put your confidence in God." The effect this ſpeech had upon the men, amounted almoſt to an heroic phrenſy, a good prognoſtication of ſucceſs.

poſed

posed himself to the hottest of the fire, in leading on his troops. The french left 3000 men dead on the field of battle; 63 pieces of cannon, a great many colours; eight french generals, 250 officers of different ranks, and 6000 private men were taken. The darkness of the night, alone saved from total destruction the scattered remains of an army, so numerous and formidable in the morning. The 6th, the conquerors pursued the run-aways to Freyburg, and the 8th and 9th to Erfurth.

His prussian majesty no sooner had pursued his enemy as far as Erfurth, than he turned back, and began a march of upwards of 200 miles, with that very army, which had before the battle been collected from places above 100 miles distant from each other. The king made a rapid march through Thuringia, Misnia, and Lusatia, in his way to fight the austrians in Silesia. He set out from Leipsick the 12th of november, with 19 battalions and 28 squadrons. Whilst this corps was on their march, marshal Keith, with another, got into Bohemia, through the defiles of Pafsberg; and marched towards Prague, taking a considerable magazine at Leitmeritz. The two austrian generals Haddick and Marshal, who were posted in Lusatia, to obstruct his majesty's march, fled before him. He arrived the 24th, at Naumburg, on the Queifs, and by making forced marches entered Silesia, and arrived at Parchwitz, near the Oder, the 28th. The prince of Bevern's army joined the king here; and soon after the garrison of Schweidnitz, which were conducting to prison by the austrians, being but weakly guarded, and hearing by accident of the victory of Rosbach, it annimated them so much, that they rose upon the escort, dispersed them, and by the greatest chance joined the king's army in its march, adding a considerable strength to it. The royal army having rested a day, marched on the 4th to Neumarck.

The

The auſtrians, in the mean time, confiding in their numbers, on his pruſſian majeſty's approach, abandoned their ſtrong camp (the ſame which the prince of Bevern had before occupied) and advanced to meet the king, with a reſolution to give him battle. The two armies met the 5th of december, near the village of Leuthen: the auſtrians were commanded by prince Charles of Lorrain, aſſiſted by marſhal Daun, the latter of whom had taken all poſſible precautions to throw a multitude of impediments in the way of his pruſſian majeſty; the ground which they occupied, had all the advantage of natural ſituation, improved to the utmoſt with great diligence and ſkill: the army was drawn up on a plain, except in ſome parts it had ſmall eminences, which count Daun had ſurrounded with artillery; ſome hills on his right and left were alſo covered with batteries of cannon; in his front were many thickets and cauſeways; but to render the whole as impenetrable as poſſible, he had felled a vaſt number of trees, and ſcattered them in the way. In this formidable ſituation was poſted 70,000 auſtrians, excellent troops, and commanded by count Daun; the only general who had ſnatched a victory from the pruſſian hero.

His majeſty heſitated not a moment; although his troops did not exceed 36,000 men, he reſolved to attack the enemy, ſo much ſuperior. From the nature of the ground, the pruſſian horſe could not act; but by a moſt judicious movement of the king's, that diſadvantage was overcome; general Nadaſti, with a corps de reſerve, was poſted on the auſtrian's left, with deſign to take the king in flank; but his majeſty, in making his firſt diſpoſitions, had foreſeen, and guarded againſt that deſign, he placed four battalions behind the cavalry of his right wing. Nadaſti, as the king expected, attacked him with great fury, but received ſo ſevere a fire from thoſe four battalions, that he retired in the greateſt diſorder;

by

by which means the king's flank being well supported and covered, acted with so much order and vigor, that the enemy's right gave way. The prussian artillery was excellently served, and having silenced that of the austrians, enabled the king to maintain those advantages, which he had gained. Never was battle fought with more obstinacy; the attacks of the prussians were incredible; and the austrians made a most gallant defence during the whole battle; they drew up all their forces again about Leuthen, which post was defended on all sides with redoubts and entrenchments: but nothing could stop the impetuosity of the prussians; they made reiterated attacks with the utmost bravey, which their enemies sustained a long time with great firmness, but at last the post was gained, and the austrians fled on all sides, the battle ending in an entire rout. The king pursued them to Lissa; 6000 were slain, 15,000 taken prisoners, 200 pieces of cannon, 60 colours and standards, and 4000 waggons of ammunition and baggage were taken. It is remarkable, that this glorious battle was fought just a month after that of Rosbach.

The fulness of the victory was soon seen in the greatness of its consequences. The austrians were pursued the day after the battle to Breslau; and that city was immediately besieged. Schweidnitz, although it was in the depth of winter, was blockaded: and the prussian parties over-ran all Silesia, recovering not only that part of it, which belonged to the king, but conquered even the austrian division, reducing the garrisons of Jagerndorf, Troppau and Tetschen. In short, the empress queen remained possessed only of the garrison of Schweidnitz, in all Silesia; the whole of which country, but a few days before was in the possession of her victorious troops. His majesty the king of Prussia, having thus gloriously ended the campaign, distributed his men into winter quarters. The austrians retired into Bohemia, with the

the shattered remains of their troops, where they also went into winter quarters. But it is time to turn our eyes towards another prospect equally advantageous to his prussian majesty.

The french army in Hanover, from the very signing the convention of Closter-seven, had been guilty of a million of unheard of excesses, and had violated the convention almost in every article. They seized the castle of Schartzfels, and pillaged it, making the garrison prisoners of war. They refused to deliver up the prisoners they had made before the convention, though this was a point expressly stipulated between the generals that settled the detail, and was exactly fulfilled on the part of the hanoverians, by the release of the french prisoners. They summoned the bailies of those districts, into which the french troops were by no means to enter, under pain of military execution, to appear before the french commissary, and compelled them to deliver up the public revenue. They appropriated to themselves part of those magazines, which by express agreement were to be left to the electoral troops. They seized the houses, revenues, and corn belong to the king of England, in the city of Bremen, in spight of the reciprocal engagements entered into, to consider that city, as a place absolutely free and neutral. The duke de Richelieu, the commander in chief, who came to lose all that the skill of d'Estrees had won, (being promoted to the chief command merely by the favour of madam de Pompadour, who hated the marshaless d'Estrees) was the author of this behaviour, so injurious to the honour of his country; his fortune, by his extravagance and vices, was very much shattered; and to repair it, he plundered the whole electorate of Hanover, with the most inflexible severity; he levied the most exorbitant contributions; and even that did not exempt the unhappy hanoverians from the insolent and brutal licentiousness of the french
soldiery.

soldiery. The capital of the electorate, was the only place which escaped from the universal rapine, by the justice, generosity, and moderation of the duke de Randan its governor, who kept up the strictest discipline; and behaved with the utmost humanity. Such instances as these, as they happen very rarely, so they ought to be transmitted to posterity to the honour of those who perform them.

There never was a more flagrant instance of what importance a regular and exact discipline is to the very being of an army, than in this under the duke de Richelieu. That general, intent only on plundering the country, relaxed every kind of military discipline; so that the numerous army, which the conduct of d'Estrees had preserved in excellent order and good spirits, through all the deserts of Westphalia, and against an enemy's army; now it was in possession of a plentiful country, without any enemy to oppose it, was reduced in its numbers, the soldiers decayed in their health and spirits, in vile order, without cloaths, and even without arms. Such was the condition of this once formidable army, when his majesty, the king of Great Britain, resolved no longer to bear the indignities which the insolence of the enemy was every day increasing. The french even went so far as to attempt taking their arms from the hanoverian and hessian troops; but this was not suffered. I have before said, that the king of Prussia had detached prince Ferdinand of Brunswick with a small army, into the country of Halberstadt, to watch the motions of marshal Richelieu; the prince finding what order the french army was in, penetrated through the northern parts of the electorate, and joined his body of prussian troops to the army of hanoverians and hessians, who instantly resumed their arms, and began to act against the french, under prince Ferdinand's command. The king published a memorial, containing the motives which obliged his troops to take arms,

setting

setting forth in the clearest light, how palpably the french had first broke every article of the convention of Closter-seven.

The prince took the command about the middle of november; by which time the army was wholly assembled. On his first motions, marshal Richelieu threatened the whole country, of which he was in possession, with fire and sword, to which no reply was made. However, on the prince's approach, the suburbs of Zell was set on fire, the bridge of the Aller burnt, and many houses reduced to ashes. His serene highness having represented to marshal Richelieu, the consequences of such a proceeding, the marshal alledged, that it was done my mere accident. The first operation of importance, which the hanoverian army undertook, was the siege of Harbourg, they became masters of the town, the 28th of november, but the french governor with the garrison retired into the castle; and defended it with the greatest bravery, till the 29th of december, when he capitulated. Marshal Richelieu, in the mean time, was collecting his troops about Zell. The 6th, the hanoverian army began their march to dislodge him, and arrived within a league of Zell the 13th; but finding that the french were too strongly intrenched to be attacked, he staid till the 21st, when he broke his camp, and returned towards Ultzen and Lunenburg, to put his troops into winter quarters.

The wonderful events, which distinguish in so remarkable a manner, the year 1757, are such, that the like is hardly to be met with in history. The king of Prussia had once more the happiness to see himself freed from all that imminent danger, which so lately surrounded him; he now felt the effects of his councils, and his labours; all his enemies were driven out of his dominions, defeated, broken, and flying every where before him; himself in quiet possession of Silesia, and his victorious troops ready to fall on
their

enemies in the next campaign, with redoubled bravery. Animated with the prefence of their fovereign, what labours are too great for pruffians to perform ? What a wonderful reverfe of fortune did this monarch fuftain, in fo fhort a fpace of time, as a fingle campaign. Triumphant at firft ; the auftrians fly before him, totally defeated, and half a kingdom conquered. The lofs of one battle turns the fcale, the king of Pruffia is defeated, the affairs of the auftrians re-eftablifhed, their armies victorious, and their enemy on the very brink of deftruction, abandoned by his allies, his dominions plundered, and laid wafte by his enemies, and himfelf at the very edge of defpair. Another battle raifes him again, and in a month's time, the auftrians, imperialifts, french, ruffians, and fwedes, all retire before him ; his dominions are freed from all his enemies ; and the force of one fmall potentate baffles all the endeavours of a confederacy of five of the greateft powers in the univerfe. How will pofterity be amazed to hear, that above half the power of Europe was united, and exerted in vain, to reduce the king of Pruffia, unaffifted by allies ! fuch are the events that happened ; fuch the actions that were performed, not in an age, but in a fingle campaign.

## CHAP. XIV.

*Affairs in England. Transactions at sea. Senegall taken. War in the East-Indies. Battles between Pocock and d'Ache. Fort St. David's taken by the french. French besiege Madrass. The siege raised. Affairs in France. In Germany. Convention between Great Britain and Prussia. French retire out of Hanover. Prince of Clermont commands the french army. Hoya and Minden taken. Generous behaviour of the duke de Randan. French army drove beyond the Rhine. Embden taken by commodore Holmes. Schweidnitz taken. King of Prussia enters Moravia. Lays siege to Olmutz. The siege raised. Retreats into Bohemia. Arrives at Frankfort on the Oder.*

THE year 1758, opened at so critical a conjuncture, that it was very reasonably expected, it would be remarkable for great and important actions. The belligerent powers of Europe, spent the winter in making the most formidable preparations, for the ensuing campaign. The immense confederacy against the king of Prussia still subsisted; and every one of the powers that formed it, seemed to be emulous who should be most forward to crush an enemy that was found more powerful, than they at first imagined. England was his only ally, and one whose assistance he had reason to hope would be very advantageous to him. The army which the king of England had under the command of prince Ferdinand of Brunswick, was of infinite service to his prussian majesty; for the french army which opposed it, it is very natural to suppose, had it had no antagonist in Hanover, would have marched against that monarch's dominions. It was resolved in England, to keep it in play, against the french, which gave occasion to a message from the king, the 18th of january, to the commons, importing, "That having ordered the army, formed last year in his electoral dominions, to be put again in motion, and to act with the utmost vigour against the common enemy, in concert with his ally the king of Prussia; and the exhausted and ruined state of the electorate and its revenues, having rendered it impossible for the same to maintain and keep together that army, until the further necessary charge of it, &c. could be laid before the house; his majesty found himself under the absolute necessity of recommending to them, the speedy consideration of such a present supply, as might enable him to subsist, and keep together the said army." In consequence of this message, the house, on the 23d, voted 100,000 l. for the end therein mentioned.

In England, we find very few events that the compass of this work will admit my speaking of. In parliament were many resolutions, which had a manifest connection with the war; of these I shall at different times take proper notice. The only military preparations of great importance in this kingdom were naval. At Portsmouth, Plymouth, Chatham, &c. several armaments were getting ready with great diligence. A squadron of eleven ships of the line, and nine frigates, had been some time in the Mediterranean, under the command of admiral Osborn, to block up M. de la Clue, who was in Carthagena, with a french squadron. On the 28th of april, Mr. Osborn fell in with another small squadron of french ships, in their way from Toulon, to reinforce de la Clue's squadron, commanded by M. de Quesne, in the Foudroyant of 80 guns, the Orpheus of 64, the Oriflamme of 50, and the Pleiade of 24. While the chief part of the english squadron continued off Carthagena, to watch the french ships there, capt. Storr, in the Revenge of 64 guns, supported by capt. Hughes, in the Berwick of 63, and capt. Evans, in the Preston of 50, took the Orpheus, commanded by M. de Herville with 500 men; capt. Gardiner, in the Monmouth of 64, supported by capt. Stanhope, in the Swiftsure of 70, and captain Hervey, in the Hampton-court of 64, took the Foudroyant with 800 men. Capt. Rowley, in the Montague of 60, and capt. Montague, in the Monarch of 74, ran the Oriflamme on shore, under the castle of Aiglos; but was not destroyed by reason of the neutrality of the coast of Spain. The Pleiade got away by out-sailing the english ships. The greatest loss sustained by the victors, was in that of the brave capt. Gardiner; lieutenant Carket commanded his ship on the captain's death, and fought the Foudroyant, with great conduct and courage; as a reward for which, admiral Osborn conferred on him the command of the ship he had conquered, and M. de Quesne, when he struck, refused to give his sword to capt. Stanhope; but gave it with great politeness to lieutenant Carket. The fleet in Carthagena consisted of one ship of 84 guns, three of 74, two of 64, two of 50, one of 36, one of 24, one of 16, and one of 14.

The english cruising squadrons, in the beginning of this year, were very successful in taking a great number of french merchantmen and privateers. We had one under vice-admiral Smith in the Downs, another under rear-admiral Cotes, in the West-Indies, who had done the english trade in those parts great service, by his conduct and bravery. Another strong squadron, under admiral Boscawen, sailed from Spithead, for north America, the 19th of february. The 12th of march, sir Edward Hawke sailed with seven ships of the line, and three frigates, from Spithead, to cruise in the bay of Biscay; the 4th of april he fell in, off the isle of Aix, with a french squadron, of five ships of the line, seven frigates, and a convoy of 40 merchantmen, to which he gave chace; the men of war fled, and the merchantmen, many of them

them were ran on shore out of the reach of the english ships, and only two or three taken. On the 7th of april, the Essex of 64 guns, and two frigates, in their way to join sir Edward Hawke, fell in with 12 sail more of french merchant's ships, escorted by a frigate of 22 guns, which the Essex took, together with five or six of the merchantmen.

In the beginning of march, a small squadron, consisting of the Nassau of 64 guns, the Harwich of 50, the Rye of 24, a sloop and two busses, under the command of captain Marsh (having on board a body of marines, under major Mason, and a detachment of artillery, under captain Walker) sailed from Plymouth for the coast of Africa. On the 24th of april, this squadron arrived off the river Senegall, got over the bar the 29th; and the next day landed 700 marines and seamen, with design to attack the french fort Lewis; but deputies arrived with articles on which they proposed to surrender, and these being agreed to, the english forces were put in possession of this most important settlement; where they found 232 french officers and soldiers, 92 pieces of cannon; with treasure, slaves, and merchandize to a very considerable value. The success which this small force met with, was of the greatest importance to the english nation, and of equal prejudice to the french: I shall speak more fully of it hereafter *.

The East-Indies, since the beginning of the war, had been a theatre fruitful in events. The year 1758, in that country, was distinguished by many acts of importance. Vice-admiral Pocock, since the death

---

* The king of the country about Senegall, was so desirous of seeing the men of war, that he swam on board, though the distance was upwards of an english mile. The officers of the ship treated him with great civility, with which he seemed vastly pleased. At parting, he told the captain, he should be extremely fond of seeing the king of England, which he thought he might do, as he had ships at his command, for if he had ships, he would go and see him.

of Mr. Watson, had commanded in chief there. Being joined by commodore Stevens in Madrafs road, on the 24th of march, with reinforcements from England, he put to fea with his fquadron * the 27th, with defign to intercept a french fquadron in thofe parts, under the command of M. d'Ache. The 29th he came in fight of them; the french admiral (whofe fquadron confifted of three fhips of 74 guns, two of 64, two of 60, two of 50, and one of 36) on feeing Mr. Pocock's fleet, formed his line, as did the englifh admiral, and bore down on the enemy; the engagement lafted but a very fhort time, before M. d'Ache broke his line, and bore away; when Pocock hung out the fignal for a general chace; but night coming on, he continued the purfuit without any effect. The firft of may, he came to an anchor near Madrafs, and was informed, that one of the french fhips of 74 guns, was fo much damaged in the action, that its captain had ran her on fhore. This victory would have been much more complete, had the captains who commanded in the rear of the englifh fquadron, done their duty; for when the admiral threw out the fignal for a clofe engagement, they kept back, and would not bear down, even after repeated fignals had been made. In admiral Pocock's letter, he beftows great encomiums on commodore Stevens, capt. Latham, and capt. Somerfet in the van; alfo, capt. Kempenfelt, the commodore's captain, and capt. Har-

* Confifting of the following fhips:

| Ships. | Guns. | Men. | |
|---|---|---|---|
| Yarmouth | 64 | 500 | Pocock. |
| Elizabeth | 64 | 595 | Stevens. |
| Cumberland | 66 | 520 | |
| Weymoth | 60 | 420 | |
| Tyger | 60 | 400 | |
| Newcaftle | 50 | 350 | |
| Salifbury | 50 | 300 | |
| Queenborough frigate | | | |
| Protector ftorefhip. | | | |

rifon,

rifon, with the reft of the officers and men on board the Yarmouth. The admiral, on his arrival at Madrafs, ordered a court martial to affemble, to enquire into the conduct of thofe captains, whofe behaviour had appeared fo faulty. In confequence of which, capt. Nicholas Vincent was fentenced to be difmiffed from the command of the Weymouth: capt. George Legge of the Newcaftle, to be cafhiered from his majefty's fervice ; and capt. William Brereton to loofe one year's rank, as a poft captain.

Mr. Pocock having repaired the moft material damages his fquadron had received, put to fea the 10th of may, with an intent to get up to fort St. David's, but was not able to effect it; he fufpected the french defigned to attack it, and knew, that if his fquadron was there, fuch an attempt would be impracticable. His fufpicions were but too true; the french army under M. Lally, had befieged it, with the affiftance of fome of the french fhips, and it furrendered the 2d of june. The 30th of may, Mr. Pocock was in fight of Pondicherry; and fome days after hearing that fort St. David's was taken, he returned immediately to Madrafs. He put to fea again, the 25th of july, in queft of the enemy, and on the 3d of auguft, by taking advantage of a fea breeze, he got the weather gage, and brought on an engagement. In ten minutes M. d'Ache bore away, keeping a very irregular line, and continuing a running fire till three o'clock, when the englifh admiral made the fignal for a general chace; and purfued them till it was dark, when they efcaped by out-failing him, and got into Pondicherry road; where they continued till the 3d of feptember, when they failed for their iflands to clean and refit; two of their fhips being in a very bad condition, and others confiderably damaged.

M. Lally, as foon as had taken fort St. David's, marched with 2500 men, into the king of Tanjour's country, to try, if poffible, to procure a fum of money

ney from him; being refused, he plundered a trading town on the coast, and besieged his capital, but meeting with a more resolute defence than he expected, he retreated about the middle of august, in great confusion, to Carrical, a french sea-port settlement; and from thence to Pondicherry, at the end of september. About the middle of december, the french army again moved from their quarters, and marched to lay siege to Madrafs: colonels Lawrence and Draper commanded there, and sustained all the attacks of the french, with the greatest conduct and bravery, making several successful sallies: but a reinforcement arriving in the port the middle of february, 1759, the enemy raised the siege, and retreated with the utmost precipitation, leaving behind them several batteries of cannon and mortars; having suffered very severely during the siege. General Lally was esteemed an officer of abilities, he had served many times with reputation in Europe; and was of greater rank than the french court usually send into this country. The bad success he met with was entirely owing to the miserable troops he commanded, and the want of the necessary support from Europe. The want of a firmness in the administration of the government of France at home, occasioned that manifest weakness which so evidently appeared in all her colonies. There were several other expeditions undertaken on both sides, in the beginning of 1759; but I shall give an account of them hereafter. The chain of affairs in India, during the year 1758, was so connected, that I could not avoid giving a history of the whole year at once. It will also appear more perspicuous to the reader.

The continent of Europe at this time, bid more fair for being the theatre of great events. Half Europe, as I before mentioned, was employed in making preparations for the ensuing campaign. The french were very diligent in putting their army on the

the Rhine, on a better footing. It will not here be amiſs to take a ſlight view of the court of France; for then the cauſe of the deſpicable figure, which the french army in Hanover made, the latter end of the laſt campaign, will more clearly appear.

Madam de Pompadour, miſtreſs to the king of France, had governed that monarch and his kingdom for 15 years, with the moſt abſolute ſway. A quarrel between her and the marſhaleſs d'Eſtrees was the occaſion of recalling the marſhal, indiſputably one of the greateſt generals in France, from his command in Hanover. The duke de Richelieu, who ſucceeded him, bought his promotion by an immenſe bribe to her. This woman ſet every thing, in the gift of the crown, up to ſale; commiſſions in the army and the navy, were at her diſpoſal. Little artifices, and petty paſſions could never make great miniſters. Yet, ſhe aſpired ſtill higher, and aſſumed all the authority of a deſpotic miſtreſs, that gave what motion ſhe pleaſed to the ſtate machine. Mean ſpirited councils naturally enough coming from her, and not the leſs followed for their being ſo; miniſters diſgraced, generals recalled, and appointed at her imperious nod, and all of theſe for the worſt, ſignalized her power and her want of judgment. In the mean time, this ſubverſion of all order and dignity threw a general languor into the adminiſtration of affairs. The ſubjects of the greateſt rank, merit, and abilities, were either driven into corners, or voluntarily ſhrank from the indignity of places, that could only be held on the ſcandalous terms of paying court to a woman, conſtantly jealous of not having enough of that reſpect ſhewn her, to which ſhe muſt have been conſcious of having ſo little title, and but the more intent on hiding that meanneſs of her's, by an inſolence ſo much fitter to prove and expoſe it. The conſequence of this muſt be, the filling the places, thus vacant, with petty characters; whoſe greateſt merit

merit could only be the having none, as no merit could there exift, but what muft be incompatible with a fubmiffion to her, or with fubminiftering to the will and meafures of a woman, that vifibly facrificed to her own private paffions, the king who was governed, and the kingdom that was difhonoured by her*. Under fuch an adminiftration, could it be wondered at, that France made fo pitiful a figure in the war fhe carried on. But the neceffity of the times called loudly for a change of minifters and meafures, and indeed the court found themfelves obliged to make fome alterations in their conduct. The duke de Bellifle, whofe abilities and conduct had gained him fo great a character, was placed at the head of the military department †; in which he

endea-

---

* The hift. de Pompadour, Vol. II. p. 131.

† On the duke's taking his place in council, as fecretary of war, he made the following fenfible and animated fpeech; which as it fets the bad ftate of the french army in a very clear light, I fhall infert it here:

"I know, faid he, the ftate of our armies. It gives me great grief, and no lefs indignation: for befides the real evil of the diforder in itfelf, the difgrace and infamy which it reflects on our government, and on the whole nation, is ftill more to be apprehended. The choice of officers ought to be made with mature deliberation. I know but too well, to what length the want of difcipline, pillaging, and robbing have been carried on, by the officers and common men, after the example fet them by their generals. It mortifies me to think I am a frenchman; my principles are known to be very different from thofe which are now followed. I had the fatisfaction to retain the efteem, the friendfhip, and the confideration of all the princes, noblemen, and even of all the common people, in all parts of Germany, where I commanded the king's forces. They lived there in the midft of abundance; every one was pleafed; it fills my foul with anguifh, to find, that at prefent, the french are held in execration; that every body is difpirited, and that many officers publicly fay things that are criminal, and highly punifhable. The evil is fo great, that it demands immediate redrefs. I can eafily judge by what paffes in my own breaft, of what our generals feel from the fpeeches they muft daily hear in Germany, concerning our conduct; which indeed would lofe much to be

compared

endeavoured to make a thorough reformation. The involving the french nation in a german war, was a measure against which this minister had before given his advice: but as it had been embraced, and his country was engaged too far to recede, he resolved to put the army in Germany on a good footing, and to prosecute the war with vigour.

Indeed the state of France, at this time, was truly deplorable; the great effort which it was resolved to make in Germany, drew off the attention of the ministry from their marine, and consequently from the due protection of their trade. The royal navy ran to ruin, and the trade of France, the sinews of their power, was cut off by the english shipping; in this condition, it was impossible to support the war vigorously in America, and the East-Indies; nay, it was afterwards found, that even the very coast of France was far from being impenetrable.

compared with that of our allies. I must particularly complain of the delays and irregularity of the posts; a service which is very ill provided for. I am likewise displeased at the negligence of our generals, in returning answers; which is a manifest breach of their duty. Had I commanded the army, a thousand things which are done, would not have been done, and others which are neglected, would have been executed. I would have multiplied my communications; I would have strong posts on the right, on the left, and in the center, lined with troops. I would have had magazines in every place. The quiet and satisfaction of the country should have been equal to their present disaffection, at being harrassed and plundered; and we should have been as much beloved, as we are at present abhorred. The consequences are too apparent to need being mentioned. I must insist on these things, because late redress is better than the continuation of the evil."

This speech is a sensible and just one. But how can we reconcile the expressions of humanity and tenderness for the conquered, and other countries in Germany, which it contains, with those we meet with in the marshal duke's letters, found among the papers of marshal Contades, at the battle of Minden?—It is in his letters we are to look for his real sentiments, not in his speeches.

The ministry in England resolved to strengthen their alliance with Prussia, b̄        ....... ....
prussian majesty. Finding
between the courts of Versa
ry day growing more firm, ...., ...., ....
safety of that monarch, as necessary to preserve the ballance of power in Europe. Pursuant to this plan, a second convention was signed the 11th of april, between the kings of Great Britain and Prussia, by which it was agreed, that the king of Great Britain should pay, on demand, to his prussian majesty 4,000000 german crowns, (670,000 l. sterling:) which sum, that monarch engaged to employ in augmenting his forces, that were to act for the good of the common cause. The two kings also agreed, not to conclude any treaty of peace, truce, or neutrality, &c. with the powers at war, but in concert, and in mutual agreement, wherein, both should be by name comprehended. On the 20th, the commons voted that sum for his majesty's service.

I left prince Ferdinand of Brunswick with the hanoverian army under his command, just retired into winter quarters, without meeting with any interruption from the french, having gained several advantages over them. Count Clermont now commanded the french army, the third commander in chief it had obeyed within a year*. Prince Ferdinand divided his troops into two bodies, the principal one under himself, marched on the right, to the country of Bremen, whilst a second body, under general Zastrow, kept on towards Gifforn. The prince made

---

* It was said, that soon after his arrival at Hanover, he wrote to his master, that he had found his majesty's army divided into three bodies, one above ground, the other under ground, and the third in the hospitals. Therefore he desired his majesty's instructions, whether he should endeavour to bring the first away, or if he should stay till it had joined the other two.

himself

himself master of Rottenburg, Otterfberg, Verden, and Bremen, by the middle of february, with little or no opposition; during his stay at the latter place, being informed, that the french general, the count de Chabot, with a strong detachment, was posted at Hoya, upon the Weser, a post of such importance, that the prince resolved to dislodge him. He pitched upon the hereditary prince of Brunswick, his nephew, to execute that service, with four battalions, and some light horse. The young prince, not 20 years of age, full of ardour to distinguish himself, took the command of those troops, and in executing his uncle's orders, displayed so much conduct and bravery, as would have done honour to the maturity of the most experienced general.

Before he came to Hoya, there was a deep and broad river to pass, without any means of crossing it, but a small float of timber, and two or three small boats, which carried about eight men each. One battalion of foot, and a squadron of dragoons were destined to make a feint attack on the left side of the Weser: the three other battalions were to pass the river, and enter the back part of the town. The passing the river on a single float took up so much time, that a long while was spent in getting less than half the corps over; by the time the first half was over, a high wind arose, which rendered the float unserviceable, and separated the prince from the greater part of his men, when the enemy he was going to attack, were more numerous than his whole party were they joined. In this dilemma, (out of which nothing but the spirit and genius of the prince could have extricated him) he took a resolution worthy of Cæsar himself; he resolved not to spend any more time, in endeavours to get over more men, but to march briskly on against the enemy, in so bold a manner as to possess them with an opinion of his strength, and attack them before they could undeceive themselves. Between four and five o'clock in the morning, he marched directly against Hoya, with a regiment of horse, part of a battalion, and a hautbitzer. When they got upon the causeway, within a mile and a half of the town, an unluckly accident happened, which might have ruined the whole enterprise, the detachment fired upon four of the enemy's dragoons that were patrolling. This firing was caught from one to another, and at last became general. This was more than sufficient to have discovered them; but putting on a bold countenance, they continued their march with the greatest diligence, and met with no obstruction, till they came to the bridge of the town, where a very smart fire well supported ensued; but the ground before the gate not being large enough for the prince to bring up all his men, he judiciously formed the resolution to turn the enemy, by attacking them in the rear; to execute which, he went a circuit round the town, with part of his men, attacked the enemy with bayonet fixed, and having drove them out of the town, with a great slaughter, rejoined his other party. Chabot threw himself into the castle, making a shew of defence, but surrendered the place, with his stores and magazines; his troops being permitted to march out, as the prince had no heavy cannon to lay a regular siege to it. This piece of service was executed the 23d of february.

Prince Ferdinand continued to advance; and the french every where to retreat. The 5th of march he laid close siege to Minden, the only place which the french possessed in the electorate of Hanover: and it surrendered with its garrison of 4000 men prisoners of war, the 14th. The hanoverian army was every where successful; the miserable condition of the french is not to be described; the total neglect of military discipline, the want of cloaths in such a rigorous season: the loss of all their baggage, and even their provisions, by the hanoverian hunters, who were cotinually

ally harrassing them: this concatination of misfortunes had so reduced their numbers, that the poor wretched soldiers were really to be pitied, had not they, by their barbarities, inflicted the same misery on the inhabitants of the country which they had evacuated. But one exception we must make to this behaviour; the duke de Randan left Hanover with all the generosity and virtue with which he had governed it. Every where else, the french generals burnt all the magazines they could not carry off; but this amiable nobleman, although he had time to do the same, left them all in the hands of the magistrates, to be gratuitously distributed amongst the poor; he employed all his vigilence to prevent his soldiers plundering, or using any violence to the inhabitants, and was himself the last man that marched out of the city. For this humane and generous behaviour, prince Ferdinand and the regency of Hanover, sent him letters of thanks; and the clergy in their sermons, did not fail to celebrate the action. In short, the duke's conduct, which did such honour to his name, and country, has made his memory for ever dear to the hanoverians, and drew tears of love and gratitude from his very enemies; which surely must give that general a much more durable satisfaction, than any he could have had from following the example of his countrymen, in satiating a brutal revenge.

After the reduction of Minden, the french army retired to Hamelen; but on the approach of the hanoverians, evacuated it, leaving their magazines and their sick behind them, not stopping till they came to Paderborn, where they fixed their head quarters the 18th of march. But the combined army arriving the next day at Melle, the french retreated as fast as they could towards the Rhine, and in their march were joined by the troops that had been at Embden, and at Cassel, and in the landgraviate

graviate of Hesse, which they evacuated the 21st. During their whole march they were closely pursued by the prussian hussars, and the hanoverian hunters, who killed and made prisoners numbers of their men. At last this once formidale army passed the Rhine, only leaving on the other side of it a strong garrison in Wesel, where the prince of Clermont fixed his head quarters.

A constant train of success at this time attended the hanoverian arms; and every where throughout the whole circle of Westphalia, the french met with the severest rebuffs. Embden was in the middle of march recovered by commodore Holmes, with a small squadron of men of war. The french garrison of 4000 men, as soon as they discovered the commodore's fleet, evacuated the place. As soon as Mr. Holmes perceived their design, he sent his armed boats to pursue them, they took too or three of the enemy's vessels; and in one of them was found the son of an officer of distinction, and a large sum of money. Mr. Holmes immediately restored the youth to his father, and offered to return the money, upon receiving the officer's word of honour, that it was his private property; a conduct which does honour to the commodore. But we must leave the operations of the armies on the Rhine, for the present, and take a view of the measures which his prussian majesty took to distress his enemies the austrians.

That monarch opened the campaign with the siege of Schweidnitz, which had been blocked up all the winter; and after 13 days siege, it surrendered the 16th of april, with its garrison, (which at the begining of the blockade was 7000 men, but reduced by sickness, &c. to 3000) prisoners of war. By the taking of this important post, the king of Prussia cleared all Silesia of the austrians. His majesty himself, in the mean time, marched with a part of his army towards Grussan and Friedland, and sent a
detachment

detachment as far as Trantenau, in Bohemia, where was an auftrian garrifon, which after a warm refiftance, was obliged to abandon the place, and fall back to their grand army at Konigfgratz, where it had been pofted fince the arrival of marfhal Daun, who fet out from Vienna the 9th of march. By this the pruffians opened themfelves a way into Bohemia, where they immediately poured in detachments of light troops, to raife contributions, and to harrafs the out-pofts of the enemy. At the fame time, general Fouquet, at the head of another detachment, marched againft the auftrian general Jahnus, who was pofted in the county of Glatz, and obliged him to abandon the pofts he had occupied in that county.

Befides the grand army in Silefia, his majefty formed another under his brother prince Henry, of above 30,000 men, in Saxony, to oppofe the army of the empire, which by means of the immenfe diligence that was ufed in collecting the troops, and by joining a body of auftrians, was again in a condition to act. Count Dohna commanded another on the fide of Pomerania; and a confiderable body was pofted between Wolau and Glogau, to cover Silefia from any inroads which the ruffians might make into it. All thefe armies were pofted in fuch a mafterly manner, as to keep open a communication with one another; and were admirably fituated for their deftined purpofes.

But the king of Pruffia's defign was very different from what the auftrians imagined; he had placed his army in fuch a pofition, that his enemies thought he would open the campaign, by marching into Bohemia. That monarch's feint took; whilft the auftrians were preparing to oppofe his march, he fuddenly made a rapid march towards Moravia, which country he entered the 3d of may. He had fome time before collected his army, amounting to about 50,000 men, near Neifs in Silefia, and marched in three days to Troppau, he divided it into two columns; marshal Keith at the head of the first column, set out the 25th of april, and took the road to Jagerndorf; and the king himself with the second, on the 27th. These two bodies entered the plain of Olmutz, one by Sternberg, and the other by Gibau. General de la Ville, who commanded a body of austrian troops in Moravia, retired on the approach of the prussians, who advanced by swift and rapid marches; de Ville threw part of his corps into Olmutz. The king had left general Fouquet in the county of Glatz, to watch the motions of marshal Daun; but finding that the austrians were beginning their march for Moravia, this general went to Neiss, and took under his convoy the artillery and stores that were requisite for besieging Olmutz, and arrived at Gibau on the 12th of may: the king advanced that day as far as Ollschau, and drove away a body of austrians, who retired from thence to Prostnitz, near which place the prince of Wurtemburg fixed his camp of four regiments of dragoons, one of hussars, and some battalions of fuzileers. The king opened the trenches against Olmutz, the 27th.

In the mean time, marshal Daun left his camp at Konigsgratz, and advanced by Skalitz, near Nachod in Bohemia, to Leutomyssel, where he encamped; but quitted it the 23d, entering Moravia by Billa, and marched to Gewicz: general Harsch commanded his vanguard, and pitched his camp at Allerheiligen opposite to Littau; and 5 or 6000 more of them advanced to Prostnitz. This situation of the austrian army did honour to marshal Daun. The country from Gewicz to Littau, in which he took his posts, was so mountainous, that it was impossible to attack him. He had the fertile country of Bohemia, from which he easily and readily drew supplies, in his back. He was also from this position enabled to harrass the prussian army before Olmutz, and to intercept the convoys

convoys which were brought to them from Silesia. His prussian majesty found a great difficulty in the siege, from the extent of the works round the city; for this obliged him to have his posts in many places very weak. Marshal Daun made the most of this advantage. In the night of the 8th of june, he attacked one of the prussian posts, penetrated through the camp, and threw succours into the city, whose garrison at the beginning of the siege consisted of 6000 men, under general Marshal. This advantage encouraged the austrians, so that scarce a night passed without some such attacks. Another circumstance which retarded the king's operations very much, was the want of forage; the austrians had destroyed all there was in the king's rout to Olmutz, so that his horse was obliged to forage at a considerable distance: which harrassed them extremely. The king of Prussia endeavoured by every art in his power to provoke Daun to a battle; but that able general knew too well the advantage of the game he was playing, to throw it out of his hands.

The marshal being informed that a great prussian convoy was to leave Troppau the 25th of june, resolved by attacking it to endeavour to force the prussians to raise the siege. The forces who escorted this convoy, consisted of eight battalions, and near 4000 recovered sick. Daun detached general Jahnus, who was at Muglitz, towards Bahrn, and ordered a detachment to march from Prerau to Stadt-Liebe, that the convoy might be attacked on two sides; and in order to deceive the prussian army, he drew near to them, very near Predlitz. But the king was too experienced a general to be deceived; he sent out general Zeithen with a strong corps to meet it. The convoy was attached on the 28th, before that general could come up with it; but the enemy were repulsed, and routed. Marshal Daun having reinforced his detachments, the convoy was again attacked, on the 29th, between Bantfch and Dornftadt. Part of it had fcarce paft the defiles of Dornftadt, when the auftrians fell upon it with their whole force. The head of the convoy was cut off from the reft: and though general Zeithen did on this occafion, all that could be expected from the moft experienced officer, yet he was obliged to abandon his waggons, and retire to Troppau. Only the head of the convoy arrived in the pruffian camp, the reft was taken by the enemy. This was a fatal ftroke; for had it arrived fafe, the place would not have held out above a fortnight longer.

The king of Pruffia directly found himfelf under the neceffity of raifing the fiege: and this neceffity was augmented, by the news which he every day received, of the near approach of the ruffian army to his dominions. Marfhal Daun had made an excellent movement, whereby he advanced himfelf to Pofnitz, in fuch an advantageous fituation, that he was able to fupport Olmutz in the moft effectual manner. But by this movement, he left the frontiers of Bohemia uncovered. The king of Pruffia in an inftant faw this advantage, and refolved to make his retreat into Bohemia: had he fallen back into Silefia, he wifely forefaw, that he fhould draw the whole auftrian army into his own dominions. To deceive marfhal Daun, he kept up an exceeding brifk fire the day before the fiege was raifed: but in the night of july 1, the king and his whole army took the road to Bohemia, and gained an entire march upon the enemy, fo that for all the utmoft efforts which they made to overtake him, he entered Bohemia without any lofs. Marfhal Keith marched by Littau to Muglitz and Tribau; the king's column marched by Konitz. The vanguard, under the prince of Anhalt Deffau, feized at Leutomiffel, a confiderable magazine. Marfhal Daun detached a large body of troops, under the generals Buccow, and Laudohn, to harrafs the king's march;

but

but they did not incommode him in the leaft. The pruffian army proceeded by Zwittau to Leutomiffel, where it halted a day, and from thence to Hohemauth. Marfhal Keith difperfed a body of auftrians at Holliz, while the king marched by Leutomiffel, and arrived the 11th at Konigfgratz, where general Buccow was with 7000 men, who were pofted behind the Elbe, and in the intrenchments they had thrown up all round the city; but he retired in a few days with his little army towards Clumetz; upon which his pruffian majefty immediately took poffeffion of that important poft, and laid all the neighbouring country under contribution: but as provifions grew very fcarce, and his prefence was wanted more and more in his own dominions, he fent lieut. general Fouquet with 16 battalions and 15 fquadrons, to occupy the poft of Nachod: the king himfelf marched to Oppotfchna; and marfhal Daun's army was encamped the 22d of july, on the hills of Libifchaw. As the king had refolved to retire into Silefia, he left the camp of Konigfgratz, the 25th, and having paffed the Mettau the 28th, encamped at Jaffina; from whence he difpatched general Retzow, towards the hills of Studnitz, from whence he drove the auftrian general Jahnus. His pruffian majefty directed his courfe through the county of Glatz, and towards the northern part of Silefia; he arrived the firft of auguft at Skalitz, and after a rapid march of 21 days, by Wifoca, Politz, and Landfhut, encamped the 22d at Frankfort on the Oder; where we muft leave him for the prefent, to take a view of the military operations between Great Britain and France.

CHAP.

## CHAP. XV.

*Expedition to the coaſt of France, under the duke of Marlborough. Stores and ſhipping at St. Maloe's burnt. Campaign of* 1758 *in America. General Abercrombie ſucceeds lord Loudon as commander in chief. Defeat at Ticonderoga. Lord Howe ſlain. Expedition againſt Cape Breton. Louiſburg capitulates. Remarks on its importance. Fort Frontenac taken. Fort du Queſne abandoned. Reflections on the ſucceſs of the campaign in America. Second expedition to the coaſt of France, under general Bligh. Cherburg taken, and its fortifications, &c. demoliſhed. Third expedition. Troops land at St. Lunar bay. Action at St. Cas. Re-embark. Reflections.*

THE miniſtry in England were divided in their opinions, as to the manner in which it was beſt to proſecute the war againſt France. Some were for making the great puſh in Germany, and improving to the utmoſt thoſe advantages which prince Ferdinand had already gained. Others were alſo for ſending ſome engliſh troops thither; but not for making it the principal theatre of our military operations, they thought that our great navy might be employed to advantage, in convoying an army over to the coaſt of France, and aſſiſting it in the attempts it ſhould make. The latter opinion prevailed, and in conſequence of it, a ſtrong ſquadron of ſhips being prepared at Spithead, with a ſufficient number of tranſports, orders were iſſued for aſſembling a body of troops on the iſle of Wight; and in the beginning of may, all the corps that compoſed this body were in motion. A battering train of artillery, and all the ordnance proper for ſuch an armament, had already been embarked at
the

the tower, and conveyed to Portsmouth in 9 transports. On the 16th, the army, consisting of sixteen battalions, and three companies of artillery, was formed on the isle of Wight; but nine troops of light horse designed for this ENTERPRIZE, were left on the Portsmouth side, for the convenience of easier embarkation. The duke of Marlborough was commander in chief; lord George Sackville was second in command, and under these was another lieutenant general, besides five major generals\*. Lord Anson and sir Edward Hawke commanded the grand fleet; and commodore Howe a smaller, who was entrusted with every thing that related to landing the troops in the enemy's dominions: for this purpose, a considerable number of flat-bottomed boats, of a new invention were provided, and nothing was wanting that could be deemed necessary to forward the execution of the enterprise. Lord Downe, sir James Lowther, sir John Armitage, Mr. Berkeley, and Mr. Delaval, persons of distinction, rank and fortune, engaged as volunteers in the service. And the whole nation formed the most ardent hopes of success in it.

The fleets † set sail the first of June; that under lord Anson separated from the rest, and bore off to-

---

\* Lieutenant general, Earl of Ancram.
Major general Waldegrave,
Major general Mostyn,
Major general Drury,
Major general Boscawen,
Major general Elliot,
Brigadier Elliot, commanding the light horse.
Lieut. Col. Hotham, adjutant general.
Capt. Watson, quarter master general, with rank of lieut. col.

† Lord Anson's consisted of one ship of 110 guns, four of 90, two of 80, three of 64, two of 60, one of 50, three of 36, and two of 20.
Commodore Howe's of one of 70, three of 50, four of 36, three of 20, nine of 16, one of 14, and ten cutters of 10. One hundred transports, 20 tenders, and ten storeships.

wards

wards the bay of Bifcay, with defign to fpread the alarm down the whole coaft of France; and to watch the motions of the fquadron in Breft harbour. The fleet under commodore Howe, with the tranfports, having on board the troops, amounting, as I faid before, to fixteen battalions, and nine troops of light horfe, was deftined for the bay of Cancalle, in the neighbourhood of St. Maloe's, where they landed on the 5th, and directly feized the pofts and villages, and the next day marked out a piece of ground for a camp, in order to fecure their retreat. The common foldiers and feamen plundered every thing that came in their way, and even murdered many of the old inhabitants in the villages, to the reproach of difcipline, and difgrace of humanity. The difembarkation being finifhed; on the 7th, the duke of Marlborough, and lord George Sackville, with the firft column of the army, began their march towards St. Maloe's: lord Ancram with the fecond column, advanced towards the fame place, by the village of Doll. The next day and night a detachment of the army burnt above 100 fail of fhipping, many of them privateers, from 20 to 30 guns, together with a great number of magazines, filled with naval ftores, at St. Servan and Solidore, a fauxbourg to St. Maloe's, with a large and open harbour. The troops alfo took poffeffion of a fort which the enemy had abandoned. During thefe tranfactions, there was a brigade left in the intrenchment at Cancalle, who continued to ftrengthen it, which was very eafily done, for there never was a finer fituation for a fmall army to make a ftand againft any fuperior number. In the mean time, the light horfe and out parties fcoured the country, and brought in a confiderable number of prifoners; but the town of St. Maloe's was too ftrong for them to attempt taking it. The 10th, the troops marched back to the landing place at Cancalle, and encamped within the intrenchments and redoubts juft finifhed;

finished; and they were re-embarked the 11th. The next day the town of Granville was reconnoitred, by a gentleman who had been formerly in that place. He perceived a camp before it, and received intelligence, that there was a confiderable body of troops there under the marſhal de Harcourt, commander of the french troops in Normandy. The 28th, they directed their courſe to Cherbourg, the bay of which is open to the ſea, without affording any ſecurity to ſhipping. Here it was reſolved to land, and a diſpoſition was made accordingly. The generals determined, that the forts Querqueville, Hommet, and Gallet, ſhould be attacked in the night, by the firſt regiment of guards. The men were actually diſtributed in the flat bottomed boats, when a very high wind aroſe, and obliged them to poſtpone the attack; and the weather continuing to be unfavourable, it was judged proper to put to ſea immediately; accordingly the fleet ſailed towards the iſle of Wight, and anchored at St. Helen's the 1ſt of july. The duke of Marlborough and lord George Sackville ſet out for London, where the king received them very graciouſly, leaving the command of the troops to the earl of Ancram. The 5th, orders came to diſembark the troops, till the tranſports ſhould be revictualled. They accordingly landed at Cowes, and marched into their old intrenchments.

Such was the reſult of this expedition to the coaſt of France. Concerning the ſucceſs of it, we ſhould obſerve, that the deſign which the engliſh miniſtry had in making the attempt was, to deſtroy the enemy's ſhipping and naval ſtores, to ſecure the navigation of the engliſh channel; and to alarm the king of France in ſuch a manner, as would oblige him to employ a great number of troops for the defence of his own coaſt; to hamper him in the proſecution of his deſigns upon Germany, and to ſcreen Great Britain and Ireland from the danger of any invaſion or inſult. It
ſhould

should also be remembered, that the success which attended the expedition, was obtained with little or no loss. But whether we may reasonably pronounce, that the good resulting from the expedition, paid for the expence we were at in forming and executing it, is a point I will not pretend to decide. Indeed the french king, while an english squadron of ships, and a strong body of troops were employed in attacking the maritime parts of France, could not send such powerful reinforcements to his armies in Germany, as if his own dominions were entirely free from such insult. Besides, this success convinced all Europe of the real superiority of the english naval power, which attacked the coasts of France, while other squadrons blocked up their ships in their own harbours.

In America it was reasonable to expect better success than our arms had hitherto met with, for the force which was employed was very formidable. Three grand expeditions were undertaken; one against Louisburg, another against Ticonderoga and Crown Point, and the third against fort du Quesne. General Abercrombie succeeded lord Loudon in the chief command, his lordship being recalled in the winter; and he resolved to command the expedition against Ticonderoga, himself. Having collected the troops together, he embarked them to the number of 6000 regulars, and 9000 provincials, with a good train of artillery, in 900 batteaus and 150 whale boats on the lake George, the 5th of july; and landed at the destined place the 6th; the general formed his troops into four columns, and marched against Ticonderoga. The enemy's advanced guard fled on his approach, deserting a logged camp, after burning their tents, &c. The country was all a wood, through which the english army continued their march; but found it impassible with any regularity for such a body of men, and the guides were unskilful, the troops were bewildered, and the
columns

columns broke, falling in upon one another. Lord Howe, at the head of the right center column, being somewhat advanced, fell in with a party of french regulars, of about 400 men, who had likewise lost themselves in their retreat, from their advanced guard: a skirmish ensued, in which the french party were defeated, with some loss. This advantage cost the engglish very dear, their loss was inconsiderable in numbers, but great in consequence. The gallant lord Howe was the first man that fell. This brave young nobleman was an honour to his country: his genius, courage and judgment displayed themselves in all his actions. His regiment was one of the best in America, owing entirely to the care which his lordship took of their discipline; and his instructing them particularly in the nature of the service, in that woody country. His death spread the greatest grief and consternation throughout the whole army, as he was deservedly and universally beloved and respected in it. Commodore Howe succeeded him in his title and in his virtues *.

General Abercrombie had taken several prisoners, who were unanimous in their reports, that the french had about 6000 men encamped before their fort at Ticonderoga, who were intrenching themselves, and

* There is something so noble and pathetic in the following advertisement, that any apology for inserting it is needless. It appeared in the public papers soon after lord Howe's death.
" To the gentlemen, clergy, freeholders and burgesses of the town, and county of the town of Nottingham,
As lord Howe is now absent upon the public service, and lieut. colonel Howe is with his regiment at Louisburg, it rests upon me to beg the favour of your votes and interests, that lieut. colonel Howe may supply the place of his late brother, as your representative in parliament.
Permit me therefore, to implore the protection of every one of you, as the mother of him, whose life has been lost in the service of his country.
  Albemarle-street,
  Sept. 14, 1758.     Charlotte Howe.

throwing

throwing up a breaſt-work; and that they expected a reinforcement of 3000 canadians, beſides indians: on this intelligence, he thought it moſt adviſeable to loſe no time, but attack them directly. Accordingly, on the 8th, he ſent Mr. Clerk the engineer, a-croſs the river, oppoſite to the fort, in order to reconnoitre the enemy's intrenchments; on his return, he reported, that an attack was practicable, if made before the intrenchments, &c. were finiſhed: the general then determined to ſtorm it that very day, without waiting for the artillery, which was not yet come up. The rangers, light infantry, and the right wing of the provincials, were poſted in a line out of cannon ſhot of the intrenchments, in order that the regular troops deſtined for the attack of the intrenchments might form in their rear. The picquets were to begin the attack, ſuſtained by the grenadiers, and they by the battalions: the whole were ordered to march up briſkly, ruſh upon the enemy's fire, and not to give their's till they were within the enemy's breaſt-work.

Theſe orders being iſſued, the whole army, except thoſe left at the landing place, for the defence of the batteaus, &c. were put into motion, and advanced againſt the fort, which the french had made as ſtrong as poſſible. It is ſituated on a tongue of land between lake George, and a narrow gut, which communicates with the lake Champlain. On three ſides, it is ſurrounded with water; and for a good part of the fourth, it has a dangerous moraſs in the front; where that failed, the french had made a very ſtrong line near eight feet high, defended by cannon, and ſecured by 4 or 5000 men. They had alſo felled a great many trees for about an hundred yards, with their branches outward. Such was the poſt which the engineer had reported to be ſo weak, that it was practicable to attack it without cannon.

The engliſh army advanced boldly towards it. When they came up, they not only perceived, how much

much stronger the enemy's intrenchments were, than they had imagined, but also felt it very severely. The troops behaved with the utmost spirit and gallantry; but found themselves so entangled amongst the felled trees, and so uncovered for want of artillery, that they suffered most terribly in their approaches; and made so little impression on the intrenchments, that the generals, seeing their reiterated and obstinate efforts fail of success, and the troops having been upwards of four hours exposed to a most terrible fire, thought it necessary to order a retreat, to save the broken remains of their army. Near 2000 men were killed or wounded in this precipitate and bad conducted attack. General Abercrombie shewed that he could retreat as fast as he could advance; for after a most speedy flight, the army arrived the 9th at their former camp, to the southward of lake George, which was the evening after the action.

In all military expeditions; but particularly those in such a country as north America, the greatest caution, prudence, and circumspection, are absolutely necessary in the conducting them. What must that general feel, who accepts employments without abilities to execute them; who receives the public money in his pay, and in return makes a sacrifice of the death of thousands of his fellow subjects, by his blunders in the field.

But the most important enterprize in north America, was the attack on Louisburg; it had been concerted by the ministry in England very early in the year; the fleet was preparing at Portsmouth some time, and consisted of 21 ships of the line, and 20 frigates *. Admiral

| Ships. | Guns. | Ships. | Guns. |
|---|---|---|---|
| * Ships. | | | |
| Namure | 90 | Terrible | 74 |
| Royal William | 84 | Northumberland | 70 |
| Princess Amelia | 80 | Vanguard | 70 |
| Dublin | 74 | Orford | 70 |
| | | | Burford |

Admiral Bofcawen was commander in chief by fea, having under him, fir Charles Hardy, rear-admiral, and Philip Durel, efq. commodore. Major general Amherft was commander in chief of the land forces, and under him, brigadier generals Whitmore, Lawrence, and Wolfe. Colonel Baftide, chief engineer, col. Williamfon, commander of the train of artillery. Admiral Bofcawen failed from England, with part of the above fleet, the 19th of february, and having joined the north american forces, at Hallifax in Nova Scotia, failed from thence the 28th of may. The land forces aboard the fleet (which confifted of 157 fail) amounted to 14,000 men. The fleet anchored in Gabarus bay, in the ifland of Cape Breton, the 2d of june. That evening the general, with brigadiers Lawrence and Wolfe, reconnoitered the fhore as near as he could, and made a difpofition for landing in three places. The enemy had made entrenchments along the fhore, mounted with cannon, and lined with a numerous infantry, where-ever there was any likelihood of the englifh attempting to land. It was the eighth before they could land their troops, the furff on fhore had been fo great, that no boat could poffibly live. During the intermediate time, the

| Ships. | Guns. | Frigates. |
|---|---|---|
| Burford | 70 | Juno |
| Somerfet | 70 | Diana |
| Lancafter | 70 | Boreas |
| Devonfhire | 66 | Faent |
| Bedford | 64 | Grammont |
| Captain | 64 | Shannon |
| Prince Frederick | 64 | Hind |
| Pembroke | 60 | Portmahon |
| Kingfton | 60 | Nightengale |
| York | 60 | Kennington |
| Prince of Orange | 60 | Squirrel |
| Defiance | 60 | Beaver |
| Nottingham | 60 | Hunter |
| Centurian | 54 | Scarborough, Hawke, Ætna, |
| Sutherland | 50 | Lightning, Tyloe. |

french

french had been making their entrenchments as strong as possible, they had cannonaded and threw shells, though ineffectually, at the ships. But on the 8th, the admiral finding that the surff was somewhat abated, the troops were assembled in the boats before break of day, in three divisions. The Kennington frigate was stationed on the left, and began the fire upon the enemy, followed by the Grammont, Diana, and Shannon frigates in the center, and the Sutherland and Squirrel upon the right: when this fire had continued about a quarter of an hour, the boats upon the left, rowed into shore, under the command of brigadier general Wolfe. The division on the right, under the command of brigadier general Whitmore, rowed towards the White Point; as if intending to force a landing there. The center division, under brigadier general Lawrence, made at the same time a shew of landing, at the fresh water cove. These two last divisions, which were only intended as feints, drew the enemy's attention to every part, and prevented their troops, posted along the coast, from joining those on the right, where the real landing was to be made.

The enemy, in the mean time, were not idle; as they had for some time expected such a visit, they were fully prepared to resist it. They had thrown up breast-works, at every probable place of landing, fortified at proper distances with cannon; besides an immense number of swivels of an extraordinary calibre, mounted on very strong perpendicular stocks of wood driven into the ground: they had also prepared for flanking, by erecting redans, mounted with cannon, in the most advantageous situations. Nothing of the kind was ever seen perhaps more complete, considering the number of men employed on them, than these fortifications. Besides, all the approaches to the front lines were rendered extremely difficult, by the trees they had laid very thick upon the shore,

T 2        round

round all the cove, with their branches lying towards the fea, for the diſtance of 20 or 30 yards. Nor could this ſtratagem be fufpected at any great diftance, as the place had the appearance of one continued green of little fcattered branches of fir: and but very few of the guns on their lines were to be diftinguifhed out of the reach of their metal; the reft were artificially concealed from view, with fpruce branches.

 The french acted very wifely, did not throw away a ſhot, till the boats were near in ſhore, and then unmafking the latent deftruction, by the removal of the fpruce branches, they directed the whole fire of their cannon and mufketry upon them. The furff was fo great, that a place could hardly be found to get a boat on ſhore. But notwithftanding the fire of the enemy, and the violence of the furff, brigadier Wolfe purfued his point, and landed juft at their left of the cove, took poft, attacked the enemy, and forced them to retreat. Many boats overfet, feveral broke to pieces, and all the men jumped into the water to get on fhore, among the firft of whom was general Wolfe. As foon as the left divifion was debarked, the center rowed to the left, and landed. After that brigadier Whitmore with the divifion of the right wing, gained the fhore amidft a continual difcharge of ſhot and fhells from the enemy's lines. And laft of all landed the commander in chief, major general Amherft, in the rear, full of the higheft fatisfaction, from feeing the refolution, bravery, and fuccefs of the troops, in furmounting difficulties and defpifing dangers. A noble fpecimen of the fpirit he had to depend on in the remaining part of the enterprize.

 The moment the troops were landed, they attacked a ftrong battery near them in flank, with fo much vigor, as foon forced the enemy to abandon it. And they fled on all fides; they were purfued till they got within cannon ſhot of the town. In a few days after the

the landing was effected, the garrison took the seasonable precaution of setting fire to the barracks, and destroying in one general conflagration all their outbuildings; and left nothing standing within two miles of the town walls.

General Amherst having traced out a camp, sent brigadier Wolfe with a strong detachment, round the north-east harbour, to a point of land; five or six ships of the line, and as many frigates, which were in the harbour, could bring all their guns to bear upon the approaches of the english, besides a battery on the island in the harbour, which did the same: to silence these, general Wolfe was detached to the light house point; where, on the 12th, he took possession of all the enemy's posts, and by his fire, he silenced the enemy's island battery on the 25th; but the ships still continued to bear upon him.

It was with infinite difficulty and labour, that a road was made from a proper landing place, for the bringing up the artillery to the camp, when landed. The ruggedness of the ground was such, that it was near a month before it was finished. The 21st of july, one of the ships that had continued firing on general Wolfe's batteries, took fire, and blew up, and the flames communicating to the sails of two others, they were also burnt to the water's edge. This was a sad accident to the enemy, as it was not to be repaired. The siege, during the first part, went on very slowly; but by the middle of july, the great abilities of the generals Amherst and Wolfe, had got the better of innumerable difficulties, and by a well concerted and continual fire, great part of the town was reduced to ashes. The admiral was also extremely attentive to employ his ships to the best advantage, and gave all the assistance in his power on every occasion, to the land forces: he had the 24th of july acquainted the general, that he intended sending 600 sailors in boats, into the harbour, to destroy, or bring away two french men of war, that yet remained. The 25th, he accordingly sent them in, under the command of the captains Laforey and Balfour; they put off about 12 o'clock at night, and by the advantage of the foggy darkness, and the inviolable silence of the people, paddled into the harbour of Louisburg unperceived. It had been before concerted, that there should be a prodigious brisk fire kept up from the trenches all night, to draw the enemy's attention from the harbour, which had a good effect. In their seeming security, after the boats had pushed almost as far as the grand battery, left the ships should be too much alarmed by their oars, they took a sweep from thence towards that part of the harbour, where they knew the ships were, and presently discovered them. Each division of the boats was no sooner within sight of the two ships, captain Laforey's of le Prudent, and captain Balfour's of le Bienfaisant, than the centinels hailed them in vain, and began to fire on them; and the two captains ordered their boats to give way along side their respective ships, and to board them immediately. In short, the men gave three cheers as they pulled up along the sides, boarded them with the greatest bravery and took them; le Prudent being on ground, they burnt her, and towed off the Bienfaisant in the midst of a most formidable fire from the mortified enemy. One of the bravest and best concerted attempts that ever was undertaken; and does equal honour to the admiral who planned it, and the captains and common men, who executed it.

The 26th, the admiral came on shore, and acquainted general Amherst, that he designed sending six of his men of war into the harbour the next day, to batter the fortifications on the sea side. He was but just come on shore, when Mr. Amherst received a letter from the governor, offering to capitulate, much on the same terms as were granted to the garrison

rison of Minorca; but, in answer to it, admiral Boscawen and general Amherst returned the following answer:

" In answer to the proposal I have just now had the honour to receive from your excellency, by the sieur Loppinot, I have only to tell your excellency, that it hath been determined by his excellency admiral Boscawen and me, that his ships shall go in to-morrow, to make a general attack upon the town. Your excellency knows very well the situation of the army and fleet; and as his excellency the admiral, as well as I, is very desirous to prevent the effusion of blood, we give your excellency one hour, after receiving this, to determine, either to capitulate as prisoners of war, or to take upon you all the bad consequences of a defence, against this fleet and army.

Boscawen,<br>Jeff. Amherst."

To which letter, the governor returned the following resolution:

" To answer your excellencies in as few words as possible, I shall have the honour to repeat to you, that my resolution is still the same; and that I will suffer the consequences, and sustain the attack you speak off.
Le chevalier de Drucour."

However, M. de Drucour changed his opinion; for as soon as Messrs. Boscawen and Amherst's letter was received into Louisburg, M. Prevot, commissary general, and intendant of the colony, brought him a petition from the traders and inhabitants; which determined him to send back the officer, who had carried his former letter to make his submission to the law of force: and accordingly the articles of capitulation

pitulation * were agreed on, whereby the garrison became prisoners of war.

On

* I. The garrison of Louisburg, shall be prisoners of war, and shall be carried to England, in the ships of his britannic majesty.

II. All the artillery, ammunition, provisions, as well as the arms of any kind whatsoever, which are at present in the town of Louisburg, the islands of Cape Breton and St. John, with their appurtenances, shall be delivered, without the least damage, to such commissaries, as shall be appointed to receive them, for the use of his britannic majesty.

III. The governor shall give his orders, that the troops which are in the island of St. John, and its appurtenances, shall go on board such ships of war, as the admiral shall send to receive them.

IV. The gate called Porte Dauphine, shall be given up to the troops of his britannic majesty, to-morrow at eight o'clock in the morning, and the garrison, including all those that carried arms, drawn up at noon on the esplanade, where they shall lay down their arms, colours, implements, and ornaments of war. And the garrison shall go on board, in order to be carried to England in a convenient time.

V. The same care shall be taken of the sick and wounded, that are in the hospitals, as of those belonging to his britannic majesty.

VI. The merchants and their clerks, that have not carried arms shall be sent to France, in such manner as the admiral shall think proper.

Louisburg, july 26, 1758,<br>Le chevalier de Drucour.

An account of the guns, mortars, shot, shells, &c. found in Louisburg.

| | | Number. |
|---|---|---|
| Iron ordnance mounted on standing carriages with beds and coins, | 36 pounders | 38 |
| | 24 | 97 |
| | 18 | 23 |
| | 12 | 19 |
| | 8 | 10 |
| | 6 | 28 |
| | 4 | 6 |
| Mortars, brass with beds, | $12\frac{1}{2}$ inches | 6 |
| | 11 | 1 |
| | $6\frac{1}{2}$ | 2 |
| Mortars, iron with beds. | $12\frac{1}{2}$ inches | 6 |
| | 11 | 4 |
| | 9 | 1 |

Muskets

( 281 )

On the 27th, three companies of grenadiers, under the command of major Farquhar, took poſſeſſion of the weſt-gate; and general Amherſt ſent in brigadier Whitmore, to ſee the garriſon lay down their arms, and poſt the neceſſary guards in the town, on the

|  |  |  | Number. |
|---|---|---|---|
| Muſkets with accoutrements, |  |  | 75,000 |
| Powder, whole barrels, |  |  | 600 |
| Muſket cartridges, |  |  | 80,000 |
| Ditto balls,—tons, |  |  | 13 |
| Round ſhot, | { | 36 | 1619 |
|  |  | 24 | 1658 |
|  |  | 12 | 4000 |
|  |  | 6 | 2336 |
| Grape ſhot, | { | 36 | 132 |
|  |  | 24 | 134 |
|  |  | 12 | 330 |
|  |  | 6 | 530 |
| Caſe ſhot | | 24 | 53 |
| Double-headed ſhot, | { | 13 | 850 |
|  |  | 12 | 153 |
| Shells, — | { | 13 inches, | 850 |
|  |  | 10 | 38 |
|  |  | 8 | 138 |
|  |  | 6 | 27 |
| Lead pig, | { | tons, |  |
| Ditto ſheet, |  |  | 27 |
| Iron of ſorts, tons |  |  | 6 |
| Wheelbarrows, |  |  | 600 |
| Shovels, wood |  |  | 760 |
| Ditto, iron |  |  | 900 |
| Pick-axes, |  |  | 822 |
| Iron crows, | { | large | 22 |
|  |  | ſmall | 12 |
| Iron wedges, |  |  | 42 |
| Hand mauls, |  |  | 18 |
| Pin mauls, |  |  | 12 |
| Maſon's trowels, |  |  | 36 |
| Hammers, |  |  | 36 |
| Axes, |  |  | 18 |

State of the garriſon.

Number of officers, 214. Of ſoldiers fit for duty, 2374. Of ſick and wounded, 443. Of the ſea officers, 135. Of private men and marines fit for duty, 1124. Sick and wounded belonging to the ſhips, 1357. Total taken priſoners, 5637.

ſtores,

stores, magazines, &c. All the french men of war that were in the harbour, were taken or destroyed. The Prudent, 74 guns, was burnt by the boats of the fleet: Entreprennant, 74 guns, blown up and burnt; Capricieux, Celebre, of 64 guns each, burnt by the Entreprannant; Bienfaisant, 64 guns, taken by the boats; Apollo 50, Chevre, Biche, and Fidelle frigates, sunk by the enemy across the harbour's mouth. Diana 36, taken by the Boreas. Eccho 26, taken by the Juno.

In this advantageous and glorious manner ended one of the most important enterprizes of the whole war; and with so trifling a loss on the side of the english, as about 400 men. The british ministry displayed their judgment in planning this attempt. The genius, conduct, and bravery of the commanders who executed it, was equalled by nothing, but the noble emulation and arduous perseverance, and the desperate courage of the troops they commanded; in particular, admiral Boscawen, and the generals Amherst and Wolfe, gained immortal honour: the former received the thanks of the house of commons.

The conquest of this valuable island was of the greatest advantage to the north american colonies: Louisburg, by its situation, was a constant repository for the french privateers, who came out from thence in great numbers, and continually infested the coasts of the english settlements. But its importance to Britain in general, is still clearer; it was the only place at which the french could cure, or from whence they could catch their cod, the fish which is taken in such great abundance in those seas. This fishery has many times been computed to bring France in upwards of 1,000000 l. sterling yearly, besides maintaining near 20,000 seamen in constant employment. This article alone sufficiently speaks its real importance. Louisburg was also the key to their settlements, on the continent of north America;

America; all the ships that went from France to Canada touched here; before they ventured into the river St. Laurence; the french soon found how great this part of their loss proved, it being very easy for the possessors of Cape Breton and Newfoundland to intercept most of the ships that go from Europe to Canada.

In the mean time general Abercrombie, to repair the misfortune he met with at Ticonderoga, dispatched lieutenant colonel Bradstreet, with 3000 troops to make an attack upon fort Frontenac; a fortress which the french had built on lake Ontario. Mr. Bradstreet, after a difficult, but well conducted march to Oswego, embarked his troops there, and landed them within a mile of fort Frontenac, the 25th of august; the garrison made little opposition, surrendering prisoners of war the 27th. It was a square fort of 100 yards, having 60 cannon, but only half of them were mounted, and 16 small mortars. Lieutenant colonel Bradstreet found in it 120 men, besides some indians, and women and children. There was an immense quantity of provisions and goods, designed for their troops on the Ohio, and their western garrisons, which the french valued at 800,000 livres. The lieutenant colonel also took 9 vessels, from eight to eighteen guns, which were all the french had upon the lake, two of them (one richly laden) were brought to Oswego, and the rest, with all the magazines, he burnt and destroyed; together with the fort, artillery, stores, &c. agreeable to the instructions the lieutenant colonel received from general Abercrombie, finishing his expedition with equal honour to himself, and advantage to his country.

But I must here make a few remarks on the general's ordering Mr. Bradstreet to destroy fort Frontenac. That post is so strong by nature, that had he ordered it to be fortified, a garrison of 3 or 400 men to be left in it, and the vessels to be preserved and kept

cruising

cruising on the lake, it has been very juftly thought that the french would have fuffered much more feverely. It could then have refifted any force they could have brought againft it; and, by its fituation, would have cut off the communication between Canada and all their fettlements on the Ohio and adjacent country, which would foon have proved a fatal ftroke to the french empire in thofe parts.

The fuccefs which lieutenant colonel Bradftreet met with at fort Frontenac, was of great affiftance to the expedition which had been undertaken againft fort du Quefne, under brigadier general Forbes. That gallant officer, with about 6000 men, after having taken the greateft pains to collect them at Philadelphia, marched from thence, the latter end of june, by Carlifle, Rayftown, and fort Cumberland. It is inconceivable what difficulties he met with in this tedious march of fome months, through an unknown woody country, continually harraffed by the enemy's indians; nothing but the moft prudent circumfpection in the general could have conducted the army fafe, through fuch an almoft impracticable rout. The 14th of feptember, major Grant, with an advanced guard of 800 men, came in fight of fort du Quefne, having marched fo forward with an unaccountable defign of taking the fort by a coup de main; and the party being very badly conducted, was defeated by the enemy, who fallied out of the fort, and attacked him, killing a great many, and difperfing the reft. However, the french found the indians wavered in their obedience, in proportion as the englifh army advanced, for general Forbes had previoufly engaged them to act a neutral part, after thoroughly convincing them in feveral fkirmifhes, that all their attempts upon his advanced pofts, were vain: this determined the french to abandon the fort, which they did: having deftroyed all the works, they fell down the Ohio the 24th of november, towards their more northern fettlements, to the number of 4 or 500 men; and the next day general Forbes erected the englifh flag on fort du Quefne, which he named Pittfburg. He directly fet about re-fortifying it, as well as circumftances would permit, and left it too ftrong to be attacked by any force which the french had in thofe parts. The general's health was fo extremely bad, as would permit him only to give the neceffary orders, and lafted juft long enough for him to fee the effects of his conduct and courage. He died on his return to Philadelphia, beloved by his friends and regreted by his enemies.

In this manner we became mafters of that important fortrefs, which was the occafion of a deftructive war being kindled, and fpread from one end of the world to the other. The lofs of it was a terrible ftroke to the french in north America; the whole country bordering on the Ohio, and its branches was directly reduced to the obedience of the englifh, as the indians, as foon as ever the french abandoned the fort, came and made their fubmiffion to the general. This conqueft, in a manner divided their fettlements of Canada and Louifiana *.    On

---

\* It is not confiftent with the fhortnefs of the plan of this work, to give an account of all the brave actions performed at fea by our privateers and fingle fhips of war; but there is fomething fo extraordinary in what captain Forreft, of his majefty's fhip Augufta, of 60 guns, effected, that it would be unpardonable to omit it; that gentleman, with the above fingle fhip, attacked and took the following fleet:

| Ships names. | Tonnage. | Guns. | Men. |
|---|---|---|---|
| Le Mars, | 500 | 22 | 108 |
| Le Theodore, | 650 | 18 | 70 |
| Le Solide | 350 | 12 | 44 |
| Le Margarite, | 350 | 12 | 51 |
| St. Pierre, | 300 | 14 | 40 |
| Maurice le Grand, | 300 | 12 | 36 |
| La Flore, | 300 | 12 | 35 |
| La Brilliant, | 200 | 10 | 20 |
| La Mannette, | 120 | 0 | 12 |
| Total | 3070 | 112 | 426 |

This

On the whole, although general Abercrombie failed in his attempt on Ticonderoga, yet this campaign in north America was extremely glorious. That moſt valuable and important fortreſs of Louiſburg, with the iſlands of Cape Breton and St. John conquered; fort du Queſne abandoned; and fort Frontenac deſtroyed: theſe are events which will adorn the annals of Britain to the lateſt poſterity. No ſucceſſes were ever more highly advantageous to Great Britain, than theſe; they were entirely national, and tended to ſecure our american ſettlements, in the greateſt degree, thoſe natural ſources of our naval ſtrength and power.

The french felt the weight of the engliſh power in every part of the world. It was now directed and put in motion by miniſters of capacity and genius. The coaſt of France itſelf had been inſulted; and it was reſolved in the britiſh cabinet to continue thoſe expeditions. Accordingly, on the 1ſt of Auguſt, commodore Howe, with his fleet and tranſports, ſet ſail from St. Hellen's, having on board the little army, which had before been under the command of the duke of Marlborough, but was commanded now by lieut. general Bligh; with his royal highneſs prince Edward, who came down from London, to be preſent at this expedition, in quality of midſhipman, and whoſe preſence diffuſed an univerſal joy amongſt the fleet and army. In a few days they came before Cherbourg, the object of the expedition; and perceived that the french had entrenched themſelves by a line running from Ecceundeville, that ſtands about two miles from Cherbourg, along the coaſt for four or five miles;

---

This is ſo very amazing, that one would think it impoſſible for one ſingle ſhip, without a friend in view, to take ſo many; but how much more ſurpriſing is it, when we know that this was performed within three leagues of one of their principal harbours, Pitit Guave in St. Domingo. This brave captain had before, in the ſame ſtation with three men of war, attacked eight french ones, and got the victory, though not with the ſame advantage as is diſplayed above.

with several batteries, at proper distances. Behind these intrenchments the french troops appeared, both horse and foot; they did not advance to the open beach, as their defences did not reach so far. The bomb-ketches lying in shore, played upon their intrenchments, not only in the usual way, but also with ball mortars, which threw a great quantity of balls; these were well directed, and seemed greatly to disconcert the french cavalry. On the adjoining fields was a great number of peasants, reaping the corn; and, in a meadow directly opposite to the forces, there was one man employed in making hay with great composure, as if the landing was not worth his notice. Prince Edward went on board the Pallas, one of the ships intended for battering the forts; afterwards visited the bomb-ketches, that he might see the manner of working the mortars.

On the 6th, the landing was effected; the flat-bottomed boats rowing towards the shore, with more regularity than appeared in the former disembarkation in the bay of Cancalle. Commodore Howe had placed the ketches and men of war so judiciously, that they covered the landing in such an effectual manner, that the enemy durst not advance beyond their intrenchments. The troops leaped into the water, and were soon formed on the beach, with a natural breastwork before them. Never did an enemy behave in a more dastardly manner; they retired with only firing a few shot, and left the english to finish their landing in the utmost security. As soon as the greatest part of the troops were landed, it was expected that they would have marched to the village of Querqueville; but the general thought proper to remain at Erville, near the place where they landed. The troops were there encamped at night, in a very irregular manner, on a spot of ground, not more in extent than 400 paces; so that had the enemy attacked them

them in the front and on the left, they would have been obliged to fight with infinite difadvantage. This ftrange conduct was quite contrary to the maxim in war, never to occupy any ground, but where you can exert your whole force to the beft advantage; and no good apology can be made, for hampering an army by a confined fituation, in the face of a retiring enemy \*.

The next day after landing, the forces entered Cherbourg without oppofition, the town being open towards the land, they proceeded to deftroy the fortifications, bafon, mole, &c. all which had been built with excellent materials, and at a vaft expence. But this fervice was not performed in the moft regular manner; the difcipline of the troops was much violated, and the inhabitants of Cherbourg, with reafon complained very much 'of the foldiers marauding; they were courteoufly heard, but received no relief. Unfortunately the troops had difcovered fome magazines of wine, which occafioned much delay in the demolition of the works, by the drunkennefs of the foldiers. But in this fcene of diffolute behaviour, the foot guards exhibited a laudable example to the reft of the troops, by the ftrictnefs of their difcipline. All the fhips in the harbour were burnt; and the town and country round it laid under contribution, and hoftages taken for 18,000 l. of it. All the cannon † were put on board a danifh fhip in the harbour, and fent under convoy to England. As foon as thefe feveral operations were executed, the troops re-embarked the 16th, with great expedition and equal fafety.

Although this expedition to Cherbourg did the french fo much damage, and was confequently fo ad-

---

\* Vide general Elliot's campaign on the coaft of France, p. 77.
† About 150 pieces. Above 6000 cannon fhot were found in Cherbourg, 50,000 lb. of gunpowder, befides a large quantity of fhells cartridges, fmall fhot, flints, &c. &c. &c.

vantageous

vantageous to us; still the MANNER in which it was conducted, reflected no great honour on the nation. Discipline, the very soul of armies, and more especially small ones, was very much neglected. Many very false steps were committed; one I have instanced: another was, the creating a delay for the sake of marching towards Cherbourg in one body, when there was no enemy to fear. The tedious manner in which the works were demolished, owing to the neglect of discipline, is so well known, that I need not repeat it. The success which attended the expedition, was much more owing to bad conduct, and cowardly behaviour of our enemies, than to any merit that can be discovered in the conducting it\*. But I should here, in justice to the commodore and sea officers, observe, that they gained great honour, by their skill in embarking and dis-embarking the troops. After having been two days in the harbour without seeing an enemy, the fleet set sail the 18th, and the 23d arrived in Weymouth road; being driven there by contrary winds.

---

\* One instance of mismanagement I must be allowed to quote: "The general, attended by some of the commanding officers, going out to reconnoitre with a detachment of grenadiers, and a party of light horse, some of the french cavalry appeared at a distance. Captain Lindsey, of the light horse was immediately ordered to attack them; at the request (as it is said) of some young gentlemen, who were desirous of seeing the horse engage: he accordingly advanced at a brisk pace, without detaching from his front and flanks; and falling in with a body of infantry, posted behind a hedge, received a severe fire, which obliged the light horse to wheel about, and retire. Captain Lindsey was mortally wounded by a musket shot, and died, universally regretted, as a worthy young man, and one of the most intelligent, active, and industrious officers in the service. What pity so much merit should have been unnecessarily thrown away, to gratify the rash impertinent curiosity of those, who had no right to dictate on such an occasion." Elliot's campaign, p. 82.

It was his majesty's instructions, that this armament, should proceed in their attempts on the coast of France; when they set sail from Cherbourg, their design was to proceed on the coast of St. Maloes; but the contrary winds detained them some time: on the 25th of august they made the french shore; and two days after anchored in the bay of St. Lunar, about two leagues to the westward of St. Maloes, and there landed without opposition. As soon as that was effected, a party of grenadiers was detached, who burned 14 or 15 vessels in the harbour of St. Briac. The 27th, 28th, and 29th were spent in reconnoitring and deliberating on what could be done. In one of these excursions, prince Edward advanced so near St. Maloes, as to expose his person to some shot from the town. A ball grazing, en ricochet, near the place where he stood, a serjeant sprung before him, to defend his royal highness with his body; the prince was so pleased with this uncommon mark of courage and attachment, that, he rewarded the man with a handsome gratification.

Nothing could give greater surprise, than the choice that was made of St. Lunar bay to land in; by its situation, it was very plain that St. Maloes was the object of the expedition; and it was very remarkable, that now their force was weaker than when under the duke of Marlborough, they should think of attacking that town, which before was too strong for more numerous forces; but there was something so extremely absurd and unaccountable in the whole management of this affair, that I cannot pretend to form any judgment on the designs of the commander.

The army was landed but a few days, when an attack on St. Maloes was found utterly impracticable; it was therefore resolved to penetrate further into the country; moving however, in such a manner

as

as to be near the fleet, in cafe it fhould be neceffary to re-embark. What the troops were to march into the country for, was very difficult at that time, or even at this, to know; for there was no other object of importance enough to be attacked, in the neighbourhood befides, St. Maloes. The march was begun the 8th of feptember; and the commodore finding the bay of St. Lunar extremely dangerous for the fhips to ride in, moved up to the bay of St. Cas, about three leagues to the weftward. The 10th, the troops had reached the village of Malignon, being continually engaged in fkirmifhing with parties of the enemy, and with fome lofs. For by this time the duke d'Aguillon, who commanded the french troops in Britanny, with an army of 12 battalions and fix fquadrons of regulars, and two regiments of militia, with a train of artillery, was advanced within fix miles of the englifh army: and, although the enemy was fo near, ftill the englifh encamped with as much fecurity and as little precaution, as if the enemy had been at the diftance of 20 leagues; and although the deferters had affured the general of their being fo near him.

The bay of St. Cas, being diftant about three miles, was reconnoitred for re-embarkation. The Coldftream regiment of guards had already poffeffed the ground to the right of the village of St. Cas, by the windmill. The bay was covered by an intrenchment, which the french had made to prevent the englifh landing; it was propofed that this fhould be turned againft the enemy, and fome progrefs was made in that work; but it was interrupted for want of tools. In fhort, the bay was found a very improper place for embarking troops; and a propofal was made, that it fhould be performed from an open fair beach on the left, between St. Cas and St. Guildo. This advice was moft unfortunately neglected; and the ill confequences foon appeared. It was determined on the 10th, in a council of war, that they fhould re-embark with all expedition.

Early in the morning on the 11th, to the aftonifhment of every mortal, the GENERAL was beat; the ASSEMBLY following as ufual; this conduct actually feemed as if the greateft pains was taken to inform the french of their departure. Had the troops decamped in the night without noife, they would in all probability have arrived at the beach before the french had known of their motions. The englifh were immediately in motion; yet, though the diftance did not exceed three miles, the halts and interruptions were fo frequent that the army did not arrive at St. Cas, before nine o'clock. The enemy did not appear till they had reached the fhore: the embarkation of the troops was immediately begun; but by fome miftake in orders, they were rowed too far in queft of their refpective fhips; fo that an unneceffary fpace of time was loft; and when they did return, they were moft infamoufly employed in carrying away horfes and cows, inftead of men; notwithftanding all the attention and care of the SEA-OFFICERS, who behaved extremely well. The french firft appeared by a windmill to the left; and played on the troops embarking, from a battery of ten guns, and eight mortars. They foon after marched down a hollow way, to attack the englifh; but as foon as they were on the beach, the fhips of the fleet played on them fo feverely, as to put them into great confufion; but they formed in a long line againft the englifh, as they came down from the hollow way. All the grenadiers of the army, and one half of the firft regiment of guards, remained on fhore, under the command of major general Dury; who was adviled to attack the enemy with bayonets fixed, before a confiderable number of them had arrived on the beach; but this

advice

advice was neglected, and the opportunity loft. The engagement began with an irregular fire from right to left; and after a short, but unequal contest, the ammunition of the english soldiers, which was far from being complete, failed; the men were then seized with a pannic, they were soon broke and fled in the utmost confusion. Sir John Armitage was shot thro' the head at the beginning of the action; many of the officers fell; and a great number of men were slain. It soon became a dreadful carnage: some ran into the sea, and endeavoured to save their lives, by swimming towards the boats, which were ordered to give them all possible assistance. Some officers swam near two miles before they were taken up; general Dury perished in the sea. The men were butchered both on the shore and in the water; many in swimming were killed by the shot and shells from the french cannon and mortars. Several of the frigates continued, during this time, to fire on the french army, and great part of the carnage was owing to that; for they being silenced by a signal from the commodore, the french officers and soldiers behaved instantly with the greatest generosity and moderation, in giving immediate quarter and protection to the conquered; such a noble behaviour as the english had very little reason to expect, in return for their marauding, pillaging, burning, and other excesses. We had a thousand choice troops killed, wounded, and taken prisoners, and considering the shot from the frigates, which made lanes through the enemy, their loss could not be much less. One instance of heroic bravery, I must be allowed to quote. Commodore lord Howe, perceiving that the sailors in the boats were a little staggered by the enemy's fire, exhibited a remarkable instance of intrepidity, by ordering himself to be rowed in his own boat through the thickeſt of the fire, and bringing off as many men as it would carry.

Such was the unfortunate end of this expedition to the coaſt of France. The loſs was but trifling; but then it caſt a difreputation on our arms; and diſpirited the people, as much as it exulted thoſe of France. It might have been more fuccefsful; nay, we may almoſt ſay it would have been ſo; had the army been conducted in a different manner; but never was ſuch weakneſs diſcovered in any military expedition. What could the general continue his operations for after the deſign upon St. Maloes was laid aſide? Why did he not re-imbark immediately, and proceed to a more proper place for making an attempt? What reaſon can be given for neglecting every piece of intelligence that was received of the enemy's force and motions; for communicating to them all thoſe midnight motions by beat of drum, when all poſſible care ought to have been taken to prevent them from procuring that knowledge? For what reaſon did the troops loiter away ſeven hours in a march only of three miles! And why were they re-imbarked at a place where no meaſures had been taken for their cover or defence? Theſe queries, I believe, will be very difficult to anſwer. In ſhort, ſuch folly and indiſcretion appeared throughout this expedition, that it is with concern, I am obliged to confefs, neither Britain nor her general gained any great honour by it. Such military enterprizes, in a country intirely unknown; and in the face of a ſuperior enemy, will never be attended with either honour or advantage to the nation, unleſs conducted by a commander of approved valour, conduct, and experience. In theſe expeditions every moment is critical; and the whole army ought on ſuch occaſions to go through all their manœuvres with the ſame alertneſs and circumſpection as if an enemy was in ſight.

fight. It should be remembered, that oftentimes every peasant in the country proves a dangerous one; and that nothing will ballance all the disadvantages, which an invading army lies under; but the greatest caution, the strictest discipline, and the never omitting to catch the decisive moment, in which every movement and action can only with propriety be made.

*Campaign on the Rhine. Army under duke Ferdinand passes that river. Battle of Crevelt. Battle of Sanderhausen. Battle of Meer. General Inhoff joins the english forces under the duke of Marlborough. Hanoverian army repasses the Rhine. Occupies the posts on the Lippe. Battle of Lanwerenhagen. The two armies go into winter quarters. Remarks on the campaign.*

THE war this campaign contained many great actions, in every part of the world; but particularly in Germany. I left duke Ferdinand of Brunſwick at the head of the hanoverians driving the french army, under the marſhal prince de Clermont, before him, which had already paſſed the Rhine. The duke prepared with all expedition to paſs it after them: and to the aſtoniſhment of all Europe he effected it in the face of a ſuperior army, and without loſs.

The 25th of may, the greateſt part of his army was encamped at Notteln; they marched from thence to Coeſveld, and the head quarters were fixed at Dulmen, the 27th. A detachment of ſeveral battalions and ſquadrons, under major general Wangenheim, aſſembled the 26th at Dorſten, with orders to advance himſelf to the gates of Duſſeldorp; and to cauſe a corps under general Scheither to paſs the Rhine at Duyſbourg. This paſſage was executed in the night, between the 29th and 30th, with ſuch ſucceſs, that Scheither having attacked with bayonets, three battalions of french who oppoſed him, entirely defeated them. On the 29th, the grand army marched
early

early in the morning from Dulmen towards Dorften, and encamped at Limbeke, from whence lieutenant general Wutgenau was detached towards Weffel, with a body of infantry and cavalry, he advanced by Raefveld and encamped at Ringenburg. In the mean time, his ferene highnefs the duke himfelf, went to Boecholt; and the advanced guard of the army marched on the 30th to Emmerick, being followed by the reft of the army, which was encamped at Vraffelt; and in the evening of the 31ft, the whole army was in motion to pafs the Rhine. The duke's defign was to crofs it at Lobit, but an unforefeen accident prevented him: however, in the night of the 1ft of June, the paffage was fuccefsfully effected near Herven.

The main army having thus paffed, the prince ordered the bridge to be carried up the river to Rees, and there laid on the 6th, whilft a corps under general Durchtlechen croffed the river in boats; as foon as the bridge was finifhed at Rees, the detachment under general Wutgenau alfo paffed the river; and next day, another under general Sporken croffed. On the 7th, the whole army marched from Goch, and encamped at Wees. The next day it proceeded to Uden, and marched to attack the enemy, who, as foon as the duke had paffed the Rhine, retired into a very ftrong camp on the eminences at Zanten; and on the 10th, the two armies were in fight of each other; the next day the prince reconnoitred the french camp, and found it acceffible only on the left, towards Guilders; by a mafterly motion, he obliged the prince of Clermont to quit this advantageous camp at Rheinburg, and to retire towards Meurs, in the night of the 12th. The duke then gave a new poffeffion to his army, by occupying fome heights, commonly called St. Anthony's mountains, having the town of Meurs in his front, at two leagues diftance, and the right towards the village of

St.

St. Jannigsberg; by the 14th of june, this position was effected; and the next day the duke was informed that the french army was advancing in four columns on his right; on which intelligence, the whole hanoverian army was immediately drawn up in order of battle. His highness went himself to reconnoitre, and distinctly saw a large body of french coming over the plain of Hulste, and marching towards Crevelt; but not knowing whether it was the whole army, or only a detachment, he halted till towards the evening, when he received certain information, that the french army had marched towards Nuys, and that the troops which he saw was a detachment sent to take possession of the post of Crevelt.

His serene highness was surprised to find that the prince of Clermont should send this detachment at so great a distance from his grand army; he wanted to penetrate into the designs of the french general, whether the prince would advance towards Crevelt, or whether the detachment there would fall back on the prince of Clermont. His highness, that he might be perfectly acquainted with the designs of that general; ordered the prince of Holstein, with three battalions and fifteen squadrons, to march early in the morning of the 18th, towards Hulste; and general Wangenheim, with four battalions and four squadrons, to cross the Rhine at Duysbourg, and advance towards Meurs; he also detached the hereditary prince of Brunswick, with 12 battalions and 12 squadrons, the 19th, towards Kempen, whilst the prince of Holstein advanced towards Hulste. The hereditary prince was also ordered, that in case he perceived no change in the disposition of the enemy's army or detachment, he should march the next day directly towards Kuremond, and endeavour to possess himself of a magazine there. Duke Ferdinand himself then reconnoitered the enemy at Kempen the next day; and perceived some movements in the camp

camp of M., St. Germain, who commanded the detachment at Crevelt, which inclined him to believe, that general intended to march againſt the prince of Holſtein at Hulſte; and was ſoon after informed, that the whole french army had quitted Nuys, and were advanced to Crevelt; this motion of the enemy was made in conſequence of the duke's detachments; and he inſtantly took ſuch meaſures, as the plan he had formed required. All the troops he could diſpoſe of were united the 20th in camp, the right of which extended towards Kempen, and the left towards Hulſte. On the 21ſt, M. de St. Germain's corps decamped, and marched towards Aurad, where it joined their grand army. In making this motion, they abandoned the town of Crevelt, which the duke immediately took poſſeſſion of. The 22d he reconnoitered the enemy on the ſide of St. Anthony, and reſolved to march the next day to attack them in their camp. His ſerene highneſs gave the command of his left wing, conſiſting of 18 battalions and 28 ſquadrons, to lieutenant general Sporken: The right wing, conſiſting of 24 ſquadrons and 16 battalions, he entruſted to the prince of Holſtein and general Wangenheim, and the infantry was commanded by the hereditary prince.

The french army was ſtrongly ſituated, their right wing extended towards a very thick wood, having in its front the village of Ravenſgaet, and the town of Crevelt; its left bordered on another thick wood, near the town of Anrad, having before the front of the whole army a ſtrong retrenchment, with a foſſe; behind which was placed their cannon.

The 23d, at four in the morning, the hanoverian army began to move; its right advanced in two columns; one by the village of St. Anthony, and the other croſſed the wood, and took the rout of Suchvelen. Its left advanced in one column, a little to the right of Crevelt. The ſtrength of the enemy's front,

front, determined the duke to make his attack at the village of Anrad; but to rise doubts in the enemy, he ordered general Sporcken, who commanded the left of his line of battle; and general Oberg, who commanded the center, (as soon as his highness himself began the attack at Anrad) to attack the front of the enemy, and do their utmost to penetrate it; recommending to them to make good use of their heavy artillery, in order to oblige the french to employ their attention as much on their right wing and center, as on their left, and to engage and divide their attention equally in three different places, which would prevent them from sending any reinforcement to the real attack, for fear of weakening themselves, in some part or other, where he might make impression.

These dispositions being made, his serene highness put himself at the head of the grenadiers of the right wing; and having arrived at Anrad, drew the whole wing up in order of battle, in the plain before that village. It was one o'clock at noon before the enemy began to act. The duke's artillery being greatly superior to that of the french, facilitated the means of his infantry's forming themselves in greater security; but this was not effected till after a cannonade, as violent as it was well supported, and the enemy's resistance was very brave: but the duke found that he must use small arms, to drive the enemy entirely from their intrenchments; wherefore the hereditary prince put himself at the head of the first line, and advanced with the whole front directly towards them; the fire then became extremely hot on each side, and neither discontinued, or in any degree diminished for two hours and an half; and about five o'clock in the afternoon, the prince assisted by the generals Kilmansegge and Wangenheim, forced two ditches in the front of the enemy, that were in a wood; and the other regiments of infantry did the same, all along

their

their front; upon which, that part of the enemy's infantry retired in the greateft confufion; but was covered by their horfe, although the hanoverian artillery kept a terrible fire on them all the while. During the whole affair, the artillery of the left and center, under generals Sporcken and Oberg, had done great execution; but as the diftance they were from the duke himfelf, made them uncertain what turn affairs had taken with him, they never ventured to attack the enemy's front oppofite to them; fo that the enemy's right wing and center retired in the greateft order towards Nueys, which was the rout of the reft of their army in the flight.

Seven thoufand of the beft troops of France were either killed, wounded, or taken prifoners in this battle: and to the great concern both of the french, and even of their enemies, the count de Gifors, only fon of the marfhal duke de Bellifle, not above 25 years of age, newly married to the heirefs of an illuftrious houfe, himfelf the laft hope of a moft noble family, was mortally wounded at the head of his regiment, which followed his heroic example, in making incredible efforts. This amiable young nobleman, who fell in his firft campaign, was one of the beft and moft accomplifhed men that did honour to his country in the prefent age *.

One capital miftake in the difpofition of the prince de Clermont, and which we have reafon to believe, in great part, occafioned his defeat, was his not pofting a ftrong corps at the entrance into the wood, on the left of Anrad. Had the flank of his left been as ftrong as his whole line of front, duke Ferdinand would never have dared to attack him.

The manœuvres of that commander, preceding the battle, were excellent; and his conduct in it, fuch as did the greateft honour to his military capacity, and the bravery of his troops: but ftill the victory, though great, was far from being either entire

* Vide appendix.

entire or decisive : the french army being near their own frontiers, were very soon strongly reinforced; so that they were enabled soon to oppose the hanoverian army again, in a defensive manner ; and even sent a considerable reinforcement to their army under the prince de Soubise, on the other side of the Rhine, which was ravaging the landgraviate of Hesse.

In the mean time, duke Ferdinand followed his blow ; and having passed the Rhine with a large detachment, appeared, on the 28th of June, before Dusseldorp, a city of great importance, situated on that river. The garrison of 2000 men, marched out on honourable terms, the 8th of July, after sustaining a very severe bombardment. * The prince left a garrison in it, and threw a bridge of boats over the river ; which he knew would be of great service to him, in case of being obliged to repass it. The army of France, with its reinforcements, received a new commander ; the prince of Clermont was removed, and marshal Contades appointed commander in chief.

Duke Ferdinand was in hopes that the prince of Ysenburg, who commanded the hessian troops against the prince de Soubise, would find him employment for some time. He resolved therefore to transfer the seat of war, from the Rhine to the Maes, think-

* Extract from a letter of the duke de Belleisle's to marshal Contades, july 15, 1758.
" You tell me, that you cannot bring yourself to imagine, that a town, such as Dusseldorp, should surrender without being besieged. We are still more surprised, that the count Clermont suffered it, having it absolutely in his power to have prevented it, by making use of the means which he had at hand ; (and it will still be the more grievous, if, what I am afraid of, we have left our artillery and military stores of all kinds there) the enemy having no troops on the right side of the river, while we had always a free communication with that city. The consequences of the loss, or keeping of Dusseldorp, were so essential and decisive, that they could not escape the general, or even private men. It was easy to foresee the embarrass it would occasion.

ing,

ing, that by carrying the war into the enemies country, he might draw the french from the Rhine, and oblige the prince de Soubife to come to the affiftance of the main army, under the marfhal Contades. To execute this plan, the duke marched towards Ruremond, the latter end of july; but the long and heavy rains, which had fell for some time paft, retarded his motions extremely; and in the mean time an unfortunate piece of news arrived, which obliged him to change his plan of operations.

The duke de Broglio had been fent by marfhal Contades, with a ftrong detachment, to reinforce the prince of Soubife in Heffe. Prince Yfenburg commanded 7000 Heffians againft him. The french, amounting to 12000 men, attacked the prince on the 23d of july, and after a moft obftinate fight, gained a victory. This affair was attended with very bad confequences; for it gave the french the poffeffion of the Wefer, and opened them a road into Weftphalia; where they might attack the reinforcement of englifh troops, under the command of the duke of Marlborough, which was marching to join prince Ferdinand. In this fituation, the prince had no other option, but a victory over the french, or to repafs the Rhine. The former was extremely difficult to attempt, for Contades declined coming to an engagement, in the moft careful manner; and it was dangerous to remain long in a pofition, where he had the french army on one wing, and the fortrefs of Guelders on the other, befides feveral pofts, within reach of obftructing the convoys and fubfiftence of his army. His highnefs determined to march back to the Rhine.

In the mean time, general Inhoff had been fome time pofted on the right of the Rhine, in a ftrong camp near Meer; with a defign to cover the bridge at Rees; to fecure a confiderable magazine; and to keep open a communication between the englifh reinforcements,

inforcements, and the duke's army; his corps did not amount to quite six battalions, and four squadrons, together about 3000 men. M. de Chevert, one of the greatest generals at that time, in the french army, had also some time before, passed the Rhine, with an intention of making himself master of Duffeldorp; but the heavy rains, and some other cross accidents, having frustrated his scheme, he instantly formed another, of more importance. It was to drive general Inhoff from his strong post; to burn the bridge at Rees; to make himself master of the magazine; and to cut off the communication of the english troops from the duke's army. A most noble and judicious project, and worthy of the general who formed it. He collected some straggling detachments, and his whole corps amounted to 12000 men.

Duke Ferdinand would have reinforced Inhoff, had it been practicable; but his army was too much fatigued, to begin such a march, as would have been necessary; and the extraordinary overflowings of the Rhine, which rendered the bridge at Rees impassable, was an additional difficulty; so that the general had no resource, but in his own good conduct, and the great bravery of his troops. On the 4th of august, he received intelligence that the enemy was to pass the Lippe, and would march to Rees directly. As he knew they might get thither by turning his camp; he resolved to decamp, to cover that place; which he accordingly did; but hearing nothing farther of the enemy, and believing his former advices false, he returned to his old camp at Meer; where he had no sooner placed his advanced guards, but they found themselves engaged with the enemy, who had advanced from Wesel.

Inhoff's front was covered with coppices and ditches; with a rising ground on his right, from whence

whence he perceived that the french were marching into that difficult ground; he resolved to attack them as soon as they entered it, well knowing the great difference there is in attacking and being attacked. He accordingly placed a regiment upon his right, in a coppice, in order to fall upon the left of the enemy when quite uncovered; and gave orders to the other regiments to march, with drums beating up to the enemy, and to attack them with bayonets, as soon as they should hear the fire of that in the coppice on the right. These judicious orders being executed by the whole corps, with the utmost spirit, had so great an effect, that after a resistance of about half an hour, the enemy left the field of battle, eleven pieces of cannon, many prisoners, and most of their ammunition and baggage, to the hanoverians, who drove them under the cannon of Wesel. General Inhoff delayed not a moment pursuing this victory, so gloriously won over so great a superiority. He directly took proper care to secure his magazines, and then quitted his post at Meer, and marched with the utmost diligence, towards the rout of the english forces, and joined them safely; an event, which had hitherto been attended with so much difficulty.

During this interim, prince Ferdinand marched his army still nearer the Maese, and encamped between Ruremond and Schwalm, the latter end of july; the enemy continuing in their camp at Dalem. The beginning of august, he marched towards Dulcken, and finding it necessary to attack the post of Watchtendonck, the hereditary prince prepared to execute that piece of service. This place is an island, surrounded by the Niers, of a very difficult approach, although without fortifications. That gallant young prince, not being able immediately to get down the bridge, the enemy had drawn up, without giving them time to recollect themselves; threw himself into the river, and passed it with some companies of grenadiers,

X

nadiers, who followed his example, and drove the french away with their bayonets; and in the evening the army paſſed the bridges there. On the 4th, it marched to Rhynberg, and in two days it reached Santen. Prince Ferdinand intended to have paſſed the Rhine at Rhynberg, but the prodigious flood in the river, occaſioned by continual rains, rendered it impracticable; and the ſame reaſon made it impoſſible to uſe the bridge at Rees. It was therefore found neceſſary to march further down; and in the night between the 8th and 9th, a bridge was laid over the river at Griethuyſen. The french foreſeeing the duke's deſign, had prepared ſome boats, of a particular invention, to demoliſh it, which they ſent down the river from Weſel; but they were all deſtroyed by ſome armed barks, before they could put their deſign in execution. In ſhort, prince Ferdinand paſſed this famous river the 10th, without the leaſt oppoſition from the french; ſo admirably had he laid his plan.

The prince, as ſoon as he was on the other ſide of the Rhine, withdrew his garriſon from Duſſeldorp; of which place the french took immediate poſſeſſion. Marſhal Contades alſo paſſed the Rhine, at Weſel, the 12th and 13th. The prince took poſſeſſion of all the poſts on the Lippe, and was able to keep the french army from attempting to penetrate any further on that ſide. Contades was encamped for ſome time between Recklinghauſen and Dortmund; and the prince between Coesfeld and Dulmen. The other diviſion of the french forces, under the prince de Soubiſe, had made but little progreſs in Heſſe Caſſel, where the prince of Yſenburg ſtill kept him at bay; but, on the 10th and 11th of ſeptember Soubiſe took poſſeſſion of Gottingen, and advanced as far as Eimbeck, near which place, the prince of Yſenburg was encamped. This general's buſineſs was to protect the courſe of the Weſer, and to cover the electorate

rate of Hanover. It was here that the hanoverian posts were weakest. The french had no hopes of penetrating into Hanover by the Lippe, which prince Ferdinand guarded himself; but it appeared more practicable to drive the prince of Yfenburg from his posts. To accomplish this, marshal Contades sent a strong detachment to the prince de Soubife, which augmented his army to 30,000 men. Prince Ferdinand aware of the enemy's design, detached general Oberg, with a strong reinforcement to join prince Yfenburg; but notwithstanding this, the whole force of the allies in Hesse did not exceed 15,000 men. Soon after Oberg's arrival near Cassel, he encamped near Lanwerenhagen, behind Lutternberg; and finding that the french were preparing to attack him, he drew up his troops in order of battle; with his right to the Fulde, and his left to a thicket upon an eminence: In this situation he was attacked on the 30th of september, by the whole french army, and after a vigorous resistance was obliged to retire, with the loss of 1500 men to Munden; but in such good order that his defeat was far from being total.

Had any but the most skilful general commanded the allied army; this unfortunate affair would, in all probability, have been of fatal confequence: but prince Ferdinand, by having established the most ready communications all along the Lippe, deprived the french of an opportunity of making use of their advantage: He marched with the utmost expedition towards Rheda, and prince Yfenburg falling back, joined him with his troops, and by this junction covered the Weser, without losing any thing on the side of the Rhine. The prince well knew, that these movements rather uncovered the electorate of Hanover: but he also foresaw, that the french would not be able to make any establishment in it; they only infested the country with their light troops, who were

sent

sent by the marshal Contades*, to carry off and destroy all the provisions and forage in that country, as well as all Westphalia. This conduct of the french general was in consequence of a plan formed between him and the duke de Belleisle, to reduce all

* The marshal duke de Belleisle, secretary at war to the french king, in a letter to marshal Contades, of the 26th of september, writes,

" You must, at any rate, consume all sort of subsistance on the higher Lippe, in the neighbourhood of Paderborn, and in the country which lies between the Lippe, Paderborn, and Warsbourg; this will be so much subsistance taken from the enemy, from this day to the end of october. You must destroy every thing that you cannot consume, so as to make a desert of all Westphalia, from Lipstadt and Munster, as far as the Rhine, on one hand, and on the other, from the higher Lippe and Paderborn, as far as Cassel; that the enemy may find it quite impracticable to direct their march to the Rhine, or the lower Roer; and this with regard to your army; and with regard to the army under M. de Soubise, that they may not have it in their power to take possession of Cassel, and much less to march to Marpurg, or to the quarters which he will have along the Lohn, or to those which you will occupy, from the lower part of the left side of the Roer, and on the right side of the Rhine, as far as Dusseldorp, and at Cologne."

On the 30th of october, he again writes:
" ——— First, You are acquainted with all our political views. Secondly, You know the present situation of all our allies. Thirdly, you know the necessity of consuming, or destroying, as far as is possible, all the subsistence, especially the forage, betwixt the Weser and the Rhine, on the one hand; and on the other, betwixt the Lippe, the bishopric of Paderborn, the Dymel, the Fulda, and the Nerra; and so to make a desert of Westphalia and Hesse," that the enemy may not be able by any means, to march, with any considerable force, either towards the Rhine or the Lohn; and that our troops may pass the winter quietly in their quarters: for, as it is now unquestionable, that we cannot make any advances into Germany this year, our principal object must be to refresh our troops, as soon as possible, that we may be able to make war the following year with more vigor, and take the field very early: it will be no small matter, if we shall be able, with a great deal of pains, constant care, and œconomy, to find the means of supporting all our horse of every kind, until the month of june." For several other extracts from these notable letters, Vide the appendix.

Westphalia,

Westphalia, Hesse, and the neighbouring countries to a desert, in order to prevent prince Ferdinand from marching in the beginning of the next campaign to the Rhine, or the Lohn, and to keep their own quarters undisturbed in the winter. But this infamous scheme was in a great part defeated by the vigilance good conduct of that gallant young prince.

In this succesful manner ended the campaign on the Rhine. I have not interrupted my narrative of it, to make way for the other military transactions in Germany, in their chronological order, as that would have rendered it more obscure, the operations of which, I have given an account, being so blended together, that they could not with propriety be seperated. Seldom has the conduct of any general appeared more conspicuously great, in a defensive campaign, than that of prince Ferdinand in this. Those admirable movements, which enabled him to pass the Rhine without loss, in the face of a superior army; to gain a signal victory over it; to maintain his ground against it, when reinforced, and rendered still more superior; to repass the Rhine with the utmost safety; and lastly, to chuse his posts in so judicious a manner on the Lippe, as to prevent the enemy from penetrating further than that river, and this even after they had gained a victory over a large detachment of his army. In short, these several actions, with a thousand skilful manœuvres that must in consequence attend them, are together justly reckoned a perfect model of a defensive campaign.

# CHAP. XVII.

*King of Pruſſia marches againſt the ruſſians. Conduct of marſhal Daun. Battle of Zorndorff. King of Pruſſia marches into Saxony. Battle of Hochkirchen. Fine march of his pruſſian majeſty to relieve Sileſia. Raiſes the ſieges of Neiſs and Coſel. Motions of marſhal Daun. Croſſes the Elbe. Marches towards Dreſden. Inveſts that city. Leipſick and Torgau beſieged. Brave conduct of count Schmettau. Suburbs of Dreſden burnt. King of Pruſſia marches into Saxony. Raiſes the ſieges of Dreſden, Leipſick, and Torgau. Auſtrians and imperialiſts retire out of Saxony. Ruſſians and Swedes retire into winter quarters. Reflections. Affairs in England. Goree taken. Reflections on the events of the year 1758.*

THE affairs of the king of Pruſſia were now greatly changed. At the beginning of the campaign, he acted offenſively, in the utmoſt extent of the word; but now he found himſelf obliged to act on the defenſive: every moment was to him critical. The ruſſians, who had been for ſeveral months marching through Poland and Pruſſia, bent their courſe at laſt, as if they deſigned to enter Sileſia; but they ſuddenly turned towards Brandenburg, and laid ſiege to Cuſtrin, a little town on the Elbe, almoſt without fortifications; but which, an army of near 90,000 ruſſians were not able in ſome weeks to reduce. We may compare their operations at this ſiege, with thoſe under Peter the Great at Narva. The ruſſians at this day, are little better than barbarians, in point of military ſkill, except ſeveral general officers, many of them foreigners; but as men they are worſe.

Theſe

These wretches, whose actions are a disgrace to human nature, had marked their road through Prussia and Brandenburg, by the most horrible barbarities; to make up for their want of skill in sieges, they had brought all their formidable train of artillery to batter this little town. They threw such an immense quantity of bombs and red hot balls into it, that it was soon on fire in every quarter; they fell like hail in the streets, and the miserable inhabitants, every where meeting danger, but no where safety, left their ruinous habitations, and fled many of them naked out of the town, on that side which was not invested. But the brave governor, with the greatest courage and fidelity, defended the ruins of the place, with the utmost firmness. The prussian general, count Dohna was posted at Francfort; but all he could do, against a force so much superior to his own, was only to observe their motions.

Never were the affairs of his prussian majesty more critical. An army of 90,000 russians, was within three days march of Berlin: in Pomerania, the swedes were greatly superior to the generals Weedel and Manteufel, who commanded the prussian troops in that province: the army of the empire, which had been reinforced with a great body of the austrians, under general Haddick, had advanced into Saxony, and every day approached nearer to prince Henry; who was strongly intrenched at Dippolswalde, with 20,000 men to cover Dresden, and commanded the course of the Elbe. Marshal Daun, foreseeing many difficulties in pursuing the king of Prussia, resolved to march into Saxony, and in conjunction with the army of the empire, under the duke of Deux Ponts, and endeavour to drive prince Henry from his strong post, and get possession of Dresden; and by that means drive the king of Prussia entirely out of Saxony, which would be depriving him of the only resource for carrying on the war. These reasons determined him.

him. He left a large body of troops under the generals Harsch and de Ville, in the southern part of Silesia, to draw the attention of the prussians that way, and marched himself towards Saxony, through Lusatia, by Zittau, Gorlitz, and Bautzen; however, he was not able to make prince Henry change his advantageous position.

In the mean time, the prussian monarch being arrived at Frankfort, lost not a moment's time to march against the russians. On the 23d of august he passed the Oder, at Gatavise; and after their prodigious march, rested his army the 24th, and in the evening advanced to Dirmitzel, where he encamped, and made his dispositions for attacking the enemy the next day; early in the morning, he broke up his camp, and marched forward, in order to wind round the enemy's left flank; in its way, the army passed the small river Mitzel: afterwards it filed off by the forest of Massin, and the village of Bazels into the plain, where both infantry and cavalry spreading themselves on the left flank, till they arrived at Zorndorff; the king then thought that he was come on the back of the enemy, and gave orders for the attack.

The russian generals foreseeing his design, had broke up the siege of Custrin, and marched towards the villages of Zwicker and Zorndorff, where the ground not admitting them to extend in front, they had drawn up their army very judiciously in four lines, forming a front on every side, and surrounded by cannon and chevaux de frize: the village of Zwicker covered their right flanks, beyond which their cavalry reached. Prince Maurice of Anhalt Dessau commanded the first line of the prussians, under the king; lieutenant general Manteufel, the left wing of infantry; and general Seydlitz conducted the cavalry of that wing.

These

These were the positions of the two armies, when the king gave the word for the attack. The russians were an enemy he had never personally engaged before; but his troops saw every where such horrid marks of their cruelty, as spurred them on with the most animated ardor to engage, and be revenged on those barbarians. Every thing that was dear to the king of Prussia depended on this day; if he lost it, the consequences must be fatal, considering the vast superiority of his enemies in Saxony. In short, all his dominions were at stake.

The battle began on the 25th of august, at nine o'clock in the morning. The prussian infantry began to attack the village under cover of an uninterrupted and terrible fire of cannon and mortars, which rained on the right wing of the russians for two hours without the least intermission. Never was there a more dreadful cannonade; the russian foot, which although raw and unexperienced, sustaned a most shocking slaughter; whole ranks fell, and their places were instantly supplied by new regiments. Their first line continued immoveable, till they had fired away all their charges, and then rushed forward on the prussian infantry; which suddenly, and with an unaccountable pannic gave way, in the presence of their sovereign, before the broken battalions of the Muscovites, and after their own cannonade had in a manner already gained the victory. This was now the critical moment, on which every thing depended; the battle was in suspence, and the prussian infantry retreating. The event of that great day depended on an instant; it was neglected by the russian general; but the king of Prussia improved it: Had general Fermor directly brought on his horse, to disperse the retiring battalions of his enemy, this day had been fatal to the prussian greatness; but the king, by a masterly and rapid motion, brought all the cavalry of his right wing to the center, which, with general Seydlitz at
their

their head, made a most furious attack upon the Muscovite foot, uncovered by their horse, and drove them back with a most miserable slaughter: this gave the repulsed infantry time to recollect and form themselves; returning to the charge with a rage, exasperated by their late disgrace, they very soon changed the fortune of the day. The russians being thrown into the most terrible confusion, plundered their own baggage, which was between the lines, and intoxicated themselves with brandy, they no longer distinguished friends from foes, but fired upon each other; and being crammed together in a narrow space, a horrible and undistinguishing carnage ensued, as well by sword and bayonet, as by the prussian artillery, charged with cartridge shot, which fired continually on them, at not 20 yards distance. Still they obstinately persisted in not quitting the ground; but one of their generals towards the evening, with a chosen corps made a judicious attack on the right wing of the prussians; that officer lost most of his men, but by drawing the king's attention that way, the broken remains of their infantry had leisure to withdraw to a new post in the night for rallying the rest of their army.

The loss of the prussians did not exceed 2000 men, killed, wounded, and prisoners; but that of the russians amounted to 10,000 dead on the spot; 10,000 wounded, most of them mortally; and about 2000 prisoners: of two particular regiments, which before the battle consisted of 4600 men, only 1500 were left. Their loss in this dreadful day, amounted in the whole to upwards of 22,000 men.

The next day, the king of prussia renewed the attack, by a very brisk cannonade; but the russians finding no safety in any thing but a retreat, marched to Landsperg on the frontiers of Poland. Never was victory more complete. An immense train of artillery, 37 colours, five standards, and several kettle-drums,

drums, and their military cheft, containing 200,000 l. fterl. were taken. Yet, the auftrians warmly afferted, that the ruffians gained the victory; but nothing fpoke fo plainly on whofe fide it fell, as its confequences; the king cleared that part of his dominions from his enemies, and was enabled to march to the affiftance of the other; general Fermor's afking leave * to bury

his

\* As foon as the battle was over, general Fermor wrote the following letter to count Dohna.

"As this day's battle hath left many dead to be buried, and many wounded men to be dreffed on both fides, I have thought proper to afk your excellency, whether it would not be fit to conclude a fufpenfion of arms for two or three days? General Brown, who is extremely weak by reafon of his wounds, having need of a room and other conveniences, which are neceffary in his prefent fituation, moft humbly entreats his majefty to fend a paffport for him and his attendants, that he may remove to a proper place. I have the honour to be, &c.

Camp, aug. 14,                      Count FERMOR."
(25 N. S. 1758.)

Count DOHNA's anfwer.

"I have the honour to anfwer the letter which your excellency was pleafed to write to me yefterday; and in confequence of it to inform you, that the king, my mafter, having gained the battle, and remained mafter of the field, his majefty will not fail to give the neceffary orders for burying the dead, and taking care of the wounded on both fides. His majefty thinks that a fufpenfion of arms is ufual in the cafe of a fiege, but not after a battle. His excellency general Brown, if ftill alive, fhall have the paffports he afks moft readily; and all poffible relief fhall be given to the other generals who are prifoners.

The cruel burning of all the villages, which is not yet difcontinued, fhews an intention not to fpare the king's eftates in any fhape: but I fhall not now enter into repetitions, on a fubject I have fo often mentioned. I fhall only defire your excellency to confider, what confequences fuch cruelties may have, if a ftop be not put to them. I have the honour to be, &c.

Camp, aug. 26,                      Count DOHNA."
1758.

Concerning what's mentioned in this letter of the cruelties of the ruffians, the following extract from the Berlin Gazette will fet it in a true light.

" The

his dead; the number of prisoners of rank that were taken; all concur, in sufficiently speaking who was victor in this bloody engagement. Among the prisoners of rank, were the generals de Soltikoff, de Chermicheaux, Manteuffel, Tieremhaufen, Chievres, &c.

In the mean time, marshal Daun, to put his design in execution of doing his utmost to drive prince Henry from his advantageous post at Dippoldswalde, encamped his army at Stolpen, to the eastward of the Elbe; he chose this position to cut off all communication between Bautzen and Dresden; it also favoured

" The Konigsberg gazette denies the cruelties with which the russians are charged, and pretends to justify those which are too notorious not to be acknowledged, by saying, that the prussians themselves have set fire to the villages to cover their march. But a reason of war ought to be distinguished from an unnecessary cruelty. The former obliged the prussians to burn the single village of Schaumbourg; but what colour can the russians give to their burning the villages of Zorndorff, Zicher, Wilkersdorff, Blumberg, Kutzdorff, Quartschen and Birckenbusch, all which were in flames at the same time, and of which, the greatest part of the inhabitants were some killed, and others thrown into the flames. The public hath already been informed, of the cruelties committed last June, by general Demikow, in Pomerania, and the New Marche. Above an hundred towns or villages were pillaged, and many women carried off and ravished. The russians also set fire to the village of Furstgnau, and killed the farmer's wife: Vorbruch, and the suburbs of Driesen, were likewise reduced to ashes. In the beginning of July, they pillaged the town of Friedeburgh, burnt the mill of Altenflies, and wounded the gardener of the bailiwic of Driesen. On the approach of the prussians, they turned the environs of Custrin into a desert, burnt the seven villages abovementioned, killed the farmer of Tamsel, and at Blumberg and Camin massacred many peasants, and even infants with their mothers, whose mutilated bodies were found in the houses and barns. The churches have not been spared; they opened even graves and vaults, to strip the dead; which they did particularly at Camin and Birckholtz, where they stripped the bodies of general Schlaberndorf, and general Ruitz, who were buried there. It will not be thought strange, that the name of barbarians should be given to persons capable of such cruelties."

the

the operations of the army under general Laudohn on the confines of Brandenburgh; and of generals Harſch and de Ville, in the ſouthern parts of Sileſia; as he drew the attention of the pruſſian forces to the northern parts of that duchy.

To defeat all theſe excellent ſchemes, his pruſſian majeſty had no ſooner fought the battle of Zorndorf, than he began a rapid march to ſuccour prince Henry: never did general make ſuch long and flying marches in ſo ſmall a ſpace of time; the king moved with ſo much celerity, that he reached Groſſen-hayn on the 9th of ſeptember, and Dreſden the 11th. As his majeſty advanced, the auſtrians withdrew from the frontiers of Brandenburgh, and even of Luſatia; and general Laudohn, who had employed himſelf in pillaging the circle of Cotbus, with the utmoſt licentiouſneſs, precipitately abandoned all the lower Luſatia, and even the fortreſs of Peitz. Marſhal Daun himſelf retired from the neighbourhood of Dreſden, and fell back as far as Littau. Indeed the duke of Deux Ponts, who commanded the army of the empire, poſſeſſed the ſtrong poſt of Pirna, and kept his ground; on the 5th of ſeptember, the ſtrong fortreſs of Sonnenſtein ſurrendered to him moſt unaccountably, after a cannonade of only one day; but this army undertook nothing further againſt the king.

As ſoon as that monarch was abſent, with the greateſt part of his army, the ruſſian general made a halt at Lanſberg, where he entrenched his army, in an inacceſſible camp. Count Dohna commanded the pruſſian troops, which the king left to act againſt the ruſſians; his head quarters were fixed at Blumberg, two leagues beyond Cuſtrin. But on the 21ſt of ſeptember, general Fermor quitted this advantageous camp, and marching by Soldin and Peritz, arrived on the 26th at Stargard in Pomerania, leaving wherever it paſſed, the uſual and diſmal marks of its preſence. Dohna followed them directly; he advanced

vanced by Necidamin, and arrived the 29th at Soldin. General Fermor left a garrison in Landsberg, but it evacuated the town on the approach of a detachment from the prussian army.

The swedes no sooner found that the king of Prussia was marching to defend Saxony against the austrians, and the army of the empire, than they thought it a proper opportunity to push the war with vigor. They began to advance very briskly, into the prussian territories. Count Hamilton who commanded their army, took up his head quarters at Fehrbellin, so that some of their advanced parties came within 25 miles of Berlin. But the king, being informed of their motions, immediately detached general Wedel, with a body of troops from Dresden, which, when augmented by some troops that joined him on the road, amounted to 11,000 men; he arrived at Berlin the 20th of september, and in two days left that city, to march against the enemy. Upon the approach of these troops, the swedish army retreated; without defending any place; they left in Fehrbellin, a garrison of 1400 men, who were driven out after some resistance, the 28th. The prince of Bevern (who had been exchanged for an austrian general taken by his prussian majesty) governor of Stetin, defended that town against them; and general Wedel continued to advance against them.

The prussian monarch himself, in the mean time, was prosecuting the war, in person, with his usual activity. Marshal Daun continued in his camp at Stolpen, from whence he had a communication with the army of the empire; the great design of this general, was to prevent the king from succouring Silesia, where the austrian generals were making great progress, and had formed the siege of Neiss. The king marched his army from the neighbourhood of Dresden, to Bautzen, a post equally advantageous for preserving a communication with
prince

prince Henry's army, for covering Brandenburg, and for throwing fuccours into Silefia. Marfhal Daun moved to the right, and encamped among the mountains of Wilten; and foon after occupied the camp of Ritlitz. The king's army marched to Hochkirchen, from whence he diflodged the auftrians, and pofted himfelf upon the eminences, which lie between Hochkirchen and Gorlitz. And during all thefe different motions, the two armies kept the moft watchful eye on each other. It was by this time found, that nothing but a decifive engagement would anfwer marfhal Daun's projects; he foon perceived, that if the king kept poffeflion of his prefent advantageous fituation, he fhould be obliged to retreat into Bohemia.

The neceffity of a battle was fo urgent, that Daun refolved to attack his pruffian majefty. He communicated his defign to the prince Deux Ponts, and having fettled meafures with him, marched in the dead of a very dark night, in three columns, towards the right of the king of Pruffia's camp. Nothing could be better contrived than this enterprize, of marfhal Daun; and it was executed with equal vigor and prudence. So wifely, that, notwithftanding the great numbers of the auftrians, the badnefs of the roads, thro' which they marched; and the darknefs of the night; yet the three columns at the fame time arrived at the pruffian camp, without being difcovered, and without confufion.

At five o'clock in the morning, of october the 4th, they began the attack, with the utmoft ardour and refolution. The pruffians had not time to ftrike their tents, before the enemy was in the midft of their camp, and had began a furious attack. The furprifed troops ran half naked to their arms; and in the beginning of the engagement, marfhal Keith was killed by two mufket balls; and prince Francis of Brunfwick had his head fhot off by a cannon ball, as

he

he was mounting his horse. The loss of two such able officers was irreparable to the king of Prussia, who now had every thing on his own hands, at the moment when he most wanted assistance. But even in the dreadful confusion which must unavoidably have ensued in his army on such an occasion, his great presence of mind, his activity, and valour, annimated his troops. Every where present, and in the hottest of the fire, he, in some measure remedied the unfortunate blow he was likely to receive. Finding himself very hard pressed, he ordered a large detachment from his left to reinforce his right wing; but at that instant, general Retzow, who commanded the left, was himself vigorously attacked by the austrians: so that little or no assistance could be afforded to the king, who was obliged to bear the brunt with his right alone, of the grand attack of the austrians where mashal Daun himself was present.

That general had entrusted the attack of the village of Hochkerchen, and its eminences, to general Laudohn, who attacked them with he greatest fury. As it was a post of such importance, that the fate of the day depended on it; the dispute was hottest there. Laudohn succeeded; but he, no sooner was in possession of it, than he was attacked with the utmost fury by the prussians; he repulsed them; a second attack was made with equal bravery; and a third, but both were also unsuccessful; the fourth attack, after a most bloody dispute they carried it; but marshal Daun determined to make every possible effort, by continually pouring fresh troops on that post, drove the prussians out of it, after reiterated attacks, and a prodigious slaughter. His majesty then despairing of the victory, ordered a retreat, which, to the astonishment of all, who knew not the excellency of the prussian discipline, was performed in good order, under the cover of a great fire of artillery placed, in the center of his camp. They lost about 7000
men

men in this bloody battle, killed, wounded and prisoners. The austrians, by their own confession, 5000; who took a great number of cannon, some colours, and a large quantity of baggage.

It was very justly a matter of wonder, that his prussian majesty, who had such a number of excellent generals under him, should be surprised in such a fatal manner; and that his out guards should not have discovered the enemy time enough to have prevented the dismal consequences that followed. As fatal as the first part of the day proved, it ought in the eye of the world, to be retrieved from dishonour, by the excellent retreat, which the prussian army made. History, I believe, can produce but few instances of an inferior army being surprised in their sleep; running half naked to their arms; recovering their order; fighting desperately for five hours; and at last making such an orderly retreat, without their enemies daring to pursue them. Nor did the greatness of the king's generalship ever appear more conspicuous; and he never found such great want of it as in this action; to have a wing of his army at a distance from his own quarters, attacked; the two commanders of it slain, in the first onset; the principal generals of it wounded; and the whole wing on the point of flight: to come himself in this critical moment, from the other wing, to restore his confused troops to order; twice to repulse the enemy; four times to attack them; and at last to make so orderly a retreat, overborn only by numbers and fatigue: these, I say, are actions which discover such a greatness of genius, such an admirable presence of mind; as was hardly ever equalled by any general.

His prussian majesty, after the action, fell back with his right wing to Weissenbourg; his left still continued at Bautzen; and the head quarters were at Doberschutz. He had been in this position but a short time, before he perceived, that marshal Daun's view, was to prevent his marching into Silesia; and that, that general had laid aside his designs on Saxony; this determined him to send for a large detachment from prince Henry's army; (which the prince brought up himself) and to march into Silesia, to raise the siege of Neifs, which the generals Harsch and de Ville were prosecuting with the utmost vigor.

His majesty found many difficulties in putting this scheme in execution. Marshal Daun lay with a superior army just in his road, whose only business was to obstruct his march. Saxony, would be left uncovered, and prince Henry, whose army was reduced by the late detachments, could make but ineffectual efforts against the united arms of the austrians and imperialists, if marshal Daun should turn his arms that way. On the contrary, if the king was to remain in his present situation, and neglect to rescue Silesia, that province would be greatly over-run by the austrians, whereby his affairs would suffer equally, with uncovering Saxony. It is for great genius's only not to be disconcerted by such dilemma's as these; instead of rendering him inactive, the king of Prussia's served only to quicken the speed of his resolution, and the vigor with which he executed it. He determined to march into Silesia.

On the 24th of october, he broke up his camp, at Doberschutz; and fetching a great compass, arrived on the 26th in the plain of Gorlitz: marshal Daun had endeavoured to seize this post before the king; but could get no further than Landscron; their granadiers and carabineers, drew up opposite to the prussian van-guard, but were defeated with the loss of 800 men. By this admirable march, Daun at once lost all the advantages which he had before gained, from the victory at Hochkirchen, and from his advantageous

vantageous posts; an open road lay before the king into Silesia, and all he could now do was to harrass his rear. His majesty pursued his march with the greatest rapidity; general Laudohn, with 24,000 men followed him with little success.

On the 28th, his majesty marched to Lauban; and in two days after entered Silesia. The 6th of november he arrived at Nossen. The siege of Neiss was carrying on with the utmost vigor; and defended with the greatest bravery; it commenced the 4th of august, and was completely invested the 3d of october. The prussian army arrived in sight of Neiss the 7th of november, general Harsh having raised the siege, and repassed the Neiss, leaving a considerable quantity of ammunition and stores behind him; general Treskow, the brave governor, sallied out upon them, and cut in pieces a body of 7 or 800 pandours. The king's presence every where relieved the whole province; a large body of austrians, who had been some time employed in the blockade of Cosel, raised it on the 9th; the austrian general fell back on the army of general Harsch, and the united corps retreated into Bohemia and austrian Silesia, with great precipitation.

Never did any general plan his schemes and execute them with greater resolution, vigor, and celerity, than his prussian majesty; this rapid march from Saxony, by which he entirely drove the austrians out of Silesia, is a remarkable instance; the prussian soldiers, with reason, expected that this would be their last operation for that campaign; but their sovereign was of a different opinion; Saxony was in danger, and it must be rescued.

Marshal Daun, soon after he had gained the advantage at Hochkirchen, determined that his greatest efforts during the remainder of the campaign, should be on the side of Silesia; and consequently his first point was, to prevent the king from marching into it: but as his majesty had entirely defeated his whole project,

project, by this rapid, march, he thought it proper to change his plan of operations, and take advantage of the king's abfence to fall on Saxony. His defign was to make himfelf mafter of the three cities of Drefden, Leipfick, and Torgau: for this purpofe he followed the king no further than Gorlitz; and when he had detached general Laudohn to harrafs his rear, he marched himfelf with all expedition towards Drefden, having paffed the Elbe at Pirna, the 6th of november. Prince Henry's army, weakened confiderably, by the large detachments which he had carried to the grand army, after the battle of Hochkirchen, was obliged to retire from its advantageous poft before Drefden, to the weftward of that city; Daun endeavoured to cut off his communication with it; but the prince threw himfelf into Drefden, and retired on the other fide the Elbe. The duke of Deux Ponts then marched, and invefted Leipfick; whilft marfhal Daun did the fame to Drefden, with 60,000 men. That city was but meanly fortified, of very great extent, and defended only by 12,000 men, which was a very poor garrifon for fo large a place, commanded by the count de Schmettau. The auftrian general appeared in fight of the city, the 6th of november; by a motion on the 7th, the governor was convinced that his defign was againft the capital.

The fuburbs of Drefden were fo extremely weak, that Schmettau found it would be impoffible for him to prevent the enemy's poffeffing himfelf of them by a coup de main. An enterprize of this nature, would have been the more eafy, as moft of the houfes of the fuburbs, from the gate of Pirna to that of Wilfdruff, abfolutely commanded the body of the town, both by their prodigious height, being fix or feven ftories high, and by their proximity to the ramparts. This laid count Schmettau under the difagreeable neceffity of burning them, for that end he filled the higheft houfes with combuftibles, and alfo thofe next to the ramparts, that his orders might be the more
speedily

speedily executed, whenever the reasons of war obliged him to issue them in his own defence: the governor made a declaration to this effect, to M. de Bose, chief cup bearer to the court of Dresden, adding, that as soon as the enemy should make a show of attacking the city, he should be obliged to set fire to the suburbs.

The suburbs of Dresden compose one of the finest cities in Europe, much superior to the part within the walls; where the most considerable of the inhabitants reside, and is also the seat of those curious manufactures, for which that city is so famous. Marshal Daun well knowing the necessity the governor would find himself under, endeavoured to intimidate him from this measure, by threatening to make him personally answerable for the steps he should take. Schmettau, with all the firmness of the bravest soldier, replied, that he would answer whatsoever he should do, and would not only burn the suburbs, in case marshal Daun advanced, but would likewise defend the city itself street by street, and at last even the castle, which was the royal residence, if he should be driven to it. The magistrates of the city no sooner were acquainted with this resolution, but they fell at the feet of count Schmettau, imploring him to change his mind; the part of the royal family that remained in Dresden, joined in these supplications, praying him to spare that last refuge of distressed royalty, and at least to allow a secure residence to those who had been deprived of every thing else. But the governor continued firm in his resolution; he answered, that their safety depended on marshal Daun, that if he attacked them, the necessity of war would oblige him to act quite contrary to the lenity of his disposition.

Schmettau had thrown up some small redoubts to cover the suburbs; these the austrians soon forced, and penetrated a good way into them; during which attack, their artillery played into the town. General Meyer, who was posted in the suburbs, gave notice to the governor the next day, that the auſtrians were erecting batteries, and making other preparations to attack the city. Whereupon, it was abſolutely neceſſary no longer to delay deſtroying the ſuburbs.

At three o'clock in the morning, of the 10th of november, general Meyer gave the ſignal, and, immediately, a place, ſo lately the ſeat of pleaſure, arts, and trade, was all in flames. Dreadful as this conflagration was, yet the good order of the pruſſian troops, and the care of the governor, prevented it from being more ſhocking than was neceſſary; very few loſt their lives. General Meyer retired into the city; and the gates were directly barricaded *.

The Saxon and auſtrian miniſters † made the moſt aggravated complaints all Europe over, of the barbarities

---

\* Vide Schmettau's memorial concerning the burning the ſuburbs of Dreſden.

† Vide M. Ponickau the Saxon reſident's memorial to the diet of the empire.

" By the violence of the flames, which was kept up by red hot balls, fired into the houſes and along the ſtreets, the whole was inſtantly on fire."—" A ſhoe-maker, who was running away with his infant on a pillow, to ſave it from being burnt to death, was met by a volunteer, who ſnatched the pillow away from him, and threw the babe into the flames."—" One man had got his things into a waggon; the pruſſians ſtopt it, covered it over with pitch, and ſet it on fire."—" By this means a multitude of people of all ages, who inhabited thoſe populous ſuburbs, periſhed amidſt the flames. The number of thoſe who were killed in the ſingle inn, called the Golden Hart, amounted to 90."—" The auſtrian army beheld theſe horrible acts, filled with indignation and rage. Its generals melting with compaſſion, tried every method to remedy them. They ſent 300 carpenters into the ſuburbs, to endeavour to extinguiſh the flames." All theſe falſities are abundantly confuted in the following authentic papers.

Letter from M. de Boſe, chief cup-bearer to the court of Dreſden, to count Schmettau.

I have the honour to acquaint your excellency, in anſwer to what you wrote me this day, I muſt own, that ever ſince you had the government of Dreſden, I informed you of all that his royal highneſs

barities exercised by the prussians in this affair. Never were there such infamous falsities trumped up, as they

ness charged me to tell you in his name, and I have likewise reported to his highness, your excellency's answers.

As to the first point, I also remember very well, that your excellency charged me, in the month of july, to represent to his royal highness, that if marshal Daun should attack the city, you must set fire to the suburbs, particularly the houses that adjoined to the ditch; into which houses, your excellency immediately ordered combustibles to be put. I also remember, that upon the follicitations, which his royal highness made, by me, to your excellency, you ordered them to be removed when marshal Daun retired; and of this I also made an humble report.

It is also true, that when marshal Daun was at Lockowitz, on the 18th of november last, your excellency charged me to acquaint his royal highness, in your name, that, if marshal Daun should approach near the town, and attack it, you should be obliged to burn the suburbs, and the houses adjoining the town ditch. Although I made several remonstrances to your excellency from the court, you declared, that you was ordered by the king your master, to defend yourself to the last extremity, and that you could not change your measures, unless marshal Daun should be prevailed with not to attack the town. To which I answered, in his royal highness's name, that he knew nothing of marshal Daun's designs; that he could not intermeddle in the operations of war, and would consequently be obliged to endure what he could not hinder.

Lastly, it is well known, that your excellency, during the fire, took every possible measure in the town, to prevent these excesses and disorders, which might have been apprehended; and his royal highness charged me to return you his thanks for it. I have the honour to be, &c.

Dec. 4, 1758. JOACHIM FREDERICK de BOSE.

Certificate of the magistrates of Dresden.

In consequence of orders received from his excellency count Schmettau, lieutenant general and governor, we certify what we know concerning the burning of the suburbs. Two persons were burnt to death, two killed, three hurt, by the fire, and two wounded by the soldiers.

We never heard, in any shape, of a waggon full. of goods, which they were endeavouring to save, and which it was pretended was covered with combustibles, and so set on fire; nor of ninety persons said to have perished at the Hart, nor of the austrian troops, who, they spread about in their memorials. They made no scruple to invent and alter facts in such a manner, as to move the greatest pity towards the sufferers, and equal indignation against his prussian majesty. But all these vile falsities were fully removed, by the authentic certificates of the magistrates, &c. of Dresden, who were perfectly acquainted with the transaction; and all the heap of inventions that had been palmed upon all Europe for truths, were instantly overthrown.

who, it is pretended, assisted in extinguishing the flames. Dresden, dec 4, 1758.

(L. S.) The magistrates of Dresden.

Certificate of the judges of the suburb of Dresden.

We the judges of the suburb of Dresden, certify, and attest, that at the time of the calamity that hath just happened, things passed in this manner. The combustibles were replaced on the 7th of november; and the magistrates ordered all the judges to attend them: accordingly, Simon Stelzner, judge; John Christian, alderman; John Michael Faber, and John Christian Kretschmar, judges, attended, and were told, (being enjoined at the same time, to ac-acquaint the other judges with it) to provide the houses with water, to give notice to the landlords, and keep the pumps ready, and endeavour to assist one another; because, if any misfortune should happen, the people of the town could not come to our assistance, nor could we go to theirs: and of this, we informed all the burghers.

On the 8th and 9th the austrian army approached the town; and on the 9th, the austrian hussars forced their way to the suburb of Pirna, and to Zinzendorf house.

On the 10th, at two in the morning, fire was set to the quarters of Pirna, Ram, and Wilsdorf, which consumed 266 houses in all.

There have been therefore in all, two persons burnt, a man and a woman greatly advanced in years, and whom it was impossible to save; two killed, and two wounded.

What has been said of a waggon is false; and it is equally false that ninety persons perished at the Hart; only four persons in all having lost their lives, as we have just mentioned. Lastly, it is false, that the austrian carpenters assisted us in extinguishing the fire. We never saw one of them.

We certify, that all the above is strictly conformable to truth.

Dec. 4, 1758.    Signed by the ten judges of Dresden.

Marshal

Marshal Daun now found that it was impossible to take Dresden by a coup de main; and besides the king of Prussia was marching back from Silesia, with great speed to succour it, he continued the siege slowly for about a week; but as regular operations took up too much time, he raised it the 17th.

I before mentioned, that his plan was to attack Leipsick and Torgau at the same time that he himself besieged Dresden. The duke of Deux Ponts commanded before Leipsick; and general Haddick, with 10,000 men before Torgau. No sooner had the king of Prussia notice of the scheme, which marshal Daun had formed, to possess himself of those cities, than he ordered count Dohna, who commanded against the russians, to march with 12,000 men, to the relief of Torgau; general Wedel, who, with a small army observed the motions of the swedes, received the same orders. The latter general threw himself into Torgau, before Haddick arrived there, and when he made his attack, he repulsed him with loss; and count Dohna being come up soon after, the two generals having joined their forces, pursued the austrians to Eulenburg. The enemy, terrified at the approach of the prussian armies, also raised the siege of Leipsick.

In the mean time, his prussian majesty was marching with the greatest speed from Silesia; so, that by the 15th of november, he arrived at Lauban; and having afterwards joined his army to the corps under the generals Dohna and Wedel, he arrived triumphantly at Dresden, the 20th. The austrian armies, commanded by marshal Daun, and that of the empire, fell back on the king's near approach, into Bohemia, without attempting any thing further. The marshal placed his troops into quarters of cantonment, in such situations as to form an immense chain of troops all along the frontiers of Silesia, and Saxony; where the imperial army joined, and continued it

through

through Thuringia and Franconia, where it was united to the quarters of the prince de Soubize, extending weftward, along the courfe of the Main and Lahn, to meet thofe of marfhal de Contades, which ftretched to the Rhine, and continued the chain along it quite to the Maefe, fo as to command the whole courfe of of the Rhine, on both fides, both upward and downward.

I left the ruffian army retreating after the battle of Zorndorf, to Stargard in Pomerania. General Fermer forefaw that he fhould be unable to keep his ground in that province during the winter, unlefs he could fecure fome fea port, by which means he might receive the neceffary reinforcements from Ruffia by fea. In purfuance to this plan, he refolved to attack the little town of Colberg on the Baltick; expecting it would be an eafy conqueft, as it was but meanly fortified. On the 3d of october, 15,000 ruffians formed the fiege; but what with their incapacity in that part of the art of war, and the brave defence made by major Heydon, the governor, this little town, fo poorly fortified, and fo weakly garrifoned, held out againft them 26 days, and then obliged them to raife the fiege, the 29th of october: and this without receiving any fuccours whatfoever from without. The ruffians, without enterprifing any thing elfe, retired in fo difgraceful a manner out of Pomerania, without having been able to mafter one place of ftrength, in either Brandenburg or Pomerania. But they deftroyed all the country as they paffed, with the moft favage fiercenefs. Nor were the ruffians the only enemy which carried on an inglorious war againft his pruffian majefty; the fwedes were driven back into their own territories, with great lofs; and feveral of their important pofts taken, before they went into quarters of cantonment. About the time that the auftrians retired into winter quarters, the french did the fame, without any moleftation from prince Ferdinand;

nand; his army was too weak for offensive operations, and the season too far advanced: so that the british troops were not employed in this campaign; but they lost their leader, the duke of Marlborough, who died of a fever at Munster, the 20th of october, contracted by the fatigues of the campaign. The prince disposed his troops in the most advantageous manner, in the bishoprics of Munster, Paderborn, and Hildesheim, and in the landgraviate of Hesse.

Before I dismiss the affairs of his prussian majesty, for this campaign, I must take notice of the change which that monarch made in his conduct, towards the unfortunate electorate of Saxony. When first he entered that country, at the beginning of the war, he declared, that he had no design to make a conquest of it, but only to hold it as a deposit in his hands for the security of his own dominions, until he could compel his enemies to agree to reasonable terms of peace; but upon his return to Dresden, after having forced marshal Daun once more to quit Saxony, he altered his resolution: he ordered his directory at war to send a decree to the deputies of the estates of the electorate, which, at the same time that it enjoined them to deliver a certain quantity of flower and forage, signified in express terms; " That though the king of Prussia had hitherto treated the electorate of Saxony as a country he had taken under his special protection; the face of affairs was now changed in such a manner, that his majesty would consider it for the future, only as a conquered country, out of which he had driven his enemies, by force of arms." This declaration was no sooner published, than the revenues of all the saxon ministers of consequence were sequestered; and as the russians had seized in Prussia, all the rents of the estates in that country, belonging to prussian officers, the same was done by the king in Saxony, in regard to the estates of saxon officers in the russian service. His majesty also ordered

ordered seals to be put on the papers of 20 persons of consequence belonging to the court of Dresden, who were, at the same time enjoined to set out for Warsaw, in 24 hours; in short, the administration of the government was thrown entirely into the hands of prussians. It has been very justly remarked on this; that as soon as the king of Prussia had declared, that he considered Saxony as a conquered country, the people had from that time a right to expect to be governed in such a manner as became a just prince; more especially when the conqueror's affairs are not in such a dangerous situation, as to require a very rigorous behaviour. When we consider the use which this monarch made of his conquest; we are no longer dazzled by the heroic qualities of his mind. He continued to exact the most severe contributions of the inhabitants; and in a manner very little becoming a lawful sovereign. He not only surrounded the exchange with soldiers, but confined the merchants to narrow lodgings, on straw beds, and by the extremity of their sufferings obliged them to draw bills on their foreign correspondents for very large sums. Dresden had been quite exhausted by former contributions, and had even suffered military execution long before: so that but little excuse can be made for these unjust and violent proceedings. What could be more unreasonable, more odious, or more cruel, than to retaliate on the unhappy saxons, some part of the excesses committed by the russians on his dominions. Such a proceeding is not consistent with that greatness of soul which one would think should attend such vast abilities, as are possessed by his prussian majesty. But let us review his actions this campaign, we shall there see his brightest side.

In the last campaign, he gained the most resplendent victories; but in this he formed and executed the most useful designs. The retreating out of Moravia in the face of a superior army, in that masterly manner,

ner, in which it was executed; his rapid march to drive the ruffians from his dominions; his gaining the battle of Zorndorf, merely by his own prefence of mind; his marching from thence to relieve Saxony, when in the mean time, the auftrians over-run Silefia; defeated at Hochkirchen, and yet acting as if he had been victorious; marfhal Daun's whole plan being to prevent his entering Silefia; he takes a great compafs round all his forces, and marching unpurfued, in the fwifteft manner, raifes the fiege of Neifs, and clears all Silefia of his enemies; from one corner of his dominions, he flies to the other; Saxony is again in danger; above an hundred thoufand of his enemies befieging three great cities in it; they no fooner invade, than he refolves to refcue; from the extremity of Silefia, he makes forced marches into Saxony, raifes the fieges of its capital, Leipfick and Torgau, drives the two armies of the auftrians and the empire entirely out of the electorate, and arrives triumphantly at Drefden; four armies, containing above two hundred and fifty thoufand men, endeavour to overwhelm his dominions, they are defeated, and drove back with difgrace; his territories are cleared, and he keeps poffeffion of Saxony itfelf. In fhort, whether we confider the rapid and vigorous marches, the artful movements, and judicious choice of pofts, in particular, or the great management, the deep laid fchemes, or the ftudied and refined conduct in general; we muft certainly allow this campaign to difplay on the part of that monarch, very great abilities, and generalfhip; greater than ever he had fhewn before.

The fingular fituation of England guarded it from thofe terrible ravages of war, which laid wafte the reft of Europe, confequently we can find but little for the fubject of a military hiftory there. Several fquadrons had been equipped, and failed in the winter, but their operations were too minute to be comprehended in the narrow plan of this work. In parliament

liament, every thing went smoothly; the voice of the minister was that of the nation; the house of commons had granted his majesty, for the war and other uses, upwards of eleven millions sterling, in the course of the year *. Nothing could have enabled the kingdom to raise such immense sums, but the flourishing and extensive commerce it enjoyed. This received a great addition by the success which commodore Keppel's squadron met with on the coast of Africa.

Mr. Keppel, having been sent out from England, with a small squadron of ships, to attack Goree, came in sight of that place the 28th of December. The Dunkirk, the Nassau, the Torbay, and the Fougeaux anchored against several batteries, on the island of Goree, and at the same time covered two bomb-ketches by their fire. The action began with a smart cannonade from the island on the ships, as they bore down, which was not returned, till they came extremely near, and then began a most dreadful fire, which in a few hours silenced the french batteries; and made such a terrible havock among their garrison, that M. de St. Jean surrendered the fortress and island, with his garrison, prisoners of war; in it was found 110 pieces of cannon and mortars.

The island of Goree consists of a low narrow piece of land, near cape Verd in Africa, West long. 17. 40. lat. 15, in the river Senegal, about half a mile long, but very narrow. Though it is in the torrid zone, yet it enjoys a cool and temperate air almost the year round; which is owing to the equality of the days and nights; and its being continually refreshed by alternate breezes from the land and sea. M. de St. Jean had embellished it with several fine buildings; and added some fortifications to it.

The conquest of these settlements on the coast of Africa, were of infinite importance to the british nation, and of near as much advantage to its commerce, as any

* Vide appendix.

any of the numerous acquisitions we have made this war. France, by means of them, brought her sugar islands to that high pitch, which they arrived at before the war. The sugar trade, and that to the coast of Africa, are so blended together, that the former cannot subsist without the latter, on account of the negroes brought from thence; the french, by means of their settlements of Senegal and Goree, raised the price of negroes upon the english, on many parts of the coast, from 6 and 7 l. per head to 20 and 30 l. And, although this great rise in their price affected the english West-indian trade so very sensibly, yet their own suffered not the least by it, by reason of their extraordinary bounties, privileges and immunities, which the french government allows for the encouragement of their african commerce. The gum Senegal is another article of great consequence, which falls into the hands of the english, by this important conquest. The african gum is exceeding useful, in several french manufactures; such as their silks, and other fabricks, which require a glossy lustre to recommend them to foreign nations; and this gum is no less useful in several english manufactures. So advantageous is it, that Mr. Postlethwait* informs us, that we have a recent instance of two merchants in the city of London, who gained above 10,000 l. by a loading of gum from Senegal, which they obtained in the year 1757, on this coast; the first cost of which cargo, on the outset, did not amount to 1000 l. There are also several other very material articles of trade, which must be chiefly in the hands of the possessors of these important settlements. Gold dust, ivory, &c. are very beneficial trades; but the vast advantage of the negroe trade is unbounded; the whole West-indies must depend greatly on those, for negroes, who possess Senegal and Goree.

* Importance of the african expedition considered, p. 4.

Never

Never was any year more glorious to Great Britain than 1758. We have many times triumphed over France, perhaps with greater eclat; but never with such real advantage to the nation. Those conquests which promote our trade, and consequently our naval power, are the most beneficial to us. The possession of Louisburg threw into our hands the whole cod-fishery, by which France maintained yearly in time of peace, near 20,000 seamen, and the profits to that nation were calculated at upwards of a million sterling; such an article, I think, to englishmen, can want no heightening. It is justly agreed, that our navy depends in great measure on our north american commerce; had the french been able to put those deep laid schemes in execution, (which I have before treated of more fully) and which depended in a great measure, on the possession of the forts Frontenac and du Quesne; our colonies would have been in the utmost danger. The conquest of those forts broke the chain, with which they had confined us, within such very narrow bounds, and threw a great part of the furr trade into our hands. The conquest of Senegal and Goree, as I have just mentioned, deprived the french of those valuable branches of commerce, the negroes gum, gold dust, and ivory. The expedition to the coast of France convinced all Europe that that kingdom was vulnerable, even at home; and the mischief it did to their trade was very considerable. Lastly, if we add the advantages gained in the East-indies, by admiral Pocock, and the vast success our shipping met with, in destroying the french commerce, by the capture of their merchant ships and men of war, we may justly conclude, that there never was a year, wherein the forces of Britain were exerted in a more glorious or advantageous manner, than that of 1758.

To what can we attribute this vast success, but to that union and harmony which subsisted in our councils? Did ever any former ministry in England carry
on

on such an extensive war as the present, without having a strong opposition in parliament to struggle with at the same time? The coalition of parties was the original cause of our success; had one ministry been in power for a few months; and then another, whose maxims were entirely opposite to those of the former, in what a confused manner must the war have been carried on? But the two parties united have triumphed over faction, perhaps more dangerous than the enemy; they have employed the forces of their country to the best advantage; the navy, that glory of Great Britain, has been exerted in the most formidable manner; and, what is unusual, we have at the same time, been equally victorious at land. They sent a british army to Germany, and at the same time another to to the coast of France, without in the least neglecting the marine. In short, Britain, this year found herself alike victorious in every quarter of the world.

Z     CHAP.

# CHAP. XVIII.

*Situation of the belligerent powers at the opening of the year* 1759. *State of the affairs of his prussian majesty. Of the empress queen. Of the empress of Russia. Of the republic of Holland. Case of the dutch ships considered. Affairs in England. In France. Expedition to the West-indies, under Hopson and Moore. Unsuccessful attack on Martinico. Basse Terre in Guadaloupe destroyed. The forces land. Basse Terre taken. General Hopson dies. Grande Terre conquered. The island capitulates. Remarks on its importance.*

THE events of the year 1758, convinced all the belligerent powers of Europe, that the fortune of the war was not to be obtained by any one victory, however considerable; but would be won by those whose resources enabled them to sustain the horrors of it longer than their enemies. It was plain, at the conclusion of the last year, that that general, whose genius furnished him with the greatest resources, was most likely to prove, in the end, victorious. It was really astonishing to see so many great victories gained by the prussian troops, without being able to procure a safe peace; when many of them would in former times, have been sufficient to transfer the empire of the world from one faction to another.

Nor was it less surprising, that the three campaigns, wherein the king of Prussia had met with such great success, did not exhaust him more. Those successes, great as they were, often times were dearly purchased; and besides these, he had met with some checks; part of his dominions had been possessed by his enemies;

the kingdom of Prussia was in the hands of the russians, part of his westphalian territories in those of the french. Many of his greatest generals were dead; and great part of those brave veterans, who had performed such unparralleled actions under him, at the beginning of the war were no more: add to this his coffers, which had been so long a filling were drained. But yet, for all this melancholy catalogue, his prussian majesty was far from being exhausted, at the close of the last campaign. Had that been his situation, let me ask the intelligent reader, whether he would have been able to drive such formidable and numerous enemies out of his german dominions. At that period, he entirely possessed the electorate of Brandenburg, Pomerania, Silesia, Magdeburg, and Halberstadt of his own dominions, Saxony, part of Mecklingburgh, and part of swedish Pomerania of his enemy's; add to this, he still received a subsidy of 670,000 l. sterling, from Great Britain; add also those great resources which he found in his own superior genius; and in the abilities of his brother Henry, seconded by a long list of able generals, who still remained to command his armies. These advantages enabled him to finish the last campaign in so glorious a manner, and to prepare with the necessary vigor for opening the approaching one.

The empress queen, during the course of the war, had met with much greater shocks than the king of Prussia; and the war felt equally heavy on her: but the resources of her power, as they are more natural than those of her enemy, so they are the more visible to the rest of Europe. Her immense territories; many of them equally fruitful and populous, enabled her to recruit all her losses. It must be a very long war that would entirely exhaust the house of Austria; her dominions are of such an immense extent; the subject so used to supply free quarter and endure military licence; her subjects so numerous, so hardy, and make such good soldiers; that it is not to be wondered at, that the empress queen was able to recruit her armies, on every shock they received: In fact, marshal Daun, very early in the new year found that he should be at the head of an army as formidable as ever.

The empress of Russia was drawn into the war by the envy which she always had to her formidable rival in the north, the king of Prussia. Never did any power enter into a war upon more unjust motives than the court of Petersburg! It was meer envy of the rising greatness of the prussian monarch. But as she had engaged, she resolved to persevere. The expence of the war fell more heavy on her enemy and the republic of Poland, than it did on herself; and, as it was an opportunity of forming her troops to service, she resolved to continue in her present system. The british minister made the greatest efforts to detach her from her alliance; but all his endeavours were vain; the court of Petersburg, notwithstanding the bad success it had hitherto met with, continued resolutely bent on the ruin of the king of Prussia.

Holland, during the greatest part of the preceding year, had been filled with nothing but remonstrances, memorials, and complaints, concerning the capture of her merchant ships by the english men of war and privateers. France, soon after their ships were seized by the english, at the beginning of the war, finding that their trade would be entirely ruined; endeavoured to obviate that stroke by her policy. She took off the tax of 50 sous per ton, which she always chuses to keep on foreign freightage: she opened even her american ports, and admitted other countries to that choice part of her commerce, which by her maritime regulations, she hath at other times so strictly kept to herself. Neutral nations seized at once on the advantage, and opened to the enemy new channels for

for the conveyance of thofe riches, by which the war was to be nurfed and protracted: Under the banner of friendfhip they thus ferved the caufe of the adverfary, whofe wealth fecured by that protection would have paffed fafe and unmolefted through the englifh fleets. Britain refolved, that her naval power fhould not be rendered ufelefs, and feized on the property of her enemy, which fhe found on board neutral fhips *.

The dutch were moftly concerned in this contraband trade; and they made terrible clamours at the capture of their fhips. The merchants of the principal cities in Holland prefented feveral memorials to the ftates general for redrefs of their grievances, offering to arm themfelves and protect their trade. The ftates remonftrated to the court of Great Britain againft this proceeding, but they met with a very cold reception. In fact, their claim was founded neither on the law of nations, nor on that of nature.

Holland, whenever fhe was engaged in war, almoft conftantly purfued the fame conduct: fhe fometimes even prohibited the commerce of neutral nations, beyond all juftice and moderation. In the year † 1599, when the government of Spain firft prohibited the fubjects of the united provinces, from trading to the ports of that kingdom, a liberty, which had unaccountably been allowed them, from the commencement of their revolt to that period; the ftates general in revenge, publifhed a placart, forbidding the people of all nations to carry any kind of merchandife into Spain. It is declared in the 41ft article of the treaty of 1674, between Great Britain and Holland, and alfo in every other commercial treaty, " That all goods are contraband, which are carried to places blockaded or in-

---

* Difcourfe on the conduct of the government of Great Britain, p. 6.
† Grotii hiftoriarum, lib. 8.

vested." To shew what opinion the dutch had of a naval blockade in 1630\*, when they pretended to have blockaded up all the coast of Flanders, and openly avowed, that they would take and condemn all neutral ships, which had the most distant appearance of being bound to the ports of that country. In 1689 †, they also declared publicly, to neutral nations, that they designed to block up all the ports of France. Now a blockade may be considered as complete by sea as land; and were not the french west-indian islands as completely blockaded, as it was possible for the dutch to blockade the ports of France? And much more; their distress and famine, for want of a communication with their mother country, fully declare, that they were invested. But besides these several reasons, I could produce many others founded intirely on the letter of the treaties subsisting between Great Britain and Holland, to shew that they have not the least right to carry the property of the enemy in their ships; but the bounds of this work will not permit me to be more particular; I must refer the reader to a very ingenious work, which canvasses the affair to the very bottom, entitled, " A discourse on " the conduct of Great Britain, in respect to neutral " nations."

If we turn our eyes towards England, and compare the state of that nation at this period, with the state it was formerly in, during the war, we shall find that the very maxims of government were changed; the constitution wore a different face. That unprecedented union, which reigned in both houses of parliament, enabled the ministry, who lived in the greatest harmony with one another, to concert those great plans of actions against the enemy, and by their penetration in the choice of commanders to ensure their

---

\* Convention between England and Holland, 1689.
† Placart of june 26, 1630.

success.

success. France, during the year, had every day found the power of the english in America to exert itself more and more: it had been like an almost smothered flame, which, when it broke through the smoke that had covered it, blazed forth with renewed violence. Those shocks, so fatal to the trade of France, which she had received in America that year, had convinced her, that it would never be possible to retrieve those losses, by her operations in that part of the world. Her great efforts must be made in Europe. Hanover was her aim on the continent, if she could keep possession of that electorate till a peace, she doubted not of being able to conclude an advantageous one. But to effect this, it required that their army in Germany should be recruited, and reinforced, that the subsidies which had been paid to Sweden, Austria, and Russia, should be regularly continued; that the king of Prussia might gain no respit. Nor was the plan which France determined to pursue, confined to Germany, she resolved to set about in real earnest, invading Great Britain; for this end, immense preparations were to made in several of the ports of that kingdom: by this means, the peace did not depend on a single stake, they had two schemes, and if either of them succeeded, their design would be entirely answered. But all these great points could not be put in execution, without great funds. It was the misfortune of the french nation at this time, to be governed by a weak and divided ministry, and a ravenous mistress, who fleeced the kingdom of immense sums every year. The destruction of their trade made money very scarce, and the necessities of the state being urgent, they were obliged to adopt a new plan of raising the revenue. Moreover Silhounate was made controller of the finances; and he immediately removed the farmers of the revenue from finding the supplies; and new methods were devised for raising money; but the great want of it still appeared, these were only temporary expedients.

But as the face of affairs in England was so much changed, so these schemes of her enemies no longer had that effect which used to attend them. At the same time that an army was maintained in Germany, and such numerous forces were kept in action in America, the East and West indies, Britain, by the good conduct of her government, was enabled to guard against any attempt that France might make to invade her. The militia act, so well known, had armed several thousand men for the defence of the kingdom, the regular troops were augmenting both in number and species; and for the first time we saw light horse and infantry. Our navy was more formidable than ever, and several squadrons were generally blocking up the ports of France, and cruising on their trade, whilst others were carrying destruction to the french colonies in every part of the world. In this situation, Britain had little to fear at this period, from the designs which that nation had formed to invade her.

One of the most considerable expeditions that was undertaken by the english ministry, in the beginning of the new year against France, was that to the West-indies. About the latter end of october 1758, commodore Hughes, with a squadron of eight ships of the line, a frigate, and four bombs, with sixty transports, set sail from Spithead, having on board the following regiments, the old buffs, Duroure's, Elliot's, Barrington's, Watson's, and Armiger's, with a detachment from the artillery at Woolwich; 800 marines were also distributed on board the men of war. The general officers employed were, major general Hopson, commander in chief; major general Barrington; colonels Armiger, and Haldane; and lieutenant colonels Trapaud and Clavering, brigadiers. The 3d of january, 1759, they came to an anchor in Carlisle bay, in the island of Barbadoes. Commodore

dore Moore, who was lying in that bay, with another small squadron, took upon himself the command of the united fleet. Having watered at Barbadoes, they set sail from thence January 13th, their armament not exceeding 5000 men complete*.

The grand object of this expedition was the island of Martinico, the first of the french sugar islands, the seat of the government, and the center of all the trade which France carries on with the West-indies: It is very strong both by nature and art. The shore on every side indented with very deep bays; the many sands round the island which are to be seen only at low water, render an approach very dangerous without good pilots. It is very fruitful, well cultivated, and watered, abounding with plantations and villages along the sea coast. Port Royal is the principal place in the island, which is considerable for its size, trade, and strength. St. Pierre is the second town which is of near as much consequence as Port Royal. The french had at this time a good number of regular forces here; besides a numerous and well armed militia, and not contemptible for their discipline.

The 15th of January, the troops were landed without opposition, on the west side of Port Royal har-

* Ships that composed the squadron.

Line of battle.

| Ships. | Guns. | Men. | Captains. |
| --- | --- | --- | --- |
| Berwick | 64 | 488 | Harman. |
| Winchester | 50 | 350 | Le Crafs. |
| Rippon | 60 | 430 | Jehkyll. |
| Bristol | 50 | 350 | Leslie. |
| Norfolk | 74 | 600 | Hughes. |
| Cambridge | 80 | 667 | Burnet. |
| St. George | 90 | 750 | Gayton. |
| Panther | 60 | 420 | Schuldham. |
| Lyon | 60 | 400 | Trelawney. |
| Burford | 64 | 520 | Gambier. |

Four frigates, four bombs, and sixty transports.

bour,

bour, after the men of war had driven the french from their batteries and intrenchments; they had frequent skirmishes with the enemy, but these did not prove so great an obstruction to the success of the troops, as the nature of the country. A multitude of deep streams of water, inclosed by steep and almost perpendicular precipices, proved a great obstacle to the march of the troops; the roads broken up, and they had five miles to march before they could get to Port Royal. General Hopson, finding these difficulties unsurmountable, sent on board the Cambridge, to acquaint the commodore, that he found it impossible to maintain his ground, unless the squadron could give him assistance, by landing some heavy cannon, &c. at the savanna, near the town of Port Royal, or that the commodore would attack the citadel in the bay, at the same time that he did it on the shore. A council of war having judged this to be impracticable, the general gave orders for the troops to retire, and they were re-embarked on the 17th. One cannot help observing in the account of this transaction, which was published in the Gazette, and which I apprehend was extracted chiefly from the commodore's letters, that there did not seem to be so perfect a harmony between the general and the commodore as is always necessary in such expeditions as these, and on which their success entirely depends.

The next day the general acquainted the commodore, that the council of war was of opinion, it would be most for his majesty's service to go to fort St. Pierre with the troops, in order to make an attack upon that place, and that no time should be lost. It was hoped that more might be done there; and accordingly the fleet came in sight of that town the 19th; forty merchantmen were then lying in the bay, and the commodore ordered two bombs to sail in near enough to do the proper execution; he sent a man of war in to sound, and ordered the Rippon to silence
a battery

a battery, about a mile and a half north of the town; and threw out a signal for the transports to come under his stern. All these dispositions seemed as if the attack was resolved on; and in fact, the commodore had assured the general, that he could destroy the town of St. Pierre, and put the troops in possession of it; but as the squadron might be considerably damaged in the attack, and the whole armament unable after it to proceed on any other material service, he represented to the general, that it would be better to proceed to the town of Basse Terre, in the island of Guadaloupe. The general concurring in this opinion, the bombs were forbid to play, the sounding ship recalled; and to the astonishment of every body, the merchantmen were left without any attack being made on them; as it was the opinion of several officers, that they might have been, at least destroyed without damaging the ships, so much as to disenable them from proceeding on their service. But it looks as if the commodore had forgot he had ordered the Rippon to engage a battery; that ship proceeded down to her station, and in a few minutes silenced it; but before she could disengage herself, four batteries more were opened, to play on the ship, which damaged her masts, sails, and rigging very much, and the captain observing the commodore above two leagues astern of him, with the rest of the fleet, and no ships but his own in the harbour, nor any coming to his assistance, concluded that the attack was laid aside, and his own ship being in great danger, ordered his boats to be manned, and towed her off.

Pursuant to the resolution agreed on at the council of war, to attack Guadaloupe, the squadron set sail, and arrived off the town of Basse Terre, the 23d of January; they found the place very formidably fortified towards the sea, as the enemy had raised several batteries at all the convenient places along the shore; and the citadel, was thought by colonel Cunningham,

the

the chief engineer, on account of its great height to be impregnable to the ships, but in this opinion he proved miftaken. The fame day the commodore ordered the attack to be made in the following difpofition: the St. George, Norfolk, and Cambridge to lay along fide the citadel, mounting 47 guns; the Lyon, a battery of nine guns; the Panther and Burford, a battery of 12 guns; the Berwick, a battery of feven guns; and the Rippon another of 6 guns. He ordered them to filence, if poffible, their refpective batteries, and to lie by them till further orders; having fhifted his broad pendant from the Cambridge, and hoifted it on board the Woolwich of 40 guns. The fhips having all taken their ftations, the cannonade began at nine o'clock, and continued with the moft unremitting fury till night; as foon as the feveral batteries were filenced, the four bombs ftood in for the fhore, and threw fhells and carcaffes into the town. The houfes and churches were every where foon in flames, the magazines of powder blown about the enemies ears, and the whole about ten o'clock blazed out in one general conflagration. It burned all night, and the following day; when it was almoft totally reduced to afhes. The lofs was immenfe, from the number of warehoufes in the town, full of rum, and other rich, but combuftible materials. It is furprifing that the fquadron fhould fuffer fo little as it did, in fuftaining fuch a terrible cannonade.

The 24th, the troops landed without oppofition, and took poffeffion of the town and citadel of Baffe Terre; the fire ftill continuing in the former. M. d'Eftreil, the governor, behaved very daftardly; inftead of exerting himfelf in the time of danger, vifiting the feveral engaged batteries, and by his prefence infpiring his people with redoubled ardor; he retired to a plantation out of gun-fhot, and remained an inactive fpectator of the deftruction of the day. Had he acted as became a brave man, fighting for his

his honour and his country, he would the next morning have taken precautions to prevent the landing of the troops, who had a difficult fhore to deal with, attended with a violent furff from the fea, and defended by entrenchments and lines every where thrown up. But this pretended fon of Mars, retired with his troops to a rifing ground, about fix miles from Baffe Terre, where he ftrongly intrenched himfelf, the fituation being very ftrong by nature. The afcent to it was very fteep. The road from the camp of the englifh troops, interrupted by broken rocks; and the ground interfected by a variety of gullies, very difficult to pafs; all which rendered an attack on it very hazardous. While the governor remained in this fituation, general Hopfon and commodore Moore fent him an offer of terms; but he returned them a very gallant anfwer, which would have done him honour, had it fucceeded as gallant behaviour.

The latter end of the month was employed in fcouring the country; and as the enemy in fmall parties were continually laying ambufcades among the fugar canes; orders were given to fet them on fire, which was very foon executed. And commodore Moore confidered, that the eaftern part of the ifland, called Grand Terre, which is the moft fertile of the whole, might be attacked with advantage, if the fort Louis was taken; refolved to detach fome men of war from the fquadron for that purpofe; accordingly the Berwick, with three frigates, three tenders, and two bombs, failed the 6th of february, and the 13th attacked the fort and the batteries near it; when, after a fevere cannonade, which lafted fix hours, a large detachment of marines, and the highlanders, landed, who drove the enemy from their intrenchments, and hoifted the englifh colours at the fort.

General Hopfon died at the camp near Baffe Terre the 27th, and the command of the army then devolved

volved on major general Barrington, who on the 1st of march, brought off all the troops, re-imbarking them on board the transports by the break of day, leaving colonel Desbrisay in the citadel, with Watson's regiment, and a detachment from the artillery. It was the general's scheme to make the attack on the side of Grande Terre; accordingly the commodore with the fleet sailed. It was the 11th before the fleet came to an anchor off fort Louis. It was here that Mr. Moore received intelligence, that Monf. Bompart, with a squadron of eight sail of the line, and three frigates, with a reinforcement of troops, was arrived at Port Royal in Martinico. The commodore directly perceived, that the french squadron might be able to throw in succours into Grand Terre, if he attempted it, without his being able to prevent it, as the squadron then lay; he took a resolution to sail immediately to prince Rupert's bay, in Dominica, as he should there have it more in his power to protect Guadaloupe. The privateers of the french took advantage of this movement; and above eleven weeks, while the two squdrons were watching one another in the two bays; they sailed out, and took above 90 sail of english merchantmen, and carried them into Martinico. Their captures occasioned heavy complaints from the british islands, for they said, (and I believe, with a good deal of reason) it was equally practicable for the english squadron to have anchored at Port Royal, as at prince Rupert's bay; by which, two ends might have been answered, the french men of war could not have got out, nor the privateer prizes have got in, and of course the latter must have been re-taken; no other harbour being then open to them except St. Pierre's or Granada, either of which, was at that time to be blockaded by a single frigate *. Had Mr. Moore

---

* Vide capt. Gardener's account of this expedition, p. 42.

made

made his appearance off Port Royal, M. du Bompart must have been reduced to the alternative of fighting a superior force, or of retiring behind the citadel into the carenage to avoid it.

General Barrington took all the precaution in his power to strengthen the fort at St. Louis; and, finding that the war in the island, was not to be prosecuted with all the troops in a body; he detached colonel Crump, with 600 men, in some of the transports, to endeavour to land between the towns of St. Anne, and St. François; colonel Crump executed this with the greatest bravery, destroying the batteries of cannon which the enemies had raised there. And as the general expected, that the enemy would weaken a strong post they had at Gosier, to reinforce St. Anne's and St. François, he went with another detachment and made himself master of it.

In the mean time, colonel Desbrisay*, who was left governor of the citadel of Basse Terre, lost his life by an unfortunate accident. A cannon being fired too near a powder magazine, the return of the wadding blew it up, and with it the governor, major Trollop, a lieutenant, and several men. Major Mel-

* Lieutenant colonel Desbrisay, was captain of foot at the battle of Val, near Mastricht, in 1747; being wounded, and lying on the ground, a french officer, contrary to the rules of war, and every generous sentiment ran him through, which unmanly example was immediately followed by the party he commanded, all of them planting their bayonets in his body. He received 15 wounds, and eight of them were judged mortal. He was afterwards in company with marshal Saxe, whose politeness in war was so well known, and who pressed him strongly to declare, who the officer was, that had used him in so base a manner, threatening to disgrace him, at the head of the regiment; but Desbrisay, though well acquainted with his name, the commission he bore, and the corps he served in, had so much greatness of mind as to decline it; he contented himself with letting his excellency know, that he was not a stranger to his person, but begged he would excuse him, from being obliged to point him out.

vil was appointed by the general to fucceed him in the government of the citadel.

The moſt confiderable force the enemy had, was collected on the mountain called Dos d'Afne. It is a poſt of great ſtrength and importance, as it forms the only communication there is between the town of Baſſe Terre and the capes Terre, the pleaſanteſt and moſt fruitful part of the iſland. It was not judged practicable to break into it this way; and all the reſt of the Baſſe Terre part of the iſland was in the enemies poſſeſſion. The general therefore formed a plan to furpriſe the towns of Petit Bourge, St. Mary's, and Guogave; but the fuccefs of this project, though well concerted, was, through the darknefs of the night, the roughnefs of the weather, and the ignorance and fear of the negroes, who were guides, entirely fruſtrated. This obliged general Barrington to attempt that by force, which could not be effected upon a fafer plan; but as he was then laid up with a fevere fit of the gout, he fent brigadier Clavering and Crump to reconnoitre the coaſt near Arnoville, and upon their report, fent them with 1400 men to land there, which they effected the 12th of april. The enemy made no oppoſition to Mr. Clavering's landing, but as his troops advanced, retired to very ſtrong intrenchments behind the river le Corne. This poſt was to them of the utmoſt importance, as it covered the whole country to the bay Mahaut, where their proviſions and fupplies of all forts were landed from St. Euſtatia, and therefore they had very early taken poſſeſſion of it, and had fpared no pains to ſtrengthen it, though the fituation was fuch, as required very little aſſiſtance from art. The river was only acceſſible at two narrow paſſes, on account of a a very deep morass; and those places they had occupied with a redoubt, and well pallisadoed intrenchments, defended with cannon, and all the militia of that part of the country. The english could only approach them in a very narrow contracted front, no wider than the roads through which they marched; and these were defended with deep and broad ditches. The artillery, consisting of six pieces of cannon, kept a constant fire on their intrenchments, to cover the attack made by Duroure's regiment, and the highlanders, who behaved with the greatest coolness and resolution, keeping up, as they advanced, a regular platoon firing. This behaviour so intimidated the enemy, that they abandoned the first intrenchment on the left. Into which the highlanders threw themselves, with part of Duroure's regiment, sword in hand, and pursued the enemy into the redoubt. The french still kept their ground in their intrenchments on the right, but on being attacked they fled, and 70 of them were made prisoners.

As soon as the ditches were filled up for the passage of the artillery, Mr. Clavering marched towards Petit Bourg; in his way, he was to cross the river Lizard; behind which, at the only ford, the enemy had thrown up very strong intrenchments, protected by four pieces of cannon, on a hill behind them. The brigadier having reconnoitred the river, found it would cost him very dear to force a passage at the ford. He therefore kept up the attention of the enemy, by firing all night in their lines; during which time, he got a couple of canoes conveyed about a mile and an half down the river, where, being launched, a sufficient number of men were ferried over, to attack them in flank, while the remainder did the same in front; but the enemy soon perceived their danger, and left the intrenchments with the greatest precipitation.

\* Z When

When the brigadier arrived at Petit Bourg, he found it fortified with lines, and a redoubt filled with cannon; but the enemy abandoned it and the port to the conquerors. On the 15th, brigadier Crump was detached with 700 men to the bay Mahaut; he found the batteries and the town abandoned. These he burnt, with an immense quantity of provisions that had been landed there by the dutch, and reduced the whole country as far as Petit Bourg. The same day, Mr. Clavering detached capt. Steel with 100 men to Guogave, to destroy a battery there: the panic of the enemy was such, that they only discharged their cannon at him, and deserted a post that might have been maintained against an army. He nailed up seven pieces of cannon, and returned the same evening.

In the mean time, the french were drawing all their force to St. Mary's, to oppose the english, and had thrown up intrenchments to strengthen the post. The brigadier immediately formed a design to get into their rear, by roads which the enemy thought impracticable; but they, perceiving his design, made a movement to oppose him, which made him resolve, without further delay, to attack them directly in front, and it was accordingly executed with the greatest vivacity, notwithstanding the constant firing, both of their cannon and musketry. They abandoned all their artillery, and fled in such confusion, that they never afterwards appeared before the brigadier. He took up his quarters at St. Mary's, and the next day entered Grande Terre, which is the richest and most beautiful part of this, or any island in the West-Indies. No less than 870 negroes, belonging to one man only, surrendered that day.

The governor of the island, finding himself so very close pressed on all sides, sent a flag of truce to general Barrington, to demand a cessation of arms, and

to

to know what terms he would grant. On the first of may the capitulation was signed; their possessions, and their civil and religious liberties were granted them.*

The capitulation was hardly signed, when the french squadron, under monf. Bompart, appeared before the island, and landed at St. Anne's, in the Grande Terre;

* Extract from the capitulation, between the governor and the english general.
II. The garrison shall be sent to Martinico.
VI. All the officers who have estates in the colony (except the governor, unless the king permits him) shall be allowed to appoint attornies to act for them until the peace; and if the island is not then ceded, they shall have leave to sell their estates, and carry off the produce.

Between the inhabitants, the english general, and commodore.

III. The inhabitants are allowed the free and public exercise of their religion; the priests and religious shall be preserved in their parishes, convents, and all other possessions.
V. The inhabitants are allowed their civil government, their laws, customs, and ordinances; justice to be administred by the same persons now in office; but when any vacancies happen, they are to be filled up by the superior council, and receive their commissions from his britannic majesty. If the island is ceded to the king of Great-Britain, the inhabitants shall have their choice, either to keep their own political government, or to accept that which is established at Antigua, and St. Christopher's.
VII If the island is ceded to his britannic majesty at the peace, it is to be subject to the same duties and imposts, as the other english leeward islands the most favoured.
XI. No other but the inhabitants residing in the island, shall possess any lands or houses before a peace; but it is ceded to the king of Great Britain, then the inhabitants shall be permitted, if they chuse it, to sell their possessions (but to none besides subjects of Great Britain) and retire where they please.
XXI The inhabitants and merchants of this island, included in the present capitulation; shall enjoy all the privileges of trade, and upon the same conditions as are granted to his britannic majesty's subjects, throughout the extent of his dominions; but without affecting the privileges of particular companies in England, or the laws of the kingdom, which prohibit the carrying on of trade in any other than english bottoms.

A a 2     the

the general of the french Carribbes, with a reinforcement from Martinico of 600 regulars, 2000 buccaneers, and 2000 stand of spare arms for the inhabitants, with artillery and mortars: had this support arrived an hour sooner, the conquest of the island must at least have been very difficult, if not impossible. As soon as he heard that the capitulation was signed, he re-embarked again.

On the signing of the articles of capitulation, the inhabitants quitted the Dos d'Asne, and returned to their plantations and houses; they began also to repair the ruins of Basse Terre; where, soon after shops were opened, and the produce of the country sold as usual, unmolested by the troops in camp or garrison, general Barrington causing the strictest discipline to be observed.

The conquest of the small island of Marigalante, on the 26th, and those of Deseada, Santos, and Petitz Terre, completed the business of the expedition; they surrendered on the same terms as Guadaloupe. So that now the french have no footing on the leeward islands. Thus was this valuable island reduced under subjection to the british crown, by the bravery of the land forces employed in the expedition. It was very odd to find how severely our West-India trade suffered from the privateers of the enemy, while commodore Moore lay with a superior squadron in those seas. Monf. Bompart was generally very near the english squadron, and effectually protected the french trade.

Gaudaloupe lies in lat. 16° 6'. long. 62°. and is about 90 leagues in compass; divided into two parts by a channel, no where above 300 feet over; the one called Grande Terre, and the other Basse Terre. Its chief produce is sugar, cotton, indigo, coffee, ginger, tobacco, cassia, bananas, pine apples, rice, maize, mandioca, and potatoes. The air is very clear and wholesome, and not so hot as in Martinico. Grande Terre is destitute of water, and
not

not thoroughly cultivated; but the case is the very reverse in Basse Terre, the water being as good there, as the soil is rich; it is very near as populous as Martinico. In short, there is nothing in this island wanting, for the convenience and delight of life, in an air more temporate and salubrious than is commonly breathed between the tropics.

As to the importance of this acquisition, I need only state a few particulars before the reader, and every intelligent person must allow it to be infinite. Guadaloup makes annually 40,000 hogsheads of sugar, which is a larger quantity than any of our sugar islands produce, except Jamaica. Besides this, the articles of cotton, indigo, coffee, and ginger, are very considerable; it also carries on a trade with the Caracca's, and other parts of the spanish main, which is a trade wholly in the manufactures of Europe, and the returns for which are made almost entirely in ready money. Without intimating the land, the houses, the works, and the goods in the island, the slaves, at the lowest estimation, are worth upwards of 1,250,090 l. sterling. The single branch of their trade, the sugars, besides the employment of so much shipping, and so many seamen, will produce clear 300,000 l. per ann. to the merchants of that nation who possesses it. Coffee, a very inconsiderable object in the british colonies, is here a very great one. They raise also great quantities of indigo and cotton, which supply materials for the best and most valuable manufactures. Another article, which makes the possession of this island so very desireable, is the conveniency of its situation, if in the hands of the french, for being a harbour for their privateers in this part of the world, as it is in the very middle of the english Leeward-islands; which made it the Dunkirk of the West-Indies.*

---

* Vide remarks on a letter addressed to two great men, p. 42.

I think

I think, thefe points confidered, every one muft allow, that the conqueft of guadaloupe was of infinite importance to this nation ; and was a particular inftance, how active and enterprifing a miniftry, at this time, guided the affairs of England, who, although they made fuch great efforts in every other part of the world againft the enemy, ftill forgot not this, but attacked them here with equal wifdom and fuccefs.

END of VOL. I.

www.ingramcontent.com/pod-product-compliance
Lightning Source LLC
Chambersburg PA
CBHW020230240426
43672CB00006B/472